リゾート&スポーツ
ファシリティ RESORT & SPORTS FACILITIES

リゾート＆スポーツ ファシリティ

目次

RESORT & SPORTS FACILITIES *EXCELLENT SHOP DESIGNS*

CONTENTS

ショップ

レストラン/複合ショップ/仮設ショップ

Stores

Restaurant/Café/Composite Shop/Temporary Shop

●本書には、'85〜88年に開業（開店）し、月刊「商店建築」に特集掲載された、リゾートホテル・アーバンリゾートホテルにフィットネスやクアハウスを含めたスポーツ施設・レジャー施設39件とリゾート感覚のレストラン・複合ショップなど21件、合計60件をセレクトし、再編集して収録しています。

●リゾートやスポーツ施設、郊外型の店舗づくりの参考に拡くご利用下さい。

●巻末に施設名（店名）別の索引を加えました。

●解説文の最後（　）は、掲載号を意味しています。
　例（88-10）は、「商店建築」88年10月号に掲載の意味です。

●解説文は掲載のさいに頁数の都合上でリライトさせていただきました。関係各位のご了承をいただきたくお願い申し上げます。

●各データ、店名、所在地、電話番号などは開業（開店）時のものです。現在変更されている場合もありますのでご了承下さい。

1990年1月 商店建築社

Shotenkenchiku Extra Number [47]
RESORT & SPORTS FACILITIES

● This book contains 39 cases of resort and sports facilities, including resort hotels, urban resort hotels, fitness and Kurhaus facilities, and 21 cases of resort type restaurants and composite shops, totaling 60 cases that opened in Japan between 1985 and 1988.
● Widely utilize this book whenever you need reference in making resort/sports facilities, or suburban shops.
● A set of data, shop name, location, telephone No., etc. denote those as of the time when the shop, etc. opened. So, in some cases, they may differ from the present data, etc.

January 1990

SHOTENKENCHIKU-SHA
Published by Shotenkenchiku-sha Co., Ltd.
7-22-36-2, Nishi-shinjuku, Shinjuku-ku, Tokyo 160 Japan

(© 1990)

平面図の略号／Abbreviation

ELV/Elevator	エレベーター	AC/Air Cleaner	エアクリーナー
WC/Water Closet	便所	RCT/Register Counter	レジカウンター
M.WC/Men's Water Closet	男子便所	Hg/Hanger	ハンガー
W. WC/Women's Water Closet	女子便所	FR/Fitting Room	フィッティングルーム
R/Register	レジスター	DT/Display Room	ディスプレイルーム
ES/Escalator	エスカレーター	SVA/Service Area	サービスエリア
PS/ Pipe Space	パイプスペース	SW/Show Window	ショーウインド
CT/Counter	カウンター	Sh/Shelf	棚

別冊商店建築 47 リゾート＆スポーツ ファシリティ　1990年 2 月15日発行

編集発行人　村上末吉　編集●辻田　博　協力スタッフ　　本文レイアウト●ぱとおく社　印刷●三共グラビヤ印刷　　　　　　製本●坂田製本
　　　　　製作●菅谷良夫　表紙デザイン●ウィークエンド　英文●海広社　　写植●福島写植　三共グラビヤ印刷　　　山田製本

発行所　株式会社商店建築社 ©
　　　　本社 東京都新宿区西新宿7-22-36-2 〒160 TEL.03(363)5770代　　支社 大阪市中央区西心斎橋1-9-28 第3大京ビル〒542　TEL.06(251)6523代
　　　ISBN:4-7858-0008-9　C2052

リゾートホテル/ *Resort Hotel*

東側から見たロケーション

The location viewed from the east side.

ラマダ ルネッサンス リゾート オキナワ

沖縄県国頭郡恩納村字山田名幸原3425-2　Phone/09896-5-0707

撮影/本木誠一

Ramada Renaissance Resort Okinawa
Onna-son, Kunigami-gun, Okinawa, Japan　Phone/09896-5-0707

南側正面入口廻り
The southern front entrance area.

ホテル棟より俯瞰したビーチ

The beach overlooked from the hotel building.

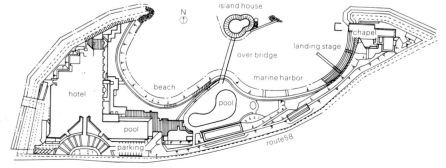

island house

N

chapel

over bridge

landing stage

marine harbor

hotel

beach

pool

pool

parking

route58

SITE PLAN　S=1:4000

右上/マリンハーバーよりオーバーブリッジごしに見たホテル棟全景
右中/遊泳のためのビーチ
右下/敷地中央に設けられたアウトドアプール

Right, top/ The entire hotel building viewed from the marine harbor across the over bridge.
Right, middle/ The beach for swimming.
Right, bottom/ The outdoor pool provided in the center of the site.

木製のオーバーブリッジでビーチと結ばれるアイランドハウス

The island house connected to the wooden overbridge across the beach.

ラマダ ルネッサンス リゾート オキナワ

このホテルは世界第3位のラマダチェーンとの業務提携をし その中でも
最高級を誇るルネッサンスクラスのホテルである。

設計のポイントとしては 本来のリゾートのあり方について今までにない
諸施設造りを計画しマリン リゾートホテルとして充実を図った。

ホテル棟は 客室すべてが東シナ海が一望できるように アトリウムを中
心に配置した。

色彩は国定公園の一画であるため白系を基調とし内部は中間色系にして
ある。　　　　　　　　　〈松野八郎綜合建築設計事務所大阪事務所〉(88-10)

監修：奥村ハウジング企画設計部

設計：建築/松野八郎綜合建築設計事務所

内装：ベント サバリン＆アソシエイツ

協力：構造/川崎建築構造研究所
　　　設備(監理)/ジュン設備研究所

施工：佐藤工業　国場組共同企画体

構　　造：SRC造(ホテル棟)

規　　模：地下1階　地上11階　塔屋1階(ホテル棟)

面　　積：敷地/27,706.0m²　建築/6,087.84m²(ホテル棟)　床/地下1階
　　　　　3,497.81m²　1階 5,107.55m²　中2階 721.13m²　2階
　　　　　3,948.27m²　3～11階　各2,517.31m²　塔屋 377.11m²　合計
　　　　　36,307.66m²(ホテル棟)

工　　期：1987年2月14日～1988年6月30日

施設概要：開業/1988年7月8日　営業時間/チェックイン　午後2時　チ
　　　　　ェックアウト　午前11時　客室数/スイート9　和室20　ツイ
　　　　　ン342　ダブル21　合計392室　料飲施設/レストラン2　日本
　　　　　料理レストラン1　カフェ1　スシバー1　バー1　ディスコ
　　　　　1　料金/スイート5～15万　和室2万7000～5万3000　ツイ
　　　　　ン2万～3万2000　ダブル2万～2万9000　経営/㈱奥村ハウ
　　　　　ジング　従業員数/391人　パート アルバイト/180人　合計571
　　　　　人

Ramada Renaissance Resort Okinawa

Opened under a business tieup agreement with Ramada chain, world's third largest hotel chain, "Ramada Renaissance Resort Okinawa" is a hotel of Renaissance class — highest in the chain.

In designing the hotel, emphasis was placed on making various unique facilities as an attractive marine resort hotel to differentiate from conventional marine resort hotels.

All rooms are arranged around an atrium so that guests can enjoy a complete view of the East China Sea.

Since the hotel is situated within a quasi-national park, the exterior is finished with white as the basic tone, and the interior is finished with a neutral tint.

Design: Hachiro Matsuno + Bent Severin & Associates

Structure : SRC (hotel building)

Scale : 1 under and 11 stories above the ground, and 1 floor on the roof (hotel building)

Area : Site/27,706 m²;　Building/6,087.84 m² (hotel building); Floor/1st basement 3,497.81 m², 1st floor 5,107.55 m², mezzanine 721.13 m², 2nd floor 3,948.27 m², 3rd to 11th floors 2,517.31 m² each, roof floor 377.11 m², totaling 36,307.66 m² (hotel building)

Term of construction: February 14, 1987 to June 30, 1988

Facilities : Opening/July 8, 1988; Open time/check-in at 2:00 p.m., check-out 11:00 a.m.; Number of guest rooms/suite 9, Japanese 20, twin 342, double 21, totaling 392; Eating & drinking facilities/restaurant 2, Japanese restaurant 1, cafe 1, sushi bar 1, bar 1, disco 1;
Charges/suite 50,000 to 150,000 yen, Japanese room 27,000 to 53,000 yen, twin 20,000 to 32,000 yen, double 20,000 to 29,000 yen; Management/Okumura Housing Co.; Number of employees/full-time 391, part-time 180, totaling 571

ホテル棟中央のアトリウムを正面入口側よりみる

The atrium in the center of the hotel building viewed from the front entrance side.

ビーチサイドハウス2階の「鉄板焼　アンヴィルハウス」の客席
The guest seat area of "Teppan-yaki (Hot plate) Anvil House" at the 2nd floor of Beachside House.

「アンヴィルハウス」のデッキテラス席
The deck terrace seat area of "Anvil House."

アイランドハウス地下1階の
「マリンディスコ　ゼファー」

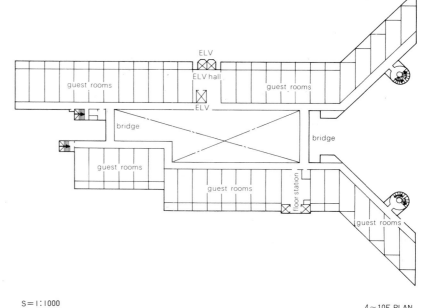

ELV

ELV hall

guest rooms   guest rooms

ELV

bridge

bridge

guest rooms

guest rooms

floor station

guest rooms

S = 1 : 1000

4～10F PLAN

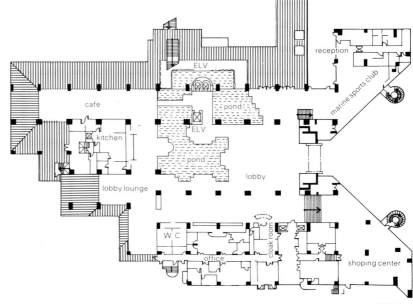

reception

ELV

cafe

pond

marine sports club

kitchen

ELV

pond

lobby lounge

lobby

W.C

cloak room

office

shoping center

1F PLAN

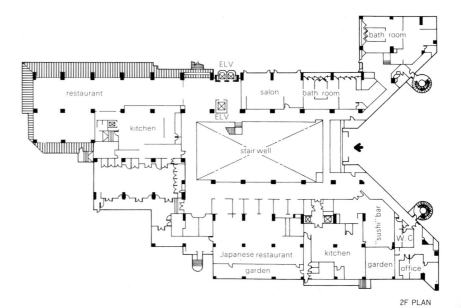

bath room

ELV

restaurant

salon

bath room

kitchen

ELV

stair well

Japanese restaurant

kitchen

"sushi" bar

W.C

garden

garden

office

2F PLAN

"Marine Disco Zephyr" at the
1st base- ment of Island House.

トロピカルな雰囲気のアイランドハウス1階「バーベキュー コラール シー ビュー」
"Barbecue Coral Sea View" at the 1st floor of Island House, giving a tropical atmosphere.

ホテル棟２階「日本料理 彩（いろどり）」

"Japanese Dish Irodori" at the 2nd floor of the hotel building.

「日本料理 彩」の庭に面した椅子席
The chair seats facing the garden of "Japanese Dish Irodori."

ホテル棟２階「レストラン フォーシーズン」
"Restaurant Four Seasons" at the 2nd floor of the hotel building.

材料仕様
屋根/アスファルト歩行用断熱防水８層下地軽量コンクリート金鏝押さえ目地切り仕上げ　外壁/コンクリート打放し下地アクリル系吹き付け塗材　外部床/コンクリート金鏝押さえ　下地木製デッキ貼り　ＯＳＣＬ　サイン/コンクリート下地御影石バーナー仕上げ　ステンレス焼き付け塗装切り文字
〈アトリウム内装〉床/コンクリート金鏝押さえ下地イタリア産御影石模様貼りバーナー仕上げ　一部スレート貼り割肌仕上げ（黒）　幅木/チーク材ＣＬ　h＝100　壁/コンクリート打ち放し補修＆ＰＢ　t＝12下地アクリル系塗料　天井/ＰＢ　t＝9下地ビニールクロス貼り　トップライト部/立体トラス　アルミサッシ　電動オペレーター付き　照明/フロアスタンド　ＦＬ間接照明　スポット　池/コンクリート下地塗布防水　天板:御影石　床/コンクリート直押さえ下地フローリング貼り　幅木/チーク材ＣＬ　h＝150　壁/コンクリートブロック積みモルタル補修下地クロス貼り　柱/鋼管下地チェリー材練り付け合板貼りマニラロープ巻　天井/合板下地藤パネル貼り　照明器具/ＦＬ間接照明　アッパーライトスポット　家具/ラタン

プールを通して建物をみる

The building viewed across the pool.

ホテル アナガ（阿那賀）

兵庫県三原郡西淡町阿那賀1109　Phone/0799-39-1111

Hotel Anaga
1109, Anaga Seidan-cho, Mihara-gun, Hyogo, Japan
Phone/0799-39-1111

撮影/福本正明

1階客室よりプールをみる

The pool viewed from the guest room at the 1st floor.

ホテル アナガ(阿那賀)

鳴門大橋の完成と明石大橋の起工を機に「ホテル アナガ」は生活レベルの変化に伴う時間の過ごし方 余暇のあり方に対応する都市感覚の長期滞在型リゾートホテルとして誕生した。

当ホテルは 鳴門大橋を正面に見る阿那賀港 約1500㎡を有する丘の上に全室南向きに建っており メインエントランスから誘導された客の視線は270度に展開し レストランから あるいは ラウンジからのガーデンプールの景色は他に類を見ない。

施設は中央にロビー ラウンジ プロショップ 宴会場等が設けられ またプールサイド ガーデンテラスは緑と花に囲まれ 非日常的空間を演出している。　　　　　　　　　〈江藤暢英/アトリエテクノフォルム〉(89-09)

設計:アトリエ テクノフォルム 間建築工房

協力:設備/山水設計

　　　構造/日浦建築設計事務所

施工:大工建設

構　　造:RC造

規　　模:地下1階 地上2階

面　　積:敷地/15,382.73㎡ 建築/2,427.01㎡ 床/地下1階　699.60㎡
　　　　　1階 2,164.37㎡　2階 1,969,39㎡　合計4,833.36㎡

工　　期:1986年5月1日～1987年4月27日

施設概要:開業/1987年7月1日　営業時間/チェックイン 午後4時 チェックアウト 午後3時　客室数/47室(内 ダブル4)　料飲施設/レストラン1(60席)　日本料理レストラン1(和室3 テーブル20席 カウンター12席)　ラウンジ 1(32席)　バーベキュー テラス 1(28席 予約制)　プールサイドバー 1(5席 7,8月のみ営業)　料金/2万(7～8月は2万7000)　経営/淡路開発興業㈱ 従業員数/49人 パート アルバイト 30人 合計 79人

Hotel Anaga

On the occasion of completed construction of Naruto Big Bridge and started construction of Akashi Big Bridge, "Hotel Anaga" came into being as a long stay type resort hotel with an urban sense responding to the latest style of spending time and enjoying leisure.

Standing on a hill near Anaga Port that is just in front of Naruto Big Bridge, this hotel secures about 1,500 m², and all rooms of this hotel face south. The guests guided from the main entrance look around in 270 degrees, and can enjoy nice scenes of a garden pool either from the restaurant or lounge.

A lobby, lounge, pro shop, banquet hall, etc. are installed in the center, while the poolside and garden terrace are surrounded with green and flowers, presenting a non-daily space.

Design: Nobuhide Eto

Structure : RC

Scale　　: 1 under and 2 stories above the ground

Area　　 : Site/15,382.73 m²; Building/2,427.01 m²; Floor/1st basement 699.60 m², 1st floor 2,164.37 m², 2nd floor 1,969.39 m², totaling 4,833.36 m²

Term of construction: May 1, 1986 to April 27, 1987

Facilities : Opening/July 1, 1987; Open time/check-in at 4:00 p.m., check-out at 3 p.m.; Number of guest rooms/47 (including double 4); Eating & drinking facilities/restaurant 1 (60 seats), Japanese restaurant 1 (Japanese room 3, table seat 20, counter 12), lounge 1 (32 seats), barbecue terrace 1 (28 seats under reserve system), poolside bar 1 (5 seats, open in July and August alone); Charges/20,000 yen (27,000 yen in July and August); Management/Awaji Kaihatsu Kogyo Co.; Number of employees/full-time 49, part-time 30, totaling 79

全景をみる　ロビーを中心に東西に客室を配している　前方に見えるのは鳴門大橋
The entire scene. The guest rooms are arranged in the east and west sides centering around the lobby. Ahead is visible the Big Naruto Bridge.

海より全景をみる

The entire scene viewed from the sea.

ロビーをみる

The lobby.

入口廻りをみる

The entrance area.

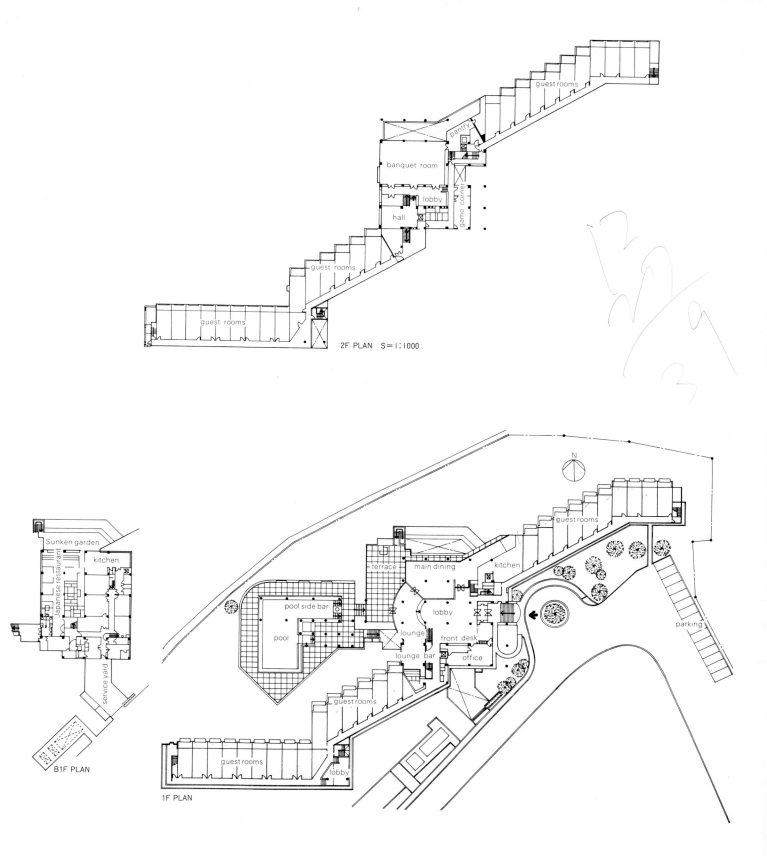

2F PLAN S=1:1000

guest rooms
pantry
banquet room
game corner
lobby
hall
guest rooms
guest rooms

N

Sunken garden
kitchen
Japanese restaurant
service yard

B1F PLAN

1F PLAN

guest rooms
terrace
main dining
kitchen
pool side bar
lobby
pool
lounge
front desk
lounge bar
office
guest rooms
guest rooms
lobby
parking

材料仕様
屋根/防水剤混入モルタル下地スペイン瓦葺き　外壁/厚付け仕上げ塗料　腰壁/丸石積み御影石ボーダーサック　アルミジュラクロン塗装　ベランダ床/防水剤混入モルタルの上モルタル鏝押
さえ　一部タイル貼り　サイン/ステンレス磨き文字　台/御影石
〈客室　廊下　供用部分〉床/特注ウールカーペット t＝8　幅木/米松CL　壁/モルタルEPローラー仕上げ　天井/PB t＝12下地ビニールクロス貼り　家具/コクヨ　アイデック　富士
ファニチャー　富士屋木工所　ホートク

ホテル正面に配置されたキャノピー　三角形は波をモチーフ　　　　The canopy installed in front of the hotel. The triangle symbolizes a wave.

三浦 シーサイド ホテル

Miura Seaside Hotel
13, Tsukui, Yokosuka city, Kanagawa, Japan　　Phone/0468-49-8686

神奈川県横須賀市津久井13番地　Phone/0468-49-8686

撮影/平沢写真事務所

キャノピー部分材料仕様
トラス/H形鋼150×100×9 フッソ樹脂塗装　L形鋼50×50×4 フッソ樹脂塗装　柱型/磁器質タイル貼り45角

ホテル全景をみる

キャノピーを１階ピロティー側よりみる
The canopy viewed from the pilotis side at the 1st floor.

２階のシーフード＆ステーキレストラン「マリーン」
The seafood & steak restaurant "Marine" at the 2nd floor.

三浦 シーサイド ホテル

夏の海は老若男女を問わず利用すべき空間であると考え それを"海老"をテーマとして全体をデザインしたが 前面に設置したキャノピーはトラス状のパーゴラとした。夏にはガーデン レストランとして利用し 冬は車路としてすぐに建物内に入ることができるという機能的な意味もある。

まだデザイン的には すぐ前にある海岸の波のイメージをキャノピーの三角形に求め 色彩も白という 空とか波といったものが連想されるような色使いをした。 〈西山泰成／原創建築設計事務所〉(87-11)

設計：原創建築設計事務所
施工：建築／日成工事
　　　内装／和光商会

構　　造：ＲＣ造
規　　模：地下１階　地上３階
面　　積：敷地／865.66㎡　建物／518.57㎡　延床／1751.45㎡
工　　期：1986年８月18日〜1987年７月６日

施設概要：開業／1987年７月９日
　　　　　経営／関矢産業㈱

Miura Seaside Hotel

Thinking that the summer sea is a space to be utilized by people regardless of age or sex, the entire structure was designed with a "lobster" as its theme. The canopy installed in the front side is formed like a trass-like pergola. It has functional implications — i.e. it is used as a garden restaurant in summer, and as a car lane in winter for easy access to the inside.

As for design, the image of waves along the seaside just before the hotel is presented by the canopy's triangle, etc., while the white color is used so that the sky, waves, etc. may be associated with.

Design: Yasunari Nishiyama

Structure : RC
Scale　　 : 1 under and 3 stories above the ground
Area　　　: Site/865.66 m²; Building/518.57 m², Total floor area/
　　　　　 1,751.45 m²
Term of construction: August 18, 1986 to July 6, 1987
Facilities : Opening/July 9, 1987; Management/Sekiya Sangyo Co.

２階よりの階段部よりロビーを見下ろす　イスラム風のアーチが象徴的
The lobby looked down upon from that staircase side close to the 2nd floor. The Islamic arch is symbolic.

葉山 ホテル音羽ノ森

神奈川県横須賀市秋谷字大崩5596-1　Phone/0468-57-0108

Hayama Hotel Otowa no Mori
5596-1, Akiya, Yokosuka city, Kanagawa, Japan
Phone/0468-57-0108

撮影/加茂一夫

２階より吹抜け空間のロビーを見下す

The lobby in the stairwell space looked down upon from the 2nd floor.

葉山 ホテル音羽ノ森

このホテルは　都心から100分前後　ＪＲ横須賀線・逗子駅より15分という交通至便なところにある。

目と鼻の先に長者ヶ崎を見下ろし　相模湾はもちろんのこと　伊豆大島　伊豆半島　さらに富士山まで一望することができる。

ロビー　フロントは徹底し　ヨーロッパから取り寄せた大理石の床。イスラム風のアーチと吹き抜けの天井。それらのコントラストによって一瞬のうちにイメージの錯覚を与えるようにした。

ダイニングルーム(レストラン潮幸)は180度の展望を得るため半円形として朝　昼　夜ともに変化する相模湾を眺望できるのが魅力である。

〈鈴木雄三/千創〉(88-06)

設計：千創
協力：日本国土開発
施工：日本国土開発

構　　造：Ｓ造
規　　模：地上３階
面　　積：敷地/1,831.77㎡　建築/1,124.90㎡　床/１階 414.90㎡(内 厨房56㎡)　２階 340㎡　３階 370㎡　合計1,124.90㎡
工　　期：1986年12月20日～1987年８月10日

施設概要：開店/1987年８月12日　営業時間/チェックイン　午後２時　チェックアウト　午前11時　客室数/22室　料飲施設/レストラン１　料金/スイート５～６万　ツイン２万2000～４万　経営/與田産業㈱　従業員数/サービス15人　厨房10人　パート　アルバイト５人　合計30人

Hayama Hotel Otowa no Mori

This hotel is conveniently situated – about 100 minutes from the center of Tokyo, and 15 minutes from Zushi Station, JR Yokosuka Line.

Just away from the hotel lies Choja-ga-Saki, and guests can also overlook Sagami Bay, Izu Oshima (Big Island), Izu Peninsula, and even Mt. Fuji.

The lobby and front floor fully covered with marble secured from Europe. The Islamic arch and stairwell. Through contrast of these elements, guests are instantly given an illusion of image.

"Restaurant Shiosachi" is situated over a semicircular space to allow guests to enjoy a view in 180 degrees of Sagami Bay whose scenery changes from morning to daytime and night.

Design: Yuzo Suzuki

Structure : S
Scale : 3 stories above the ground
Area : Site/1,831.77 m²; Building/1,124.90 m²; Floor/1st floor 414.90 m² (including kitchen 56 m²), 2nd floor 340 m², 3rd floor 370 m², totaling 1,124.90 m²
Term of construction: December 20, 1986 to August 10, 1987
Facilities : Opening/August 12, 1987; Open time/check-in at 2:00 p.m., check-out 11:00 a.m.; Number of guest rooms/ 22; Eating & drinking facilities/restaurant 1; Charges/suite 50,000 to 60,000 yen, twin 22,000 to 40,000 yen; Management/Yoda Sangyo Co.; Number of employees/service 15, kitchen 10, part-time 5, totaling 30

海側に半円形に突き出したレストランの客席　　　　　　　　The restaurant's guest seat area projected semicircularly towards the sea side.

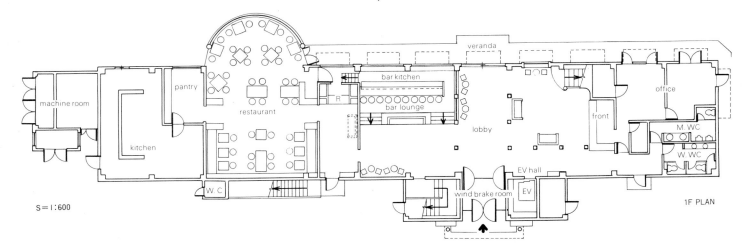

machine room

pantry

kitchen

restaurant

W.C

S=1:600

veranda

bar kitchen

R

bar lounge

lobby

front

office

M.WC

W.WC

EV hall

wind brake room

EV

1F PLAN

材料仕様

屋根/外断熱アスファルト露出防水　一部スパニッシュ洋瓦葺き　外壁/大型ＡＣＬ板下地吹き付けタイル仕上げ　一部インド砂岩 t＝25貼り　外部床/ピンコロ石貼り　サイン/ステンレスＨＬ仕上げ　文字真鍮（ＦＬ内蔵）　床/1階：ロビー　大理石貼り（カビストラ：イタリア産）　レストラン　テラゾタイル貼り（フェレマーブル）　2階　3階：じゅうたん敷　幅木/木製ウレタン仕上げ　h＝150　壁/1階：軽鉄ＰＢ t＝12下地漆喰仕上げ　2階　3階廊下部：漆喰仕上げ　腰壁/インド砂岩乱れ貼り　天井/軽鉄 t＝12下地クロス貼り　回り縁　スプルスラッカー仕上げ　レストラン貝殻形天井:石膏仕上げ

24

リゾートホテル / *Resort Hotel*

正面入口側のキャノピーとオフ ホワイトのホテル外観をみる

The canopy in the front entrance side and off-white hotel appearance.

ハイランドリゾート

山梨県富士吉田市上吉田5597-4　Phone/0555-22-1000

撮影/平沢写真事務所

Highland Resort

5597-4, Kami-Yoshida, Fuji-Yoshida city, Yamanashi, Japan
Phone/0555-22-1000

右上/ハイランドリゾート全景をみる
右下/トップライトのキャノピーのある正面入口をみる

Right, top/ The entire highland resort scene.
Right, bottom/ The front entrance with the top light canopy.

上/１階ロビー全景をみる
下/プールの水平に逆さ富士が映り込んだリゾート感覚溢れる３階室内プールをみる
Top/ The entire lobby scene at the 1st floor.
Bottom/ The 3rd floor indoor pool full of resort sense in whose water an inverted image of Mt. Fuji is reflected in parallel with the poolside.

上/12階のメインダイニングフロア中央の円形ソファ席をみる
下/地下１階のバーカウンター席をみる
Top/ The circular sofa seat in the center of the 12th floor main dining hall.
Bottom/ The bar counter seat area at the 1st basement.

大宴会場　　　　　　　　　　　　　　　　　　　　　　The large banquet hall.

1階のカフェレストラン　　　The cafe restaurant at the 1st floor.

チャペル　　　　　　　　　　　　　　　　　　The chapel.

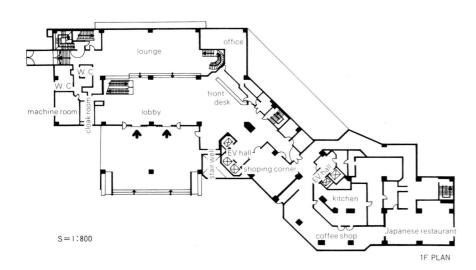

S＝1:800

1F PLAN

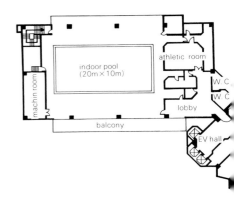

1階の日本料理「力車」
The Japanese restaurant "Rikisha" at the 1st floor.

スイートルーム
The suite room.

ハイランドリゾート

このホテルは 中央高速道路・河口湖インターチェンジの近く 周囲には雄大な富士山 富士急ハイランド 富士吉田市街の眺望景観の恵まれた環境に位置している。

基本構想は ヤング層を対象に観光の拠点としてのリゾートホテルの機能と 併せて地域への社会的貢献を考慮したシティ ホテル機能を兼ね備えたホテルをつくることにあった。

プランニングは 開放感のあるロビー ラウンジを中央に配し 西側にエスカレーター2基により国際会議 結婚式等のイベントに対応できる大宴会場 会議室へ。東側にはシースルーエレベーターで富士山を望みながら客室棟へアプローチするように配した。

〈斎藤民雄/朝吹一級建築士設計事務所〉(86-09)

トータルデザイン コーディネート:大石 尚
設計:朝吹一級建築士設計事務所
施工:鹿島建設横浜支店

構 造:SRC造
規 模:地下3階 地上12階
面 積:敷地/32,000㎡ 建築/3,039㎡ 床/地下3階 796.81㎡ 地下2階 2,928.12㎡ 地下1階 376.11㎡ 1階 1,986.34㎡ 2階 1,581.70㎡ 3階 813.11㎡ 4階 1,725.67㎡ 5～10階 各808.35㎡ 11階 820.50㎡ 12階 800.78㎡ 塔屋 197.07㎡ 合計16,876.31㎡
工 期:1984年6月1日～1986年2月15日

施設概要:開業/1986年3月22日 営業時間/チェックイン 午後2時 チェックアウト 正午 客室数/176室(ロイヤルスイート1 スイート3 和室6 ファミリールーム7 ツイン112 ダブル37 シングル10) 料飲施設/レストラン1(116席) カフェレストラン1(90席) 日本料理レストラン1(80席) バー1(50席) カクテルラウンジ1(30席) 料金/ロイヤルスイート 10万 スイート5万 和室3～5万 ファミリールーム2万7000～3万8000 ツイン1万7000～2万4000 経営/ハイランドリゾート㈱

Highland Resort

This hotel is favorably situated near Kawaguchi-ko Interchange of Chuo Speedway, and guests can enjoy a grand view of Mt. Fuji, Fujikyu Highland and streets of Fuji-Yoshida City.

The basic idea was to create a hotel having functions of a resort hotel that serves as a center of tourism for the young and also functions of a city hotel that can contribute to community welfare.

With the open lobby/lounge in the center, two escalators are provided in the west side to lead guests to a large banquet hall/board room that can accept events, such as an international conference and wedding. Another see-through elevator is arranged in the east side to allow guests to approach the guest room building while enjoying a view of Mt. Fuji from the elevator.

Design: Nao Oishi & Tamio Saito

Structure : SRC
Scale : 3 under and 12 stories above the ground
Area : Site/32,000 m²; Building/3,039 m²; Fooor/3rd basement 796.81 m², 2nd basement 2,928.12 m², 1st basement 376.11 m², 1st floor 1,986.34 m², 2nd floor 1,581.70 m², 3rd floor 813.11 m², 4th floor 1,725.67 m², 5th to 10th 808.35 m² each, 11th floor 820.50 m², 12th floor 800.78 m², roof floor 197.07 m², totaling 16,876.31 m²
Term of construction: June 1, 1984 to February 15, 1986
Facilities : Opening/March 22, 1986; Open time/check-in at 2:00 p.m., check-out at noon; Number of guest rooms/176 (royal suite 1, suite 3, Japanese room 6, family room 7, twin 112, double 37, single 10); Eating & drinking facilities/ restaurant 1 (116 seats), cafe restaurant 1 (90 seats), Japanese restaurant 1 (80 seats), bar 1 (50 seats), cocktail lounge 1 (30 seats); Charges/royal suite 100,000 yen, suite 50,000 yen, Japanese room 30,000 to 50,000 yen, family room 27,000 to 38,000 yen, twin 17,000 to 24,000 yen; Management/ Highland Resort Co.

材料仕様
屋上/アスファルト防水3層下地コンクリート押さえ プール屋根/打り板:s=60 石綿フェルトt=5貼り 一部トップライト アルミ枠8自然発色 外壁/磁器質タイル貼り(50×100貼り)
〈車寄せ回り〉 屋上/アスファルト防水3層 軽鉄コンクリート下地 エポキシ系塗装 トップライト/アルミ枠 網入りガラスt=10 Fix 床/御影石t=30貼り アスファルト防水下地 ジェット仕上げ 柱/大理石貼り 天井&廂裏/3.アルミスパンドレル貼り パラペット笠木/カラーアルミパネル貼り
〈ロビー〉 床/テラゾブロック化粧貼り 幅木/大理石貼り 壁/大理石貼り テラゾブロック貼り(柱部) 天井/PB下地 石綿吸音板キューブ型t=9貼り 一部石綿吸音板貼り
〈1階 カフェレストラン「ザ ブライトン ベル」〉 床/楢フローリング 一部大理石貼り 壁/PBt=12下地 寒冷紗VP 一部大理石貼り 天井/PBt=12下地VP
〈1階 日本料理「力車」〉 床/玄昌石貼り300角 一部玉砂利敷 幅木/御影石貼り h=50 腰h=800 杉板貼り 壁/PBt=12GL工法下地 ビニールクロス貼り 天井/ジュラクサテン吹き付け 網代貼り 一部竿天井(杉t=900 100×50貼り)
〈12階 メインダイニング「ル トラン ブルー」〉 床/じゅうたん敷 壁&天井/PBt=12下地VP
〈客室〉 床/じゅうたん敷 壁&天井/ビニールクロス貼り

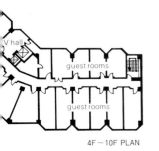

4F～10F PLAN

西欧の"舘"をイメージした外観をみる

湯ヶ嶋高原倶楽部ホテル

静岡県田方郡天城湯ヶ嶋町持越2571-10　Phone/05588-5-0333

撮影/平沢写真事務所

Yugashima Kogen Club Hotel
2571-10, Amagi Yugashima-cho, Tagata-gun, Shizuoka, Japan　　Phone/05588-5-0333

ゴルフコースの中央に建つホテル

The appearance imaging a West European "mansion."

吹抜けの中庭をみる

The courtyard in the stairwell area.

The hotel built in the center of the golf course.

正面入口外観をみる

The front entrance appearance.

上／1階プロムナードの右手にあるティーラウンジよりショップのファサードをみる
下／3階のダイニングルーム

Top/ The shop's facade viewed from the tea lounge in the right side of the 1st floor promenade.
Bottom/ The dining room at the 3rd floor.

上／地下1階のレストラン
下／1階の日本料理店

Top/ The restaurant at the 1st basement.
Bottom/ Japanese restaurant at the 1st floor.

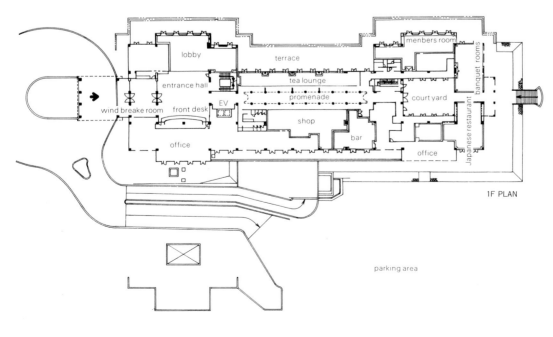
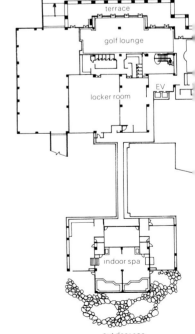

1F PLAN

湯ヶ嶋高原倶楽部ホテル

この倶楽部は　現代人の日常的体験にはない非日常的な開放感と情緒性が体験できるものを自然と科学を共生させる　ことによって実現させることを目指した。

建物のイメージは　世紀末から今世紀初頭にかけて　アメリカ東部で多大な喝采を浴びた建築集団＝マッキム　ミード　アンド　ホワイト事務所の古典的な美観のなかに　現代を超えた情感をただよわせる人間的なイメージの広がりを　建築という媒体を介して　よみがえらせた。

インテリアデザインは　1920年代後半から30年代の人間とモノの関係が見直された　アール　デコを基調とした壮麗な内部空間を実現させた。

〈松本留樹/オールファッションアート研究所〉(86-09)

企画　　　　　：日誠総業
総合プロデュース：松本瑠樹＆オールファッションアート研究所
ＣＩ　　　　　：電通
設計　　　　　：住友建設一級建築士事務所
施工　　　　　：住友建設静岡支店

構　　造：ＲＣ造
規　　模：地下１階　地上４階
面　　積：敷地/1,556,665.17㎡　建築/4,338.75㎡　床/地下1階 3,781.12㎡　1階 2,445.32㎡　2階 2,040.65㎡　3階 1,833.55㎡　4階 401.76㎡　合計10,502.40㎡
工　　期：1985年5月1日～1986年4月30日

施設概要：開業/1986年5月23日　営業時間/チェックイン　午後3時　チェックアウト　午前11時　客室数/50室(ロイヤルスイート2　スイート4　ツイン40　ダブル2　シングル2)　料飲施設/レストラン2(190席)　ティーラウンジ1(24席)　日本料理レストラン1(44席)　中国料理レストラン1(78席)　バー1(26席)　施設/ゴルフコース(18ホール)　テニスコート　料金/会員制　(　)内はビジター料金　ロイヤルスイート/5万(15万)　スイート/3万(7万)　ツイン/6000～1万2000(2～3万)　ダブル/6000(1万6000)　シングル/3000(7000)　経営/㈱湯ヶ嶋高原倶楽部

Yugashima Kogen Club Hotel

This club is aimed to serve as a place where modern people can experience something that makes us feel open or rich — something that cannot be experienced in daily life — by causing nature and science to go together.

The building's image is based on a classical beauty realized by Mckim Mead & White Office, an architects' group hotly accepted in the East from the end of the 19th century to the beginning of this century, and the designer revived a sentimental, humane image that transcends time, through an architecture as a medium.

The interior design is based on an image of art deco that appeared in the latter half of the 1920s to the 30s when relations between man and thing were reviewed, giving rise to a splendid interior space.

Design: Ruki Matsumoto & Kenichi Kumazawa

Structure : RC
Scale　　 : 1 under and 4 stories above the ground
Area　　 : Site/1,556,665.17 m²;　Building/4,338.75 m²;　Floor/ 1st basement 3,781.12 m², 1st floor 2,445.32 m², 2nd floor 2,040.65 m², 3rd floor 1,833.55 m², 4th floor 401.76 m², totaling 10,502.40 m²
Term of construction: May 1, 1985 to April 30, 1986
Facilities : Opening/May 23, 1986; Open time/check-in at 3:00 p.m., check-out at 11:00 a.m.; Number of guest rooms/50 (royal suite 2, suite 4, twin 40, double 2, single 2); Eating & drinking facilities/restaurant 2 (190 seats), tea lounge 1 (24 seats), Japanese restaurant 1 (44 seats), Chinese restaurant 1 (78 seats), bar 1 (26 seats); Sports/ golf course (18 holes), tennis court; Charges/membership system; figures in ( ) show visitor charge, royal suite 50,000 (150,000) yen, suite 30,000 (70,000) yen, twin 6,000 to 12,000 (20,000 to 30,000) yen, double 6,000 (16,000) yen, single 3,000 (7,000) yen; Management/Yugashima Kogen Club Co.

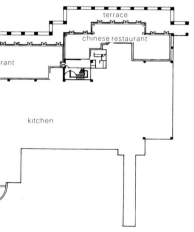

B1 PLAN　S＝1:1000

材料仕様

屋根/天然スレート t ＝6葺き(玄昌石/東北天然スレート工事)　外壁/モルタル鏝塗下地　特注タイル貼り　ペディメント(三角の切妻壁)/漆喰塗　独立柱/花崗岩　外部床/磁器タイル貼り100角

〈1階　エントランスホール〉床/大理石市松模様貼り　幅木/大理石貼り　壁/インド砂岩貼り(割肌　砂擦り)　天井/蛭石吹き付け　プロムナード上部/アスベスト成形板下地リシン吹き付け　フロントカラー/大理石

〈1階　ロビー〉床/ウールカーペット t ＝10敷　一部大理石貼り　幅木/ウォールナット練り付けCL　壁/寒冷紗下地EP　一部インド砂岩貼り　天井/蛭石吹き付け　木製化粧梁/セラミック系人造木材下地　化粧単板貼り仕上げ

〈1階　ティーラウンジ〉床/大理石市松模様貼り　幅木/大理石貼り　レンガタイル貼り　壁/レンガタイル貼り　一部プラスター壁装　インド砂岩貼り　回り縁/ニヤトOS　CL

〈1階　ショップ〉床/楢フローリング t ＝15貼り　一部カーペット敷　幅木/ラワンOSCL　壁/プラスター塗装　腰/タモ練り付け合板貼りOSCL　天井/蛭石吹き付け

〈1階　日本料理「石楠花」〉床/炉器質タイル貼り　板の間/栗小幅板貼り　OSCL　幅木/ニヤトポリウレタン塗装　壁/聚楽鏝押さえ　天井/蛭石吹き付け　回り縁/ニヤトウポリウレタン塗装　板の間/柾目練り付け合板目透し貼りOSCL

〈3階　メインダイニングルーム「ロサージュ」〉床/ウールカーペット T ＝10敷一部楢フローリング　ウレタン塗装　幅木/マホガニー練り付け　壁/プラスター塗装　腰/マホガニー練り付け合板貼りOSCL　天井/蛭石吹き付け　化粧モール/マホガニー練り付けSOCL

〈地下1階　レストラン「アルペンローズ」〉床/ゴルフ用ナイロンカーペット t・＝10敷　一部フローリング t ＝15貼り　ウレタン塗装　幅木/タイル貼り　壁/プラスター化粧目地仕上げ　腰:タイル貼り　天井/蛭石吹き付け　化粧モール/マンガンシロOSCL

〈地下1階　中国料理「紅長寿」〉床/ゴルフ用ナイロンカーペット t ＝18敷　一部大理石パターン貼り　幅木/ニヤトウOSCL　壁/クロス貼り　天井/クロス貼り　回り縁　化粧モール/ニヤトウOSCL　ガラススクリーン/エッチング仕上げ

〈客室〉床/ウールカーペット t ＝7敷　一部楢フローリング/アガチスOP　壁＆天井クロス貼り

1階エレベーターホールよりプロムナードをみる　彫刻はR.ガルフ作「マーメイド」
The promenade viewed from the 1st floor elevator hall. The sculpture is "Mermaid" produced by R. Gulf.

既存東館より増築部分大浴場の屋上庭園をみる
左側の既存西館とはブリッジで結ばれている

The roof garden on the big bathroom that has been extended, as viewed from the existing East Building which is connected to the existing West Building in the leftside through the bridge.

撮影/福本正明

西館よりみた増築部分大浴場の屋上庭園　池の水は循環して浴場階のレベルに達する
The roof garden on the extended big bathroom, as viewed from the West Building. The pond water is circulated, reaching the bathroom floor level.

兵衛向陽閣

神戸市北区有馬町丸山1904　Phone/078-904-0501

Hyoe Koyokaku
1904, Maruyama Arima-cho, Kita-ku, Kobe city, Hyogo, Japan
Phone/078-904-0501

和風で構成した"一の湯"からみた庭 "一の湯"と"二の湯"の二つの大浴場は朝夕で男女別がチェンジし 一泊で二つの浴場スタイルが楽しめる
The garden viewed from "Ichino-yu" (1st bathroom) arranged in Japanese style. "Ichino-yu" and "Nino-yu" (2nd bathroom) change in male and female use between morning and evening, so that guests can enjoy two styles of bathroom during a night's stay.

屋上庭園より滝を伝わって池へ落ちる水の流れ
The flow of water dropping along the waterfall from the roof garden.

ローマ風大浴場の"二の湯"
"Nino-yu" — a big Roman style bathroom.

"二の湯"景観を展望できるようにフロアレベルが設定されている　　　The floor level is set so that the "Nino-yu" scenery may be overlooked entirely.

"一の湯"全景

The entire view of "Ichino-yu."

"二の湯"浴室手前の小路に面した休息スペース
The rest space facing the lane in front of the "nino-yu" bathroom.

大浴場入口ホールの待合と奥へ続く堀割り
The waiting room in the entrance hall of the big bath room, and the canal leading to an inner area.

兵衛向陽閣

太閤秀吉の好んだ有馬温泉は全国に名だたる温泉地である。心尽くしの
サービスと味わい深い料理を提供する旅館が多く建ち並び「兵衛向陽閣」
もその一つである。施設も 南 東 西 西新館からなり 大小多数の
宴会場 料亭 娯楽室 ボーリング場 そして大浴場と かなり充実を
みせている。しかし その歴史の積み重ねが施設の拡張を余儀なくし
反面 部分的に立ちおくれを生じている。
今回の改築と増築は これらに対応すべく 旅館にとって欠くことのでき
ない要素である大浴場と 心臓ともいえる厨房の老朽化及び規模的支
障に対して行なわれた。　　〈山本勝昭/山本勝建築設計室〉(88-06)

設計:山本　勝建築設計室
協力:構造/大橋構造設計事務所
　　　設備/石井設備設計
施工:鴻池組

構　　造:RC造
規　　模:地下2階　地上1階(増築部分)
面　　積:敷地/17,925.27m²　延床/15,222.46m²(内　増床面積 2,689.31
　　　m²/浴槽階 1,034.29m²　改装床面積 624.52m² プラザ パート
　　　II)
工　　期:1986年11月4日～1987年7月4日(増築部分)
　　　1987年8月1日～1987年9月30日(改装部分)

施設概要:開業/1987年7月11日(大浴場)　1987年10月1日(プラザ パー
　　　トII)　営業時間/チェックイン　午後3時　チェックアウト
　　　午前10時　客室数/165室　料金/1万5000～3万5000　経営/兵
　　　衛旅館別館向陽閣　風早喜一　従業員数/293人　パート/95人
　　　合計388人

Hyoe Koyokaku

Arima Onsen (Hot Spring) used to be frequented by Taikou (General) Hideyoshi, and has been one of the most famous hot spring resorts in Japan. There are many traditional hotels entertaining guests with hospitable service and tasty dishes. "Hyoe Koyokaku" is one of them. The facilities consist of south, east, west and new west hotels, and also of small to large banquet halls, restaurants, amusement rooms, bowling alley, and large bathrooms. However, because of its long history, this time-honored hotel had to expand its facilities, leaving some of the old facilities intact.
The current rebuilding and extension were carried out in view of superannuation and insufficient space of big bathrooms and kitchen that are the indispensable hotel elements.

Design: Katsuaki Yamamoto

Structure : RC
Scale : 2 under and 1 story above the ground (extended part)
Area : Site/17,925.27 m²; Total floor area/15,222.46 m² (including extended floor 2,689.31 m²/bathroom floor 1,034.29 m², renovated floor area 624.52 m² (Plaza Part II)
Term of construction: November 4, 1986 to July 4, 1987 (extended part)
　　　August 1, 1987 to September 30, 1987 (renovated part)
Facilities : Opening/July 11, 1987 (large bathroom), October 1, 1987 (Plaza Part II); Open time/check-in at 3:00 p.m., check-out at 10:00 a.m.; Number of guest rooms/165; Charges/15,000 to 35,000 yen; Management/Hyoe Ryokan Bekkan Koyokaku, Kiichi Kazehaya; Number of employees/full-time 293, part-time 95, totaling 388

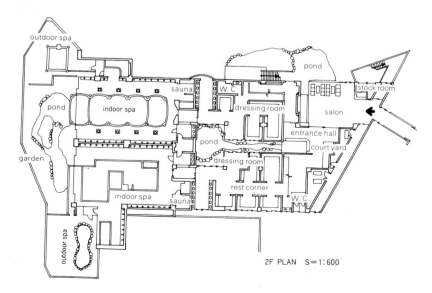

2F PLAN　S=1:600

材料仕様
〈1階大浴場「一の場」〉床/青石水磨き　一部赤御影石ジェットバーナー
仕上げ　浴槽内/石英岩　浴槽縁/錆び御影石水磨き　壁/錆び御影石水磨き
天井＆梁形/アルミ加工品にジュラクロン塗装　天井/アルミスパンドレル
にジュラクロン塗装　トップライト:ガラスブロック　照明器具/防水型F
L　一部白熱燈
〈1階大浴場「二の湯」〉床/石英質砂岩　一部赤御影石ジェットバーナー
仕上げ　浴槽内:御影石ジェットバーナー仕上げ　浴槽縁/大理石水磨き
壁/大理石本磨き　天井/梁型:アルミ加工品にジュラクロン塗装　天板:ア
ルミスパンドレルにジュラクロン塗装　トップライト:アルミ加工枠特注網
入り型ガラス＋樹脂系ステンドグラス　照明器具/特注白熱燈

アーバン リゾートホテル／*Urban Resort Hotel*

東京湾に面したファサード

The facade facing Tokyo Bay.

撮影／鳴瀬　亨

メインエントランス側のファサード

The facade in the main entrance side.

東京ベイ ヒルトン インターナショナル

千葉県浦安市舞浜1-8　Phone/0473-55-5000

Tokyo Bay Hilton International

1-8, Maihama, Urayasu city, Chiba, Japan　　Phone/0473-55-5000

上/屋外プール　プールサイドにはプール スナック バーが併設されている
下/2階より1階「ベイラウンジ」をみる

Top/ The outdoor pool. The pool snack bar is open along the poolside.
Bottom/ ''Bay Lounge'' at the 1st floor, viewed from the 2nd floor.

2階・大宴会場「クリスタル」前より「ベイラウンジ」をみる　　　　　　　　　"Bay Lounge" viewed from the 2nd floor big banquet hall "Crystal."

1階・イタリアンレストラン

Italian restaurant at the 1st floor.

東京ベイ ヒルトン インターナショナル
このホテルは インターナショナルに識別できる日本のデザイン表現を
目指した。すなわち ヒルトンホテルは 海外展開の施設コンセプトに
機能面では仕様を守りながら 建設地の特徴を生かしたデザインをする
という基本的姿勢がある "祭り" "海" "江戸" "東京" といったデザイン
コンセプトを提案する中で これら個性のあるデザインを展開している。
配置計画としては 全客室が海と東京ディズニーランドに面し ロビー
からは海を臨み 振り返れば シンデレラキャッスルが見える立地を100
％生かした計画といえる。 〈森一朗/日本設計事務所〉(88-09)
設計:建築/日本設計事務所
　　　内装/日本設計事務所　チャダ シンビエダ アソシエイト
協力:照明/石井幹子デザイン事務所　チャイルズ アソシエイト
　　　造園/愛植物設計事務所
施工:清水建設　竹中工務店　日本建設　三井建設 J.V.

構　　造:地下/SRC造　一部RC造　地上/SRC造　一部S造
規　　模:地下1階　地上11階　塔屋1階
面　　積:敷地/59,504.20m²　建築/20,065.21m²(隣接　NKホール含む)
　　　　床/地下1階 12,190.51m²　1階 8,671.62m²　2階 8,713.28
　　　　m²　3階 5,534.12m²　4～11階 4,609.83m²　塔屋 405.63m²
　　　　合計72,393.80m²
工　　期:1986年8月12日～1988年6月30日

施設概要:開業/1988年7月2日　営業時間/チェックイン 午後3時 チ
　　　　ェックアウト　正午　客室数/770室　料飲施設/レストラン5
　　　　日本料理レストラン1　中国料理レストラン1　ラウンジ2
　　　　バー1　料金/デラックス スイート18万　スーベリア スイー
　　　　ト 1ベッドルーム5万5000　2ベッドルーム7万5000　スイー
　　　　ト 1ベッドルーム5万　2ベッドルーム7万　和室 4万2000
　　　　～5万(6人まで)　エグゼクティブ フロア/1人2万3000 2
　　　　万6000　2人2万7000 3万　スタンダード1人1万6000　2
　　　　人1万9000　スーベリア 1人1万9000　2人2万2000　デラ
　　　　ックス 1人2万2000　2人2万5000　駐車場/400台収容　経
　　　　営/東京ベイヒルトン㈱

Tokyo Bay Hilton International

In designing this hotel, it was intended to express something through
which Japan may be identified internationally. That is, in its overseas
development, Hilton Hotel chain makes it a basic concept to keep to
the basic specifications for functions, but utilize features of the place
for construction. Observing this concept, "Tokyo Bay Hilton International" was designed by incorporating "festival," "sea," "Edo,"
"Tokyo," etc. as characteristic design elements. In overall hotel
arrangement, all guest rooms are designed to face the sea and Tokyo
Disneyland, and from the lobby the sea can be overlooked. When
looked back upon, Cinderella Castle is visible. Thus, the eventful
location is fully utilized.

Design: Nihon Architects, Engineers & Consultants, Inc.

Structure : Basement/SRC (RC in part); Above the ground/SRC
　　　　　　(S in part)
Scale 　　: 1 under and 11 stories above the ground, and 1 floor on
　　　　　　the roof
Area 　　: Site/59,504.20 m²; Building/20,065.21 m² (including the
　　　　　　adjacent NK Hall); Floor/1st basement 12,190.51 m²,
　　　　　　1st floor 8,671.62 m², 2nd floor 8,713.28 m², 3rd floor
　　　　　　5,534.12 m², 4th to 11th floor 4,609.83 m² each, roof
　　　　　　floor 405.63 m², totaling 72,393.80 m²
Term of construction: August 12, 1986 to June 30, 1988
Facilities : Opening/July 2, 1988; Open time/check-in at 3:00 p.m.,
　　　　　　check-out at noon; Number of guest rooms/770; Eating
　　　　　　& drinking facilities/restaurant 5, Japanese restaurant 1,
　　　　　　Chinese restaurant 1, lounge 2, bar 1;
　　　　　　Charges/deluxe suite — 180,000 yen; superior suite —
　　　　　　1 bedroom 55,000 yen, 2 bedrooms 75,000 yen; suite —
　　　　　　1 bedroom 50,000 yen, 2 bedrooms 70,000 yen; Japa-
　　　　　　nese style room 42,000 to 50,000 yen (up to 6 persons);
　　　　　　executive floor — single 23,000 to 26,000 yen, 2 persons
　　　　　　27,000 to 30,000 yen; standard — single 16,000 yen,
　　　　　　2 persons 19,000 yen; superior — single 19,000 yen,
　　　　　　2 persons 22,000 yen; deluxe — single 22,000 yen,
　　　　　　2 persons 25,000 yen; Parking lot/400 cars accommo-
　　　　　　dated; Management/Tokyo Bay Hilton Co.

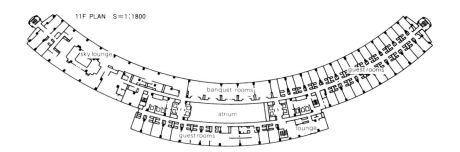

11F PLAN S=1:1800

sky lounge
banquet rooms
atrium
guest rooms
guest rooms
lounge

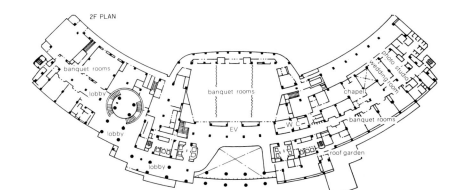

2F PLAN

banquet rooms
lobby
banquet rooms
EV
WC
chapel
photo studio
wedding room
banquet rooms
roof garden
lobby
lobby
lobby

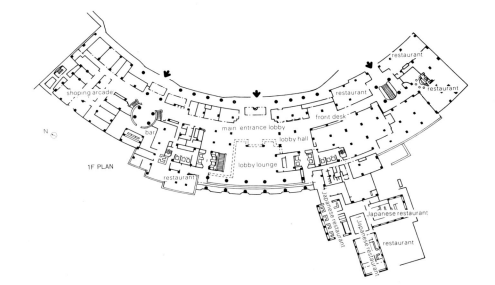

N

shoping arcade
bar
restaurant
restaurant
restaurant
restaurant
front desk
main entrance lobby
lobby hall
lobby lounge
restaurant
Japanese restaurant
Japanese restaurant
restaurant

1F PLAN

1/1階　中国レストラン
2/11階　スカイラウンジ
3/2階　中宴会場
4/客室（スタンダード）

1/ Chinese restaurant at the 1st floor.
2/ Sky lounge at the 11th floor.
3/ The medium-size banquet hall at the 2nd floor.
4/ The guest room (standard).

材料仕様

屋根/アスファルト防水コンクリート金鏝押さえ　低層部/アスファルト露出防水砂利敷　外壁/モザイクタイル貼り　アルミサッシュラクロン焼き付け塗装透明ガラス　エントランス/真鍮サッシ本磨き透明ガラス　外部床/磁器タイル貼り　エントランス：御影石ジェットバーナー仕上げ　一部本磨き仕上げ　サイン/ステンレス塗装仕上げ

〈エントランスホール〉床/大理石 t＝25本磨き仕上げ　壁/大理石 t＝25本磨き仕上げ　天井/PBt＝9下地ビニールクロス貼り

〈客室〉床/コンクリート金鏝下地じゅうたん貼り　幅木/塩ビ系幅木　h＝60　壁/PBt＝12二重貼り及びコンクリート下地ビニールクロス貼り　天井/PBt＝9下地ビニールクロス貼り

〈大 中 小宴会場〉床/コンクリート金鏝下地じゅうたん貼り　幅木/桜練り付けCL　h＝150　壁/PBt＝9＋t＝12下地クロス貼り　桜練り付けCLミラー貼り　天井/PBt＝9下地EP　PBt＝9下地ビニールクロス貼り　一部ミラー貼り及びアルミルーバー

アーバン リゾートホテル / *Urban Resort Hotel*

西側に設けられた宴会場への入口廻り

The entrance area leading to the banquet hall in the west side.

第一ホテル東京ベイ

千葉県浦安市舞浜1-8　Phone/0473-55-3333

Dai-ichi Hotel Tokyo Bay
1-8, Maihama, Urayasu city, Chiba, Japan　　Phone/0473-55-3333

撮影/T.ナカサ＆パートナーズ

コートヤード全景   The entire courtyard scene.

宴会場の屋根に設けられたドルフィンの彫刻
The dolphin sculpture installed on the banquet hall's roof.

第一ホテル 東京ベイ

このホテルは「東京ディズニーランド」に隣接し　東京湾ウォーターフロント開発計画の一翼を担う浦安ホテル群の中にあって　最高水準の都市型リゾートホテルとして建設された。

基本設計はベケット社によってなされ　装飾的な舗装がされたクロイスター状のコートヤードを中心に　これを囲むヴォールト天井の回廊のまわりに　レストランをはじめとするアメニティ空間が配されている　客室構成は　このコートヤードを囲むようにコの字型に海に向かって開いて配置されており　428室の規模となっている　コートヤードに立つと南側の宴会場の屋根が青い海　うねる大波のように浮かんでおり　波頭には神聖なドルフィンの彫刻が躍動している。

〈佐野幸夫/鹿島建設建築設計本部〉(88-09)

設計:建築/鹿島建設建築設計本部　ベケット インターナショナル
　　　内装/メディア ファイブ　魁総合設計事務所　イリア
施工:建築/鹿島建設建築設計本部
　　　内装/鹿島建設建築設計本部　イリア

構　　造:SRC造　一部RC造
規　　模:地下1階　地上11階　塔屋1階
面　　積:敷地/21,157㎡　建築/6,629.54㎡　床/地下1階　6,809.37㎡
　　　　1階 5,881.44㎡　2階 6,056.11㎡　3階 2,871.37㎡ 4～7階
　　　　各3,026.14㎡　8階 2,983.99㎡　9階 2,847.81㎡　10階
　　　　1,228.72㎡　11階 1,075.78㎡　塔屋 306.05㎡ 合計42,165.20
　　　　㎡
工　　期:1986年9月1日～1988年6月30日

施設概要:開業/1988年7月8日　営業時間/チェックイン 午後3時　チェックアウト　正午　客室数/428室(モデレイトタイプ　ツイン52室　ダブル14室　スーペリアタイプ ツイン120室 ダブル24室　デラックスタイプ ツイン119室　ダブル42室　和室12室　和室スイート3室　ジュニアスイート ツイン10室　ダブル20室　シニアスイート4室　エグゼクティブスイート6室 アンバサダースイート1室 ロイヤルスイート1室)　料飲施設/レストラン1　日本料理レストラン1　中国料理レストラン1　ティーサロン1　バー1　料金/モデレイトタイプ1人2万2000　2人 2万6000　スーペリアタイプ1人 2万6000　2人 3万2000　デラックスタイプ 1人 3万 2人 3万6000　和室4万　和室スイート 5万5000　ジュニアスイート ツイン 5万5000　ダブル 5万　シニアスイート 6万5000　エグゼクティブスイート 7万5000　アンバサダースイート 10万 ロイヤルスイート 35万　駐車場/190台収容 経営/東京ベイ第一リゾート㈱

1階・オールディダイニング

Dai-ichi Hotel Tokyo Bay

Located among a group of hotels in Urayasu that is adjacent to "Tokyo Disneyland" and forms part of Tokyo Bay Waterfront Development Program, this hotel was constructed as a first-rate urban resort hotel.

The basic design was undertaken by Becket. A cloister-like, decoratively paved courtyard in the center is surrounded with a vaulted corridor along which restaurants and other amenities are placed. The guest rooms (as many as 428) are arranged in the form of ⊐ facing the sea, just surrounding the courtyard. Standing on the courtyard, the roof of the southern banquet hall is floating like swelling waves in the blue sea, with the carved sacred dolphins alive on the crest.

Design: Kajima Construction Inc./Becket International

Structure : SRC (RC in part)
Scale　　: 1 under and 11 stories above ground, and 1 floor on the roof
Area　　 : Site/21,157 m²; Building/6,629.54 m²; Floor/1st basement 6,809.37 m², 1st floor 5,881.44 m², 2nd floor 6,056.11 m², 3rd floor 2,871.37 m², 4th to 7th floor 3,026.14 m² each, 8th floor 2,983.99 m², 9th floor 2,847.81 m², 10th floor 1,228.72 m², 11th floor 1,075.78 m², roof floor 306.05 m², totaling 42,165.20 m²
Term of construction: September 1, 1986 to June 30, 1988
Facilities : Opening/July 8, 1988; Open time/chieck-in at 3:00 p.m., check-out at noon; Number of guest rooms/428 (moderate type – twin 52, double 14, superior type – twin 120, double 24, deluxe type – twin 119, double 42, Japanese style 12, Japanese suite 3, junior suite – twin 10, double 20, senior suite 4, executive suite 6, ambassador suite 1, royal suite 1); Eating & drinking facilities/restaurant 1, Japanese restaurant 1, Chinese restaurant 1, tea salon 1, bar 1;
Charges/moderate type – single 22,000 yen, 2 persons 26,000 yen; superior type – single 26,000 yen, 2 persons 32,000 yen; deluxe type – single 30,000 yen, 2 persons 36,000 yen; Japanese style 40,000 yen; Japanese suite 55,000 yen; junior suite – twin 55,000 yen, double 50,000 yen; senior suite 65,000 yen, executive suite 75,000 yen, ambassador suite 100,000 yen, royal suite 350,000 yen; Parking lot/190 cars accommodated; Management/Tokyo Bay Dai-ichi Resort Co.

The all-day dining hall at the 1st floor.

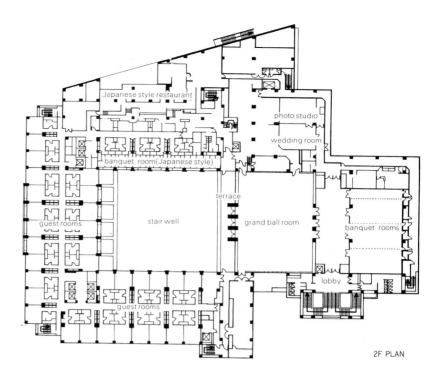

2F PLAN

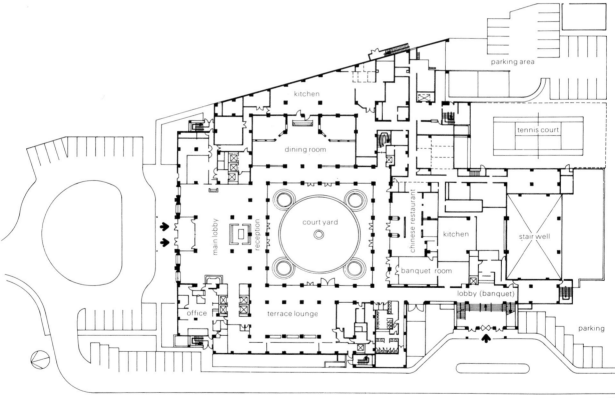

1F PLAN S=1:1000

材料仕様
屋根/アスファルト断熱防水の上コンクリート押さえ　一部カラーアルミ葺き　外壁/磁器タイル貼り45×95　一部砂岩貼り　吹き付けタイル　アルミサッシ電解着色　キャストアルミジ
ュラクロン焼き付け塗装　外部床/車寄せ:インターロッキングブロック　歩道:磁器タイル貼り　車道:アスファルト舗装　コートヤード/大理石テラゾ現場研出し
〈ロビー〉床/大理石本磨き　カーペット　幅木/大理石本磨きh＝150　壁&天井/ＰＢ下地ＡＥＰ　モールディング:アルミ下地処理の上ＯＰ
〈回廊〉床/大理石本磨き　幅木/大理石本磨き　h＝150　壁/ＰＢ下地ＡＥＰ　天井/石膏現場施工ＡＥＰ
〈客室〉床/カーペット　幅木/木製ＳＯＰ　h＝130　壁&天井/ＰＢ下地ＡＥＰ　モールディング/アルミ下地処理の上ＯＰ

地下１階・会員制ヘルスガーデンの屋内プール

The indoor pool at the 1st basement membership health garden.

１階回廊よりコートヤードをみる
The courtyard viewed from the 1st floor corridor.

３階・茶室
The tearoom at the 3rd floor.

国立京都国際会館からみた南面外観全景
The entire south side appearance viewed from Kokuritsu Kyoto Kokusai Kaikan (National Kyoto International Conference Hall).

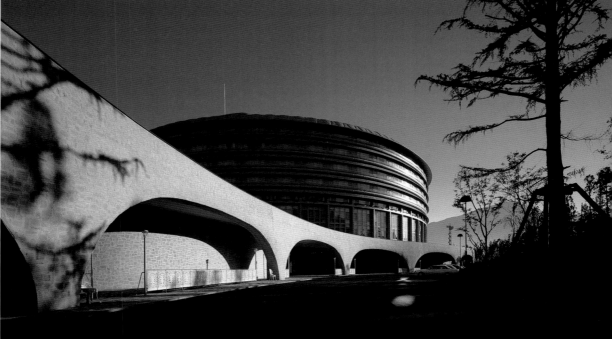

撮影／藤原 弘

エントランス アプローチ側より南面の高層宿泊棟と低層棟をみる
The south side high-rise hotel building and low building viewed from the entrance approach side.

京都宝ヶ池 プリンスホテル

京都市左京区宝ヶ池　Phone／075-712-1111

Kyoto Takaragaike Prince Hotel
Takaragaike, Sakyo-ku, Kyoto city, Japan　Phone／075-712-1111

1階ロビーより階段吹抜け部の柱とシャンデリアをみる

The stairwell pillar and chandelier viewed from the 1st floor lobby.

1階中庭に面して配された"すし 天ぷら"コーナーの座敷席

Japanese seat area of "Sushi · Tenpura" corner facing the 1st floor courtyard.

1階北側奥のフランス レストランの個室

The private room in the French restaurant at a northern inner part of the 1st floor.

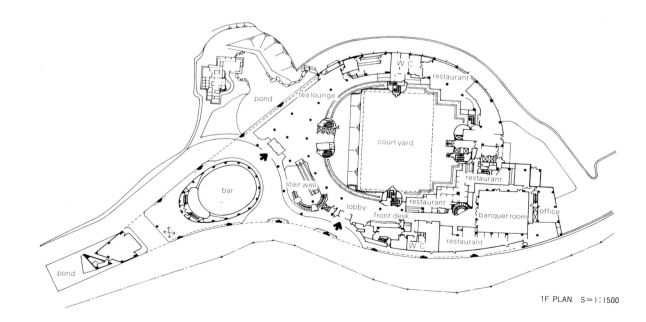

1F PLAN S=1:1500

東側より中庭を通して西側宿泊棟をみる

The west side hotel building viewed from the east side through the courtyard.

地下2階の宴会場　ゴールドルームの壁面ディテール　故・村野藤吾の残されたスケッチによるもの
The banquet hall at the 2nd basement. The wall details in the gold room; based on the sketch of late Togo Murano.

左頁下/宿泊棟と池を隔てた西北側に別棟として建てられた"茶寮"
Left page, bottom/ "Tea Ceremony House" built independently in the northwestern side across the pond from the hotel building.

京都宝ヶ池 プリンスホテル

このホテルは　隣接する国立京都国際会議とその周辺に宿泊施設がないために　地元行政側からの要請があったこと　もう一つは　京都におけるハイエスト クラスの社交場を備えたリゾート型の一流ホテルをというオーナー側の基本姿勢から生まれた。

周辺地域は京都の風情を残す美しい環境でもあり　地上に高くボリュームのある建築は避け　天井高及び広さの必要な宴会施設は地下2階レベルまで下げ　地上一階の長く広い低層部と中庭を持つ地上8階の楕円型宿泊棟を柔らかな曲線でデザインした。

また　ホテル棟と池を隔てて建つ"茶寮"は　本格的なお茶会ができるホテルの施設では関西でも数少ないものである。

〈近藤正志/村野・森建築事務所〉(87-01)

基本設計：村野藤吾
設　計：村野・森建築事務所
施　工：竹中工務店

構　　造：SRC造
規　　模：地下2階　地上8階　塔屋2階
面　　積：敷地/29,238.84㎡　建築/7,045.26㎡　床/地下2階 7,886.40
　　　　　㎡　地下1階 4,027.79㎡　1階 6,042.19㎡　2階 2,631.17㎡
　　　　　3・4階　各2,617.17㎡　5〜8階　各2,746.07㎡　屋階 307.69㎡
　　　　　合計37,113.86㎡
工　　期：1984年8月17日〜1986年10月6日

施設概要：開業/1986年10月9日　営業時間/チェックイン 正午 チェック
　　　　　アウト　正午　客室数/322室（ツイン252室　ダブル42室 スイ
　　　　　ート21室　ロイヤルスイート7室）料金/ツイン3〜3万6000
　　　　　ダブル3〜3万3000　スイート7〜8万　ロイヤルスイート
　　　　　18〜20万　経営/㈱プリンスホテル

This hotel was born in response to the local administrative request for construction a hotel, since there were no hotel facilities around the adjacent Kokuritsu Kyoto Kokusai Kaikan (National Kyoto International Conference Hall), and also to the owner's basic request for creating a first-rate resort type hotel equipped with one of the highest class social clubs in Kyoto.

Since the surrounding area is in a beautiful environment rich with elegant Kyoto elements, a highrise, voluminous structure was avoided. The banquet facilities that require a high ceiling and wide space, were lowered to the 2nd basement, and the 8-storied oval hotel building with lengthy and wide lower segments and a courtyard were designed by using gentle curves.

A "tea ceremony house" separate from the hotel building can be used for a full-scale tea ceremony – one of the few such hotel facilities in Kansai district.

Design: Togo Murano

Structure : SRC
Scale : 2 under and 8 stories above the ground, and 2 roof floors
Area : Site/29,238.84 m²；Building/7,045.26 m²；Floor/2nd basement 7,886.40 m²，1st basement 4,027.79 m²，1st floor 6,042.19 m²，2nd floor 2,631.17 m²，3rd and 4th floor 2,617.17 m² each, 5th to 8th floor 2,746.07 m² each, roof floor 307.69 m², totaling 37.113.86 m²
Term of construction: August 17, 1984 to October 6, 1986
Facilities : Opening/October 9, 1986; Open time/check-in at noon, check-out at noon; Number of guest rooms/322 (twin 252, double 42, suite 21, royal suite 7; Charges/twin 30,000 to 36,000 yen, double 30,000 to 33,000 yen, suite 70,000 to 80,000 yen, royal suite 180,000 to 200,000 yen; Management/Prince Hotel Co.

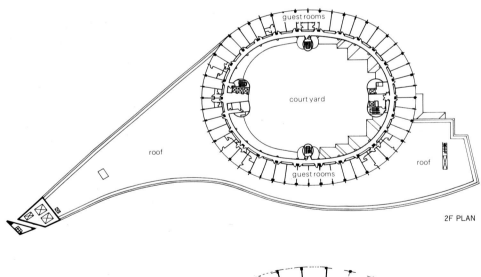

2F PLAN

材料仕様
高層大屋根/銅板緑青着色一文字葺き　廂:銅板一枚葺き瓦棒押さえ　低属屋根/御膳ブロックの上に植栽　外壁/高層部:エポキシ樹脂系吹き付けタイル　セメントスタッコ押さえ　低層部:インド砂岩塗り込み　エポキシ樹脂系吹き付けタイル　外部床/ピロティ歩道:丹波石乱れ貼り　車道:御影石切り石敷
〈主要飲食部分内装〉 プリンスホール/床:じゅうたん敷　壁:裂地貼り　天井:上部 壁紙 下部複層塗材吹き付け　ゴールドルーム/床:桜寄木網代貼り　壁:ガラスモザイク　天井:複層塗材吹き付け　レストラン ボーセジュール/床:じゅうたん敷　壁:レンガタイル 不燃米松合板　天井:不燃米松合板　寿司 天麩羅コーナー/床:ゴムタイル　通路:じゅうたん置敷　壁:ジュラクサテン吹き付け　天井:裂地貼り

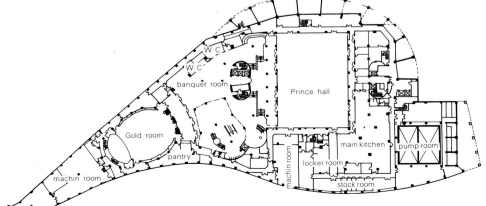

B2F PLAN

アーバン リゾートホテル/ *Urban Resort Hotel*

アーク森ビルよりみた外観及びロケーション

The appearance and location viewed from Ark Mori Building.

東京全日空ホテル

東京都港区赤坂1-12-33　Phone/03-505-1111

撮影/本木誠一

ANA Hotel Tokyo
1-12-33, Akasaka, Minato-ku, Tokyo, Japan　　Phone/03-505-1111

4階吹抜側よりガーデンプールをみる

The garden pool viewed from the 4th floor stairwell.

37階・"スカイバー"

"Sky Bar" at the 37th floor.

吹抜けを通して2階アトリウムラウンジをみる

The 2nd floor atrium lounge viewed through the stairwell.

56

アトリウムラウンジを通して人工滝をみる　天井にはスカイライトを設け　刻々と変化する室内空間を演出している
The artificial waterfall viewed through the atrium lounge. The skylight on the ceiling helps in presenting the ever-changing indoor space.

3階・日本料理店　　Japanese restaurant at the 3rd floor.

3階・コンチネンタルキュイジーヌ
The continental cuisine at the 3rd floor.

スカイライトとグリーンで南欧風の中庭をモチーフに表現した3階の"レストラン"
The 3rd floor "Restaurant" expressing a South European courtyard with the skylight and green.

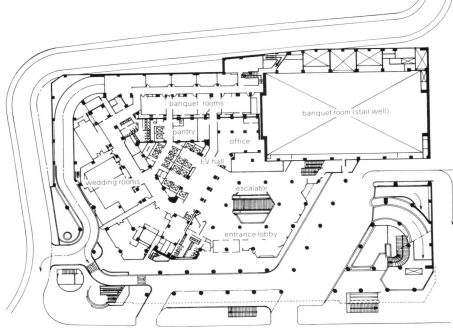

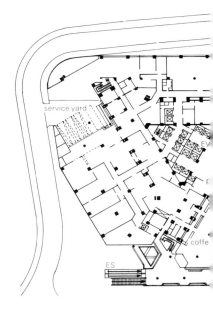

1F PLAN S=1:1200

東京全日空ホテル

"水と緑と光"のテーマに沿って2200㎡の面積と3層吹抜け分の高さを持ったこのホテルのアトリウムは 天の川と呼ばれる大照明とスリガラススクリーンを通したスカイライトの組合せによって 明るさに満ち 変化に富み 室内空間のイメージを超えた空間となった。
中央にはカスケードを設け 天の川の横の流れに対し縦の流れをダイナミックに構成している。アトリウムの中にはコーヒーショップとラウンジがあり アトリウムに開かれたバーや中華レストランなど7つの飲食施設がこのアトリウムに面し 利用する人々がそれぞれの目的に向いながら アトリウムの眺めを享受できるようにしている。

〈川村真兄/観光企画設計社〉（86-09）

設計：建築/観光企画設計社 構造/構造計画研究所 設備/建築設備設計
　　研究所 内装/観光企画設計社 他
協力：照明/石井幹子デザイン事務所 造園/石勝エクステリア 岩城造園
施工：大成建設

構　　造：S造 地下RC造 地下 地上一部 SRC造
規　　模：地下3階 地上36階 塔屋2階
面　　積：敷地/10,984.69㎡ 建築/8,940.98㎡ 床/地下3階1,977.63㎡
　　　　 地下2階 2,893.30㎡ 地下1階 9,025.60㎡ 1階 4,169.85㎡
　　　　 2階 6,523.40㎡ 3階 5,019.44㎡ 4階 1,557.75㎡ 基準階
　　　　 1,489.95㎡ 塔屋1階 321.55㎡ 2階 228.08㎡
　　　　 合計 98,331.68㎡
工　　期：1983年11月16日～1986年3月31日

施設概要：開業/1986年6月7日 営業時間/チェックイン 正午 チェック
　　　　 アウト 正午 客室数/900室 料飲施設/レストラン バー12
　　　　 料金/シングル1万7500 ツイン2万1000～2万4000 ダブル2
　　　　 万1000～2万4000 和室5万5000 スイート4～20万 エグゼ
　　　　 クティブ ダブル2万5000 ツイン2万6000～2万8000 スイー
　　　　 ト 4万1000～5万6000 駐車場/500台収容 経営/全日空エン
　　　　 タープライズ㈱

ANA Hotel Tokyo

This hotel's atrium pursues the theme "Water, Green and Light," and with 2,200 m² of space and height through three stories, it is very bright and rich with variety due to the combination of huge lighting called the "Milky Way," and skylight through frosted glass, going beyond an image of indoor space.
The cascade is provided in the center, dynamically forming a vertical flow against the horizontal flow of Milky Way.
Inside the atrium are a coffee shop and lounge, and also facing the atrium there are seven eating facilities, including a bar and Chinese restaurant, thus allowing guests to enjoy viewing the atrium while pursuing their own purposes.

Design: Yozo Shibata

Structure : S; basement RC; part of basement and above the ground SRC
Scale : 3 under and 36 stories above the ground, and 2 roof floors
Area : Site/10,984.69 m²; Building/8,940.98 m²; Floor/3rd basement 1,977.63 m², 2nd basement 2,837.30 m², 1st basement 9,025.60 m², 1st floor 4,169.85 m², 2nd floor 6,523.40 m², 3rd floor 5,019.44 m², 4th floor 1,557.75 m², standard floor 1,489.95 m², roof floor — 1st roof floor 321.55 m², 2nd roof floor 228.08 m², totaling 98,331.68 m²
Term of construction: November 16, 1983 to March 31, 1986
Facilities : Opening/June 7, 1986; Open time/check-in at noon, check-out at noon; Number of guest rooms/900; Eating & drinking facilities/restaurant · bar 12; Charges/single 17,500 yen, twin 21,000 to 24,000 yen, double 21,000 to 24,000 yen, Japanese style 55,000 yen, suite 40,000 to 200,000 yen, executive — double 25,000 yen, twin 26,000 to 28,000 yen, suite 41,000 to 56,000 yen; Parking lot/500 cars accommodated; Management/ANA Enterprise Co.

材料仕様
屋根/アスファルト防水の上タイル貼り 一部銅板貼り 軽量コンクリート鏝押さえ 外壁/磁器質山形三丁掛けタイル貼りPC板及びオムニア板打ち込み アルミ自然発色カーテンウォール 一部ステンレスサッシ 御影石本磨き 外部床/三角タイル貼り 一部御影タイル貼り 客室/床：コンクリート金鏝押さえ カーペット敷 壁：ビニールクロス貼り 天井：PB t＝21 三重貼りの上ビニールクロス貼り 幅木：ソフト幅木 化粧回り縁：特殊プラスチックスペンキ仕上 飾り柱 梁：木製ペンキ仕上 地下1階/大宴会場「鳳」/床：コンクリート金鏝押さえ カーペット貼り 壁：PB t＝9＋t＝12クロス貼りバーズアイメイプル練り付け 一部熱線吸収板ガラス 2階 アトリウムロビー/床：コンクリート金鏝押さえ大理石貼り 壁：PB t＝15バーズアイメイプル練り付け 天井：PB t＝9＋12クロス貼り 3階 日本料理「雲海」/床：コンクリート金鏝押さえカーペット貼り 一部玄昌石貼り 壁：聚楽塗 一部インド砂岩貼り 天井：PB t＝9＋12クロス貼り 杉柾目練り付け 36階 スカイバンケットルーム/床：カーペット貼り 壁：PB t＝9＋t＝12クロス貼り 大理石貼り 天井：PB t＝9＋t＝9クロス貼り 照明器具：ダウンライト 一部シャンデリア

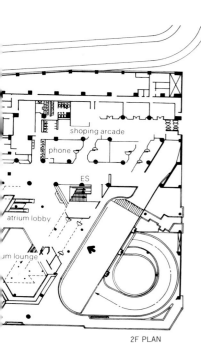

2F PLAN

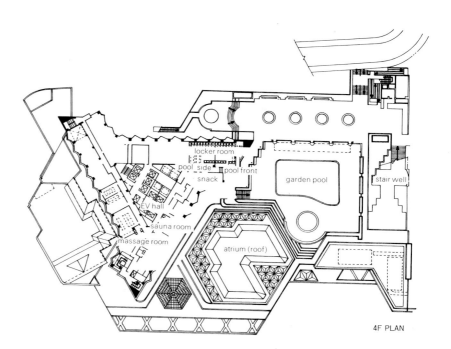

4F PLAN

アーバン リゾートホテル/ *Urban Resort Hotel*

大通公園からみた北側外観全景

The entire north side scene viewed from the Ohdori (Main Street) Park.

札幌後楽園ホテル

札幌市中央区大通西8丁目　Phone/011-261-0111

撮影/安達　治

Sapporo Korakuen Hotel
8-chome, Ohdori-nishi, Chuo-ku, Sapporo city, Japan
Phone/011-261-0111

アトリウムロビーの中央に配されたメッシュのベンチ
The meshed bench set in the center of the atrium lobby.

アトリウムロビーよりシースルーのエレベーターを見上げる　　　　　　　　　　　Looking up at the see-through elevator from the atrium lobby.

爽やかなパステルカラーで統一された2階のレストラン　　　　　　The 2nd floor restaurant uniformly finished with refreshing pastel colors.

"コンフォール"が面する1階北側の石庭

上/"コンフォール"のアトリウムロビーに面した客席
下/1階正面エントランスのネオンドーム

The stone garden in the north side of the 1st floor which the atrium lounge faces.

Top/ The guest seat area facing the atrium lobby of the atrium lounge.
Bottom/ The neon dome at the 1st floor front entrance.

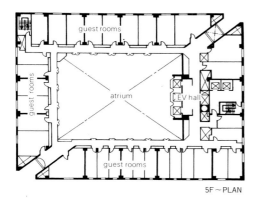

guest rooms

guest rooms

guest rooms

atrium

EV hall

guest rooms

5F～PLAN

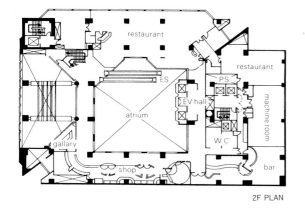

restaurant

restaurant

ES

PS

atrium

EV hall

W.C

machine room

gallary

shop

bar

2F PLAN

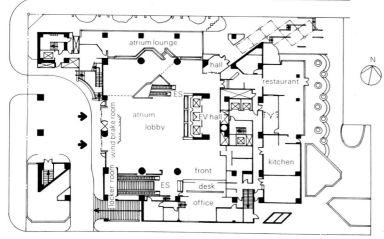

atrium lounge

hall

restaurant

ES

EV hall

atrium lobby

kitchen

locker room

wind brake room

front

ES

desk

office

N

1F PLAN S=1:800

材料仕様
屋根/コンクリート直下地ウレタンボードt＝28アスファルト3層防水砂付きルーフィン
グ 外壁/モルタル下地磁器タイル貼り45三丁掛けリブ付き 開口部:アルミサッシ二次
電解発色横軸回転及び内倒し 外部床/モルタル下地磁器タイル貼り
〈アトリウム〉床/軽量コンクリート下地石英石貼り モザイクタイル貼り 幅木/大理
石貼り 壁/コンクリート下地大理石貼り 高層部:コンクリート下地吹き付けタイル仕
上 天井/ガラス繊維布 フレーム/スチールSOP

札幌後楽園ホテル
"札幌市の象徴である大通公園に面する核として地域社会の発展に寄与
する（建築主）"ホテル事業を通して地域に貢献したい"(ホテルテナン
ト）という両者の基本コンセプトを踏まえ 総合設計制度を採用し 街
区と建築物の快適な調和を目指した。
シティホテルはその性格上 都市生活そのものに密着した機能を担って
いる。その存在が都市環境に与えるインパクトはかなり大きい と言え
るだろう。
そこで このホテルを設計するにあたり 世界屈指の美しい都市公園と
の相乗効果を図り"地域性豊かな文化 健康と憩いとの調和"をテーマ
とした。 〈神田 孜・熊本 努/竹中工務店設計部〉(88-09)
設計:竹中工務店
施工:竹中工務店 清水建設 地崎工業共同企業体

構 造:S造 RC造 SRC造
規 模:地下4階 地上14階 塔屋3階
面 積:敷地/4,567㎡ 建築/2,353㎡ 床/地下4階～地下1階8,592.80
㎡ 1階 1,761.44㎡ 2階 1,435.99㎡ 3階 1,619.63㎡ 4階
1,228.71㎡ 5階 1,234.34㎡ 6階 1,219.66㎡ 7階 1,225.17㎡
8階 1,217.43㎡ 9階 1,224.89㎡ 10階 1,219.94㎡ 11階
1,234.34㎡ 12階 1,219.66㎡ 13階 1,219.94㎡ 14階1,234.34
㎡ 塔屋1～3階 481.07㎡ 合計27,369.35㎡
工 期:1987年7月24日～1988年5月19日

施設概要:開業/1988年6月20日 営業時間/チェックイン 午後1時 チ
ェックアウト 午前11時 客室数/305室 料金/シングル1万1500
～ ツイン1万8000～ ダブル1万7500 ラージツイン1万9000
～ デラックスツイン2万8500 和室2万8500～ ブライダルル
ーム3万 ジュニアスイート3万～ スイート7万～
経営/㈱札幌後楽園ホテル 従業員数/305人

Sapporo Korakuen Hotel

In view of the basic concept aimed at by the owner of the building,
i.e. "intended to contribute to development of community as a core
of facilities facing 'Ohdori Park that is a symbol of Sapporo City',"
and that envisaged by the hotel tenants, i.e. "intended to contribute
to community through hotel service," the planner employed a comprehensive design system pursuing comfortable harmony of building
with street.
Because of its nature, a city hotel has functions closely related to the
very urban life, and its existence will have a significant impact upon
the urban environment.
Thus, in designing this hotel, expecting a multiplying effect in conjunction with Ohdori Park, one of the world's most beautiful parks,
its theme was set at "Culture Rich with Local Features and Harmony
of Health with Leisure."

Design: Takenaka-komuten

Structure : S; RC; SRC
Scale : 4 under and 14 stories above the ground, and 3 roof floors
Area : Site/4,567 m²; Building/2,353 m²; Floor/1st to 4th
basement 8,592.80 m², 1st floor 1,761.44 m², 2nd
floor 1,435.99 m², 3rd floor 1,619.63 m², 4th floor
1,228.71 m², 5th floor 1,234.34 m², 6th floor 1,219.66
m², 7th floor 1,225.17 m², 8th floor 1,217.43 m²,
9th floor 1,224.89 m², 10th floor 1,219.94 m², 11th
floor 1,234.34 m², 12th floor 1,219.66 m², 13th floor
1,219.94 m², 14th floor 1,234.34 m², 1st to 3rd roof
floors 481.07 m², totaling 27,369.35 m²
Term of construction: July 24, 1987 to May 19, 1988
Facilities : Opening/June 20, 1988; Open time/check-in at 1:00
p.m., check-out at 11:00 a.m.; Number of guest rooms/
305;
Charges/single – from 11,500 yen, twin – from 18,000
yen, double – 17,500 yen, large twin – from 19,000
yen, deluxe twin – 28,500 yen, Japanese style – from
28,500 yen, bridal room – 30,000 yen, junior suite –
from 30,000 yen, suite – from 70,000 yen; Management/
Sapporo Korakuen Hotel Co; Number of employees/305

玉砂利を敷きつめた庭をもつ3階の日本料理店

The 3rd floor Japanese restaurant having a garden covered with pebbles.

地下2階の大宴会場

The large banquet hall at the 2nd basement.

正面外観をみる

The front appearance.

ホテル新潟

新潟市万代5丁目11-20　Phone/025-245-3331

Hotel Niigata
5-11-20, Bandai, Niigata city, Japan　Phone/025-245-3331

撮影/エスエス

1階・ラウンジ

The lounge at the 1st floor.

ホテル新潟

新潟駅より徒歩7分ほどの場所に位置する老舗「ホテル新潟」の旧館跡地に計画された。客室数186室 フランス料理を供する メインダイニング「舞」から老舗の伝統を継承する割烹「万代」まで幅広い飲食施設。また国際会議が開催できる1100㎡の大宴会場をはじめとする大小11室の宴会場を具備している。個性的な曲線の外観は夕日が沈む佐渡ヶ島を望み 残照を受けて黄金色に輝き 印象的である。そして一歩足を踏み入れると やさしく 爽やかなフュージョンが流れる。全館を通じ 飲食施設のカジュアルとフォーマルの差別化 及び宿泊部門と宴会部門の分離を明確に打ち出し 各施設の独自性を高めるよう心がけた。

〈田中幸男・三宅正芳/鹿島建設建築設計本部〉(88-09)

設　　　計:鹿島建築設計本部
設計監理:川崎エンジニアリング　鹿島建設建築設計本部
施　　　工:福田組　鹿島建設共同企業体

構　　　造:RC造　SRC造
規　　　模:地下1階　地上16階　塔屋1階
面　　　積:敷地/7,906㎡　建築/4,480.61㎡　床/地下1階 1,668.28㎡
　　　　　1階 4,147.85㎡　2階 3,977.84㎡　3階 4,177.30㎡　4階
　　　　　2,508.78㎡　5階 847.31㎡　6～15階各819.13㎡16階 515.12㎡
　　　　　塔屋　176.43㎡　合計26,210.21㎡

工　　　期:1986年8月22日～1988年3月31日

施設概要:開業/1988年4月18日　営業時間/チェックイン 正午　チェックアウト 午前11時　客室数/186室(シングル66　ダブル10　ツイン100　デラックスツイン3　スイート5　和室2)料飲施設/カフェ&レストラン2(144席)日本料理レストラン 2(157席)　中国料理レストラン1(82席)ラウンジ2(92席)料金/シングル8000～1万　ツイン1万3000～1万6000　ダブル 1万3000　デラックスツイン2万5000　スイート3万8000～15万　和室3万5000　駐車場119台収容　経営/㈱ホテル新潟

Hotel Niigata

Construction of this hotel was planned on the site of the old established "Hotel Niigata" that is situated about 7 minutes by walk from Niigata Station. Having 186 rooms, it also is provided with a wide range of eating/drinking facilities, including the main dining "Mai" that serves French dishes and Japanese cuisine "Bandai" that serves traditional Japanese dishes, as well as with 11 banquet halls varying in size, including a large 1,100 m² banquet hall where an international conference can be held. Featuring the uniquely curved appearance, the hotel commands a fine view of Sado Island against the setting sun, and impressively sparkles with the afterglow. Taking a step inside the hotel, a sweet, refreshing fusion is on the air. Throughout the hotel, eating/drinking facilities are differentiated between casual and formal types, and the hotel and banquet departments are clearly separated, so that the uniqueness of each type is stressed.

Design: Kajima Construction, Inc.

Structure : RC, SRC
Scale : 1 under and 16 stories above the ground, and 1 floor on the roof
Area : Site/7,906.00 m²; Building/4,480.61 m²; Floor/1st basement 1,668.28 m², 1st floor 4,147.85 m², 2nd floor 3,977.84 m², 3rd floor 4,177.30 m², 4th floor 2,508.78 m², 5th floor 847.31 m², 6th to 15th floor 819.13 m² each, 16th floor 515.12 m², roof floor 176.43 m², totaling 26,210.21 m²
Term of construction: August 22, 1986 to March 31, 1988
Facilities : Opening/April 18, 1988; Open time/check-in at noon, check-out at 11:00 a.m.; Number of guest rooms/186 (single 66, double 10, twin 100, deluxe twin 3, suite 5, Japanese style 2; Eating & drinking facilities/cafe & restaurant 2 (144 seats), Japanese restaurant 2 (157 seats), Chinese restaurant 1 (82 seats), lounge 2 (92 seats); Charges/single 8,000 to 10,000 yen, double 13,000 yen, twin 13,000 to 16,000 yen, deluxe twin 25,000 yen, suite 38,000 to 150,000 yen, Japanese style 35,000 yen; Parking lot/119 cars accommodated; Management/Hotel Niigata Co.

ル エルミタージュ

私は海外旅行が好きで　世界各国のホテルをみてきたが　そのほとんど
がセンスとゆとりを持ち　行き届いたサービスがある。その点　日本の
ホテルの多くは　サービス業ではなくて　レンタルルーム業という感じ
を受ける。
ヨーロッパの４つ星クラスのホテルは大きくてもせいぜい200室　これが
サービスをする限度である。その点　ホテルはサービス業の極致　と言
われるが　大規模主義ではとても行き届いたサービスは無理である。
このように欧州ホテル旅行の実感から生まれたのがこのホテルである。
〈斉藤憲彦/日本ビルマネージメント〉(86-09)

企画：日本ビルマネージメント
設計：内装/長島商業建築設計事務所
施工：建築/村本建設
　　　内装/大丸装工部

構　　　造：ＲＣ造
規　　　模：地下１階　地上７階
面　　　積：敷地/310.81㎡　建築/214.26㎡　床/地下１階 188.04㎡　１階
　　　　　　185.55㎡　２３階 各194.75㎡　４〜７階 各91.45㎡
　　　　　　合計1,128.89㎡
工　　　期：1984年６月25日〜1985年11月15日

施設概要：開業/1986年３月14日　営業時間/チェックイン　正午　チェッ
　　　　　クアウト　正午　客室数/24室　料飲施設/レストラン２ ラウ
　　　　　ンジ１　料金/２万5000〜５万　経営/㈱マネジメント　従業員
　　　　　数/20人　パート アルバイト６人　合計26人

L'Ermitage

As I'm very fond of travelling overseas, I have seen many hotels in
different countries across the world. Most of them have a fine sense
in a composed atmosphere, and offers hospitable service. Differing
from them, many of Japanese hotels are left not like hotel business,
but like rental room service.
A four-star class hotel in Europe has 200 rooms at most, as this is
the limit do hospitable service. This is inevitable to hotels that are
said to be the culmination of service business. In Japan where hotel
management clings to a large-scale system, hospitable service is quite
impossible.
This hotel was brought into being reflecting the impressions I had
during my European hotel inspection tour.

Planner: Norihiko Saito

Struction : RC
Scale　　: 1 under and 7 stories above the ground
Area　　 : Site/310.81 m²;　Building/214.26 m²;　Floor/1st base-
　　　　　ment 188.04 m², 1st floor 185.55 m², 2nd to 3rd floor
　　　　　194.75 m² each, 4th to 7th floor 91.45 m² each, totaling
　　　　　1,128.89 m²
Term of construction: June 25, 1984 to November 15, 1985
Facilities : Opening/March 14, 1986;　Opening/check-in at noon,
　　　　　check-out at noon; Number of guest rooms/24; Eating &
　　　　　drinking facilities/restaurant 2, lounge 1;
　　　　　Charges/25,000 to 50,000 yen; Management/Management
　　　　　Co;　Number of employees/full-time 20, part-time 6,
　　　　　totaling 26

材料仕様

〈客室〉床/じゅうたん敷　壁　天井/クロス貼り

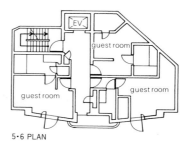

5・6 PLAN

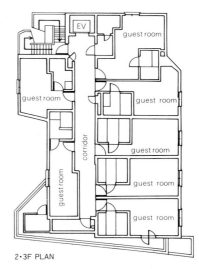

2・3F PLAN

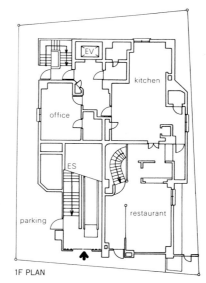

1F PLAN

B1F PLAN　S＝1:300

地下1階・ロビーエレベーター廻りをみる

The lobby elevator area at the 1st basement.

地下1階・エレベーター右の小ラウンジ
The small lounge at the right side of the 1st basement elevator.

バスルーム
The bathroom.

地下1階のレストラン

The restaurant at the 1st basement.

ツインルームⅡ

The twin room Ⅱ.

アーバン リゾートホテル / *Urban Resort Hotel*

道路越しに南側正面外観をみる　安田銀行当時は中央スパンに入口があった
The south side front appearance viewed across the road. In the days of Yasuda Bank, the entrance was open in the center span.

外観とロケーション 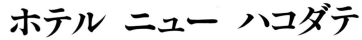 The appearance and location.

ホテル ニュー ハコダテ

北海道函館市末広町23-9　Phone/0138-22-8131

撮影/安達　治

Hotel New Hakodate
23-9, Suehiro-cho, Hakodate city, Hokkaido, Japan　Phone/0138-22-8131

74

上/入口わきに配されたレストラン
下/客室
Top/ The restaurant located beside the entrance area.
Bottom/ The guest room.

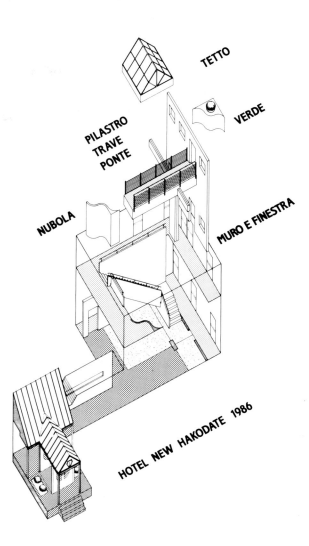

ホテル ニュー ハコダテ
「ホテル ニュー ハコダテ」の建物の本体は1932年に現在の富士銀行の
前身である安田銀行の店舗として建てられたものである。
今回の改装は 荒 知幾のデザインに基づいて 前回の銀行からホテル
へと全く異なった方向に沿って行なわれた。
イタリアでスーパースタジオと共働きの経験のある彼は 今回の改装と
並行して工事が進められた隣接地でのテナントビルの建設をにらんだ上
で 2つの建物を総合していくような緊張感のあるボリュームとしてエ
ントランス部分を両建物に挟まれたスペースに新たに設計した。これに
よって ホテルの2つのファサードの3スパンの大オーダーを全面的に
開放すると同時にオーダーの間へ 縦長のサッシを挿入することで 建
物における大オーダーの存在を一層深く印象付けることに成功した。
〈菊地理夫/横浜工学院〉（86-09）

設計/スタジオ トモ アラ アソシエイツ 施工/熊谷木工

構　　造：SRC造 一部S造
規　　模：地上3階
面　　積：床/1階 392m² 2階 318m² 3階 64m²（内 厨房30m²）
　　　　　合計774m²
工　　期：1986年4月25日～6月30日

施設概要：開業/1986年7月6日 営業時間/チェックイン 午後3時 チ
　　　　　ェックアウト 午前10時 客室数/22室 料飲施設/レストラン
　　　　　1 バー1 料金/シングル8500 ダブル1万5000 ツイン1
　　　　　万7000 経営/フジヤ企画㈱ 従業員数/9人

Hotel New Hakodate

The main part of "Hotel New Hakodate" is a building constructed in 1932 as an office of Yasuda Bank, predecessor to the present Fuji Bank.
Based on Tomoiku Ara's design, the current renovation was carried out in quite a different direction towards the hotel from the previous bank.
Having once worked with a super studio in Italy, he took into account construction of a tenant building on the adjacent land that has taken place in parallel with the current renovation, and newly designed an entrance portion in a space sandwiched by both buildings to give a voluminous impression like uniting the two buildings in a tense atmosphere. While fully opening the hotel's facade in big three-spanned order, a lengthly set of sash has been inserted between the order, there by succeeding in impressing the existence of the big order in the building more deeply.

Design: Tomoiku Ara

Structure : SRC (S in part)
Scale : 3 stories above the ground
Area : Floor/1st floor 392 m², 2nd floor 318 m², 3rd floor 64 m² (kitchen 30 m²), totaling 774 m²
Term of construction: April 25, 1986 to June 30, 1986
Facilities : Opening/July 6, 1986; Open time/check-in at 3:00 p.m., check-out at 10:00 a.m.; Number of guest rooms/22; Eating & drinking facilities/restaurant 1, bar 1; Charges/single 8,500 yen, double 15,000 yen, twin 17,000 yen; Management/Fujiya Kigyo Co.; Number of employees/9

1階中央ロビー上部吹抜けをみる　　　　　　　　　　　　The upper stairwell at the 1st floor center lobby.

1階ロビー奥から入口アプローチ通路方向をみる

The entrance approach aisle viewed from an inner part of the 1st floor lobby.

新設された入口廻り　左側に同じ経営のファッションビルが隣接する

The newly installed entrance area. The fashion building under the same management is adjoining in the left side.

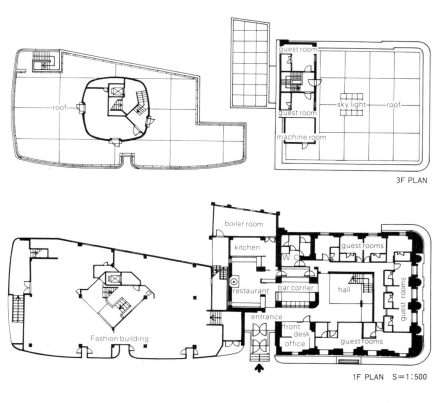

3F PLAN

1F PLAN　S＝1：500

材料仕様
屋根/トップライト部分：スチールフレーム　クロスワイヤーガラス　外壁/外部サッシ：スチールサッシ　ハーフミラーペアガラス　エントランス：鉄骨組キャノピー　銅板葺き　床/御影石　フローリング　幅木/ステンレスHL　壁/合成樹脂系塗料　ラッカー塗装スクラッチ仕上　天井/EP塗装

スポーツ＆レジャー　ファシリティ
Sports & Leisure Facilities

スポーツクラブ／フィットネスクラブ／クアハウス
テニスクラブ／ゴルフクラブ／レジャー＆アーバン
リゾート　ファシリティ／ディスコ

*Sports Club / Fitness Club / Kurhaus / Tennis Club
/ Golf Club Leisurex Urban Resort Facilities / Disco*

フィットネスクラブ／*Fitness Club*

10階・クラブハウスよりプール全景をみる

The entire pool scene viewed from the 10th floor club house.

リボン川崎

神奈川県川崎市川崎区1-11　川崎西武 9 〜 10階
Phone／044-245-3330

撮影／鳴瀬　亨

Re-Born Kawasaki
1-11, Nisshin-cho, Kawasaki-ku, Kawasaki city,
Kanagawa, Japan　　Phone/044-245-3330

ダイビングプール側よりプール全景をみる
The entire pool scene viewed from the diving pool side.

上/ジム（188.1㎡）と連続して設けられたスタジオ（171.6㎡）
下/9階・エントランスロビー

Top/ The studio (171.6 m²) installed in a row with the gymnasium (188.1 m²).
Bottom/ The entrance lobby at the 9th floor.

上/エントランスロビーよりプールをみる
下/エントランスロビー側のプールの一部はアクリル板で　その断面をみせる演出がなされている
Top/ The pool viewed from the entrance lobby.
Bottom/ Part of the pool in the entrance lobby side uses acrylic plates whose cross section is made visible.

リボン川崎

このフィットネス クラブはＳＥＩＢＵにとって４つ目である。
従来のトレーニングに主体を置いたフィットネス クラブとは異なり"遊び心"を優先させ スポーツを通じてコミュニケーションづくりを目的とするアーバンリゾート型のプロトタイプである。
このヒトとのコミュニケーションの場となるためには 一時の話題性だけではなく 常に情報発信性を持つ可変空間の機能を兼ね備える必要がある。また ビルの９〜10階という立地上 環境演出はあくまで"非日常性"をテーマとした心と体のリラックスを求めて自然の素材 自然の造形を生かしたインテリアである。〈中田雅博/西武百貨店 高野治/竹中工務店設計部 福谷正典/竹中工務店開発計画本部〉
(88-06)

企画：西武百貨店販売促進部　竹中工務店設計部
設計：竹中工務店設計部　アイ アンド エス環境企画事業部
協力：ウルトラボックス　環境庁デザイン研究所
施工：竹中工務店　大林組　鹿島建設　銭高組 J.V.

面　　積：床/8階 131㎡（プール機械室）9階 1,084㎡　10階 1,255㎡
　　　　　合計2,470㎡
工　　期：1987年10月1日〜1988年3月8日

施設概要：開業/1988年3月11日　営業時間/午前10時〜午後10時 定休日
　　　　　/毎月第2木曜日 施設/リゾート型プール（全長20m 最大幅
　　　　　10m 水深1.2mのシェル型変形プール）ダイビングプール
　　　　　（全長7m 幅4m 水深3.8m）ジム スタジオ クラブ
　　　　　ハウス（バスルーム サウナ）システム/会員制 経営/㈱川崎
　　　　　西武百貨店 従業員数/インストラクター20人 事務部門15人
　　　　　クラブハウス10人 合計45人

Re-Born Kawasaki

This fitness club is the fourth one for Seibu. Differing from conventional fitness clubs which are mainly intended for training, this club is intended to be a prototype of urban resort club that gives priority to the "spirit of play" and thereby helps in making communications through sports.
In order to serve as a place for communications with man, it is important not merely to offer topics temporarily, but also serve as a function of variable space from which information is despatched. Since the club is situated at the 9th and 10th floors of a building, its environment is basically presented as being a "non-daily" space where you can relax the body and heart surrounded with an interior using natural materials and elements.

Design: Takenaka-komuten

Area　　　: Floor/8th floor 131 m² (pool's machine room), 9th floor 1,084 m², 10th floor 1,255 m², totaling 2,470 m²
Term of construction: October 1, 1987 to March 8, 1988
Facilities : Opening/March 11, 1988; Open time/10:00 a.m. to 10:00 p.m.; Closed regularly on/2nd Thursday of every month; Resort type pool (total length 20 m, max. width 10 m, water depth 1.2 m – shell type deformed pool), diving pool (total length 7 m, width 4 m, water depth 3.8 m), gymnasium, studio, club house (bathroom, sauna); System/membership; Management/Kawasaki Seibu Department Store; Number of employees/instructor 20, clerical sector 15, club house 10, totaling 45

材料仕様
〈エントランスロビー〉床/タイルカーペット 壁/軽鉄下地坑火石貼り 天井/軽鉄下地ＰＢ t＝12ＥＰ
〈クラブハウス〉床/カーペット 寄木フローリング 幅木/木製ＯＰ h＝60 壁/軽鉄下地ＰＢ t＝12ＥＰ模様塗 天井/軽鉄下地ＰＢ t＝12ＥＰ
〈プール〉床/樹脂塗床 一部豆砂利洗い出し 壁/軽鉄下地坑火石貼り 一部吹き付けタイル 天井/軽鉄下地プール用石綿吸音板 t＝15貼り プール（ダイビングプールとも）：コンクリート下地グラスコーティング3層の上樹脂コーティング 透明部分/アクリル板 t＝75 一部 t＝85

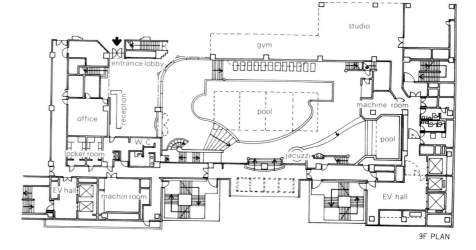

9F PLAN

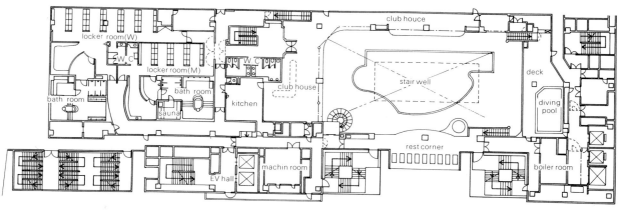

10F PLAN　S＝1:600

1階のダイビングプール（5m×12m 深さ5mと1.2m）をみる

The diving pool at the 1st floor (5 m × 12 m; 5 m and 1.2 m deep).

アイランド

京都市伏見区竹田小屋ノ内町１丁目－１
Phone/075-623-0055

撮影／藤原　弘

Island

1-1, Takeda Koyanouchi-cho, Fushimi-ku,
Kyoto city, Japan　　Phone/075-623-0055

1階のショップより吹抜けを通してダイビングプールをみる
The diving pool viewed from the 1st floor shop across
the stairwell.

地階のレストラン「クラブ アイランド」をみる

The restaurant "Club Island" at the basement.

スキューバダイビング風景

A scuba diving scene.

アイランド

この施設は京都南インターの南側に位置し マリンスポーツ その中でもスキューバダイビングというスポーツを多くの人たちに知ってもらい楽しんでもらうために計画された。

従来あるダイビングショップがその必要な機能内の一部(ショップのみ)しか備えておらず ダイバーに不便を強いているのが現状であるのに対して 当ショップでは必要な機能はすべて(ソフト ハード共に) 提供し遊びのスペースをも提供しようとのことである。海をテーマにシーフードメニューを中心に アダルトな雰囲気で食事ができ お酒も飲めるレストラン&バーを隣に設置し ダイバーの憩いの場 そしてダイビングを知らない人たちの 窓口になるようにと設計が進められた。

〈松丸敏之/相原デザイン事務所〉(86-07)

企画:相原正俊
設計:相原デザイン事務所
協力:野間 昭(レストラン&バー)
施工:建築/エイ・アンド・ビー
　　　内装/大晃建設

構　造:RC造　一部S造
規　模:地下1階 地上4階
面　積:床/地階 342.52㎡(レストランバー 113.82㎡ 内 厨房 35.1㎡) 1階 166.95㎡ (レストランバー 8.75㎡) 合計509.47㎡
工　期:1986年1月15日〜4月10日(レストランバー 3月5日〜4月3日)

施設概要:開業/1986年4月13日 営業時間/午前11時〜午後9時 定休日/なし 業務内容/スキューバダイビング スクール スキューバダイビング器材 ツアーの提供 マリンウェア アクセサリーの販売 システム/会員制 経営㈱エイ アイ ティー 従業員数/サービス5人 パート アルバイト6人 合計11人

Island

Situated in the south side of Kyoto Minami Interchange, "Island" has been provided to teach many people about marine sports, including scuba diving, among others, and thereby enable them to enjoy them. Differing from conventional diving shops which are equipped with only part (i.e. shop facilities alone) of necessary functions, and very inconvenient to divers, this shop comes with all necessary functions of both hardware and software, and also offers an enjoyable space for play. Adjacent to it, a restaurant & bar is open pursuing the sea as its theme, and mainly serves seafoods so that guests can enjoy eating and drinking. Thus, "Island" was designed to serve as a rest place for drivers and also as a school for beginners.

Design: Toshiyuki Matsumaru

Structure : RC, S in part
Scale : 1 under and 4 stories above the ground
Area : Floor/basement 342.52 m² (restaurant & bar 113.82 m², including kitchen 35.10 m²), 1st floor 166.95 m² (restaurant bar 8.75 m²), totaling 509.47 m²
Term of construction: January 15 to April 10, 1986 (restaurant & bar; March 5 to April 3, 1986)
Facilities : Opening/April 13, 1986; Open time/11:00 a.m. to 9:00 p.m.; Fixed close/nil; Service/scuba diving school, offering scuba diving kits and tour, selling marine wear and accessories; System/membership; Management/A. I. D Co.; Number of employees/service 5, part-time 6, totaling 11

材料仕様

外壁/ALC板二丁掛けタイル貼り 外部床/磁器質タイル貼り100角 サイン/スチールメラミン焼き付け仕上 切り文字切り抜き文字FL内蔵 レストラン バーサイン/ボンデ鋼板焼き付け仕上 床/ショップ:Pタイル市松貼り300角 プール:モザイクタイル貼り50角 レストラン バー/楢材フローリングOS染色仕上 一部玉砂利洗い出し 100角と200角タイル砕いて圧着貼り 壁/ショップ:PBt＝12下地 クロク貼り プール:モルタル下地ボンタイル吹き付け仕上 腰:モザイクタイル貼り50角 レストラン バー:モルタル金鏝押さえパテしごきEP吹き付け 一部木毛板t＝12圧着貼り EP吹き付け仕上 天井/ショップ:軽鉄下地ジプトーン貼り 吹き付け仕上 プール:軽鉄下地バスリブ貼り レストラン バー:PBt＝12下地 寒紗 パテしごきEP吹き付け仕上 照明器具/ショップ&プール:DL SP ハロゲンランプ 水銀燈リフレクター 間接照明 カウンター/トップ:ガラス&コーリアン 腰:デコラ貼り分け スクリーン/スチール板t＝3サンダーブラッシュ仕上 一部玉砂利洗い出し仕上

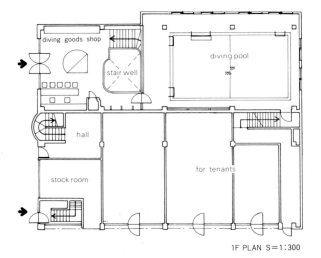

1F PLAN S=1:300

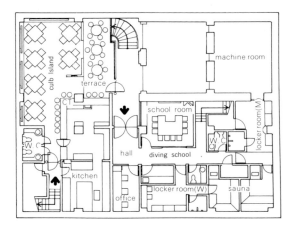

B1F PLAN

外観全景をみる　ウォータースライダーが曲線を描いて外部に突出している　1階はスーパーや飲食店のテナントが入っている
The entire appearance. The water slider is projected outside curvilinearly. The 1st floor is occupied by tenants, such as supermarket and restaurants.

撮影/加斗タカオ

2階のインドア温水プール　　　　　　　　　　　　　　The heated indoor pool at the 2nd floor.

ライフシティ とみだ

愛知県海部郡美和町大字篠田五ノ坪60　Phone/052-443-0088

Life City Tomida
Miwa-cho, Ama-gun, Aichi, Japan　　Phone/052-443-0088

スイミングスクールでは日本で初めて採用した西ドイツ製のウォータースライダー（全長82ｍ　傾斜角９％）
West German water slider employed for the first time in Japan (82 m in total length; angle of inclination 9°).

右上/ウォータースライダーのスタート地点
右下/同じく　そのゴール地点
Right, top/ The starting point of the water slider.
Right, bottom/ The goal of the water slider.

ライフシティ とみだ

名古屋の西 県道名古屋・萱津線 田園や山が広がる自然豊かな立地に
1階ショッピングセンター 2～3階にスイミング アスレチッククラ
ブを設けるという異種用途の企画ですすめた。
1階ホールから3階を吹き抜け 階段により各階を有機的に結び 外壁
をカーテンウォールにして遮蔽感をなくし 開放的な空間とした。また
日本で初めてのドイツ製ウォータースライダーをオールシーズン使用し
遊びを建築に反映 時を超え親から子へ語り継がれることを願いつつメ
ビウスの輪を思い曲線に使用し 建物の内から外へ外から内へとダイナ
ミックな躍動感を演出した。　　　　　　〈山田洋之/匠設計室〉(86-07)
設計:匠設計室
協力:熊沢慈孝 岩泉忠明 構造/野田建築事務所
施工:川村工務店

構　　造:RC造
規　　模:地上3階 塔屋1階
面　　積:敷地/3,246.34㎡ 建築/1,664.98㎡ 床/1階テナント部分
　　　　1,476.38㎡ 2階 1,480.62㎡ 3階 692.06㎡ 塔屋 52.97㎡
　　　　合計3,702.03㎡
工　　期:1985年2月1日～8月30日

施設概要:開業/1985年9月12日 営業時間/午前10時～午後9時 定休日
　　　　/年間11日 施設/ウォータースライダー(全長 82m)付き室内
　　　　温水プール(26m×6コース) エアロビクス ダンススタジオ
　　　　アスレチック トレーニングルーム サウナ システム/会員
　　　　制 経営/㈱とみだ 富田兼松 従業員数:コーチ10人 オフィ
　　　　ス8人 合計18人

Life City Tomida

In the west of Nagoya, along the prefectural Nagoya-Kayatsu road
rich with natural features such as rural fields and mountains, "Life
City Tomida" has opened as a place for different uses, i.e. a shopping
center at the 1st floor, and a swimming athletic club at the 2nd and
3rd floors.
Providing a stairwell at the 1st floor hall through the 3rd floor, and
systematically linking the three floors through the staircase, the outer
wall has been finished as a curtain wall to create an open space by
removing a shielding sense. Japan's first German water slider has also
been employed for year-round use, in order to reflect the spirit of
play in architecture, and wishing to transmit this space from parents
to children transcending time, curves imaging Möbius band have been
used to present a dynamic interaction from the inside to outside and
from the outside to inside of the building.

Design: Hiroyuki Yamada

Structure : RC
Scale　　 : 3 stories above the ground, and 1 roof floor
Area　　 : Site/3,246.34 m²; Building/1,664.98 m²; Floor/1st floor
　　　　　for tenants 1,476.38 m², 2nd floor 1,480.62 m², 3rd floor
　　　　　692.06 m², roof floor 52.97 m², totaling 3,702.03 m²
Term of construction: February 1 to August 30, 1985
Facilities : Opening/September 12, 1985; Open time/10:00 a.m. to
　　　　　9:00 p.m.; Closed regularly on/11 days a year; Equip-
　　　　　ment/heated indoor pool (26 m × 6 courses) with water
　　　　　slider (82 m in total length), aerobics dance studio,
　　　　　athletic training room, sauna; System/membership;
　　　　　Management/Kanematsu Tomida, Tomida Co.; Number
　　　　　of employees/coach 10, office staff 8, totaling 18

材料仕様

屋根/塗膜防水 外壁/コンクリート打ち放し 吹き
付けタイル貼り 外部床/磁器質タイル貼り カラー
コンクリート平板 床/長尺ビニール床シート フロ
ーリング ブロック 幅木/ビニール幅木 堅木 壁
/モルタルEP モルタル下地ビニールクロス貼り
天井/化粧石膏ボード 石膏ボード下地クロス貼り
カウンター/メラミン化粧板貼り アルミスクリーン
ウォータースライダー/ロルバ(安全素道)

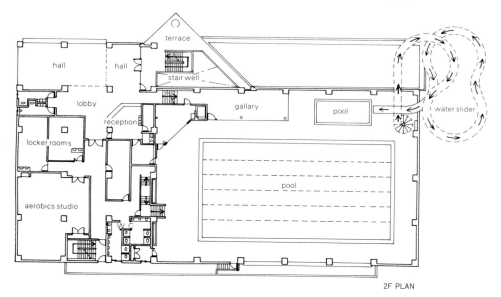

3F PLAN

2F PLAN

１階・エントランスの夜景

A night scene of the 1st floor entrance.

４階・リフレッシュ エリアのラウンジをみる
The lounge of the refreshing area at the 4th floor.

４階・フィットネス エリアのトレーニングジムをみる
The training gymnasium at the 4th floor fitness area.

アクア スパ

東京都世田谷区瀬田４丁目15-30　瀬田パークアベニュー１階・４階
Phone/03-700-3444

Aqua Spa
4-15-30, Seta, Setagaya-ku, Tokyo, Japan　　Phone/03-700-3444

撮影/原　栄三郎

上/メインロビーをみる
下/4階・スウェット エリアの男子用風呂をみる。
Top/ The main lobby.
Bottom/ The bath for males at the 4th floor sweat area.

エアロビクス スタジオ　　　　　　　The aerobics studio.

4階・アクア スタジオ エリアをみる　手前がジャグジー

The aqua studio area at the 4th floor; the Jacuzzi in your side.

アクア スパ

この施設は世田谷の高台にあり 旧徳川邸ゆかりの庭園をそのまま生かした自然環境の中で水の特性を応用して健康促進させる 新しいタイプのメンバーズクラブである。

その施設は メディカルエリア フィットネスエリア エステティックエリア アクアエリア スウェットエリア リフレッシュエリア と大きく6つに分けられ 最新の保健医学に基づいた総合的なメディカルチェックシステムを採用し ストレス 体力 栄養 体型 体調等 健康状態のトータルなチェックと 無理のないトレーニング プログラムによる肉体的効果の追求と 整理 精神面からの多彩なアプローチによる相乗効果を通じ 日常味わうことのできない運動の醍醐味を得ることのできる施設である。 〈塩見一郎/インテリアデザインオフィス ノブ〉(86-07)

設計：インテリアデザインオフィス ノブ
施工：小松建設工業

面　　積：床/1階 648m²　4階 2,934m²　合計3,582m²
工　　期：1984年9月1日～1985年5月25日

施設概要：開業/1985年5月27日　営業時間/午前10時～午後10時 定休日/毎月第2月曜日 施設/メディカル ストレス チェック トレーニングジム エアロビックス スタジオ ジャズダンス スタジオ エステティック サロン アクアスタジオ パノラマ バス ジャグジー システム/会員制 経営/南西㈱ 従業員数/インストラクター15人 フロント8人 合計23人

Aqua Spa

Situated on the heights of Setagaya Ward, "Aqua Spa" is a new-type members club standing in a natural environment of an old garden connected with the Tokugawa residence, aimed to promote our health by means of characteristics of water.

This center consists of six major areas – medical area, fitness area, aesthetic area, aqua area, sweat area and refreshing area. By employing a comprehensive medical check system based on the latest medical knowledge of health, "Aqua Spa'" serves as a place for a) totally checking the health conditions, such as stress, physical strength, body shape and condition, b) pursuing the physical effect of moderate and adequate training programs, and c) also making various physiological and mental approaches. Thus, the members can enjoy the real charm of exercises that is unattainable in daily life.

Design: Koji Yoshio

Area : Floor/1st floor 648 m², 4th floor 2,934 m², totaling 3,582 m²
Term of construction: September 1, 1984 to May 25, 1985
Facilities : Opening/ May 27, 1985; Open time/10:00 a.m. to 10:00 p.m.; Closed regularly on/2nd Monday every month; Equipment/medical stress check, training gymnasium, aerobics studio, jazz dance studio, aesthetic salon, aqua studio, panorama bath, Jacuzzi; System/membership; Management/Nansei Co.; Number of employees/instructor 15, reception desk 8, totaling 23

材料仕様
〈フロント〉 床/パターンカーペット貼り 壁＆天井/ＰＢ下地パテ塗装
〈ロッカー室〉 床/カーペット貼り 壁＆天井/ＰＢ下地パテ塗装
〈メディカル〉 床/楢材フローリング パターン貼り 染色ウレタン 壁＆天井/ＰＢ下地 パテ塗装 〈スタジオ〉 床/カーペット貼り 壁/ミラー貼り 天井/ＰＢ下地パテ塗装 〈ジム〉 床/カーペットパターン貼り 壁/ＰＢ下地パテ塗装 一部ミラー貼り 天井/ＰＢ下地パテ塗装 〈エステティック〉 床/楢材フローリング 染色ウレタン 壁/ＰＢ下地 ヘシャンクロス パテ塗装 目地:木製塗装 天井/ＰＢ下地パテ塗装 〈プール〉 床/御影石パターン貼り プール内:タイル貼り 壁/モルタル パテ塗装 幕板:楢材染色 天井/軟質繊維板下地 寒冷紗パテ塗装 〈脱衣室〉 床/藤貼り 壁/ＰＢ下地ヘシャンクロス パテ塗装 〈スウェット〉 床/大理石パターン貼り 壁/タイルパターン貼り100角 天井/軟質繊維板下地 寒冷紗パテ塗装 〈リフレッシュ〉 床/パターンカーペット貼り 壁/ＰＢ下地 パテ塗装 腰:楢材パネル 染色ＣＬ仕上 天井/ＰＢ下地パテ塗装 照明器具/特注

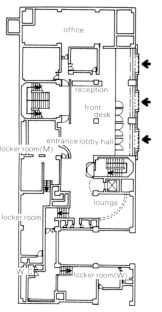

1F PLAN　S=1:600

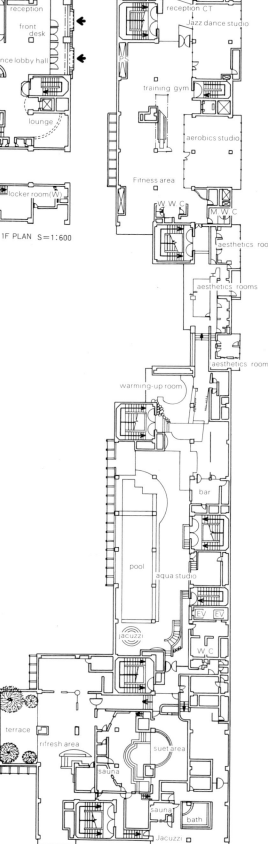

4F PLAN

入口廻り

The entrance area.

東側ファサード

The east side facade.

ダイヤモンドスポーツクラブ　アトラス

横浜市神奈川区沢渡 5　Phone/045-324-3600

撮影/本木誠一

Diamond Sports Club Atlas
5, Sawatari, Kanagawa-ku, Yokohama city, Kanagawa, Japan
Phone/045-324-3600

1階から4階までをストレートにつなぐ階段　壁面のアートは"アトラスの海"　作・佐伯和子
The staircase connecting the 1st through 4th floors straight.　The art on the wall is the "Sea of Atlas" by Kazuko Saeki.

3階・プール全景

A whole view of the pool at the 3rd floor.

上/5階・ランニングトラック全景
下/4階・アスレチックルーム
Top/ A whole view of the running track at the 5th floor.
Bottom/ The athletic room at the 4th floor.

上/2階・コーヒーショップ
下/2階・メンバーズサロン
Top/ The coffee shop at the 2nd floor.
Bottom/ The members salon at the 2nd floor.

この施設は 横浜駅西口より 徒歩10分のところに位置し 公園と学校
に挟まれた静かな地域である。
会員制の都市型複合スポーツクラブとして プレステージの高さを大切
にし 単にスポーツトレーニングによる健康維持だけではなく 休養
社交 文化 ビジネスにわたる幅広い機能を持っている。また 会員の
良さを十分に楽しんでもらうために 会員の資格は厳選されている。

〈中田敏彦/大林組東京本社一級建築士事務所〉(88-06)

設計:大林組東京本社一級建築事務所
施工:大林組東京本社 相鉄建設 J.V.

構　　　造:ＳＲＣ造　一部ＲＣ造
規　　　模:地下1階 地上4階 一部5階 塔屋1階
面　　　積:敷地/3,540.17㎡　建築/2,571.18㎡　床/地下1階 1,406.40㎡
　　　　　1階 2,513.94㎡　2階 1,633.64㎡　3階 2,284.04㎡　4階
　　　　　1,475.31㎡　5階 299.76㎡　合計9,613.09㎡
工　　　期:1986年6月1日～1987年5月25日

施設概要:開業/1987年6月1日　営業時間/午前10時～午後10時 定休日
/毎月第3水曜日　施設/1階　駐車場(45台収容) スカッシュ
ラケットボール コート インドアゴルフルーム アトラスホ
ール 2階 コーヒーショップ メンバーズサロン プレイル
ーム エグゼクティブルーム エステティック サロン 3階
スイミング プール(25m×10m) 浴室 サウナ マッサージ
ルーム レストルーム 4階 アスレチック ルーム エアロ
ビクス スタジオ(2) スキューバダイビング プール 5階 ラ
ンニング トラック システム/会員制 経営/横浜地下街㈱
従業員数/インストラクター46人 フロント19人 オフィス11
人 合計76人

Diamond Sports Club Atlas

This sports club is open in a quiet area sandwiched by a park and
school, and about 10 minutes by walk from the west exit of Yokohama Station.

As an urban composite membership sports club, "Diamond Sports
Club Atlas" makes much of high prestige, and is equipped with a wide
range of functions not merely for maintaining the health through
sports training, but also allowing the members to take rest, enjoy
social life, acquire culture and even have business opportunities.
In order to allow the members to fully enjoy their privileges, member
qualification is very strict.

Design: Toshihiko Nakane

Structure : SRC, RC in part
Scale : 1 under and 4 stories above the ground, and 1 roof floor
Area : Site/3,540.17 m²; Building/2,571.18 m²; Floo/1st basement 1,406.40 m², 1st floor 2,513.94 m², 2nd floor
1,633,64 m², 3rd floor 2,284.04 m², 4th floor 1,475.31
m², roof floor 299.76 m², totaling 9,613.09 m²
Term of construction: June 1, 1986 to May 25, 1987
Facilities : Opening/June 1, 1987; Open time/10:00 a.m. to 10:00
p.m.; Closed regularly on/3rd Wednesday every month;
Equipment/1st floor – parking lot (accommodating 45
cars), squash rackets ball court, indoor golf room, Atlas
Hall; 2nd floor – coffee shop, members salon, play room,
executive room, aesthetic salon; 3rd floor – swimming
pool (25 m × 10 m), bathroom, sauna, massage room,
rest room; 4th floor – athletic room, aerobics studio (2),
scuba diving pool; roof floor – running track; System/
membership; Management/Yokohama Chikagai Co.;
Number of employees/instructor 46, reception desk 19,
office staff 11, totaling 76

材料仕様
ヴォールト屋根/フッソ樹脂鋼板　外壁/タイル貼り　一部リシン吹き付け　サッシ:アルミジュラクロン塗装　外部床/大型特殊タイル
〈ロビー〉 床/大型特殊タイル 壁/ＰＢ寒冷紗ＶＰ 天井/石綿吸音板
〈プール〉 床/セラミックタイル 壁/モルタル鏝押さえ アクリルウレタン塗装 天井/耐湿石綿吸音
〈アスレチックルーム〉 床/ラバークッションロールカーペットt=20 壁/ＰＶ ＶＥＰ 天井/ケイ酸カルシウム板ＶＥＰ

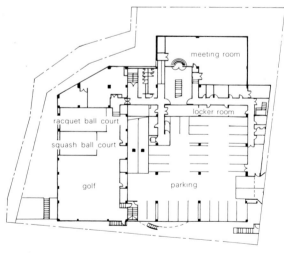

1F PLAN　S=1:1000

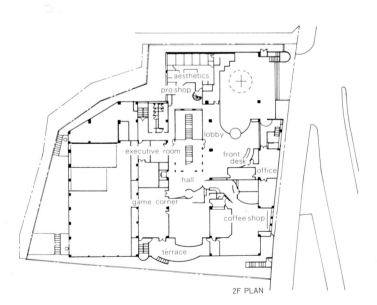

2F PLAN

地下鉄・東西線高架下からみた外観

The appearance viewed from beneath the elevated track of Subway Tozai Line.

スウェット

千葉県市川市末広丨丁目2-丨　Phone/0473-99-0121

撮影/平沢写真事務所

Sweat

1-2-1, Suehiro, Ichikawa city, Chiba, Japan　　Phone/0473-99-0121

正面入口
The front entrance.

1階・プール　イスラム教のモスクをデザインモチーフとしている

The pool at the 1st floor; the design motif is an Islamic mosque.

1階・レストラン

The restaurant at the 1st floor.

デザインの傾向として若者を対象とするクラブイメージと判断し そうした方向のインテリアを展開させてみた。

現代の日本の若者を相手にする場合 ヨーロッパの格調高い落ち着いた雰囲気を表現しても受け入れ難いと判断したからである。

一般に ヨーロッパのクラブでは 受付とフロント回りはメンバーに理解できればよく 一般の人々が初めて来ても 分かりにくいぐらいのレイアウトが良いとされているが ここでは若い人たち さらにはメンバー以外の人びとがビジターとして訪れることも考えられるので そうした限られた高級クラブのイメージはやめ 親しみやすい 大衆的な開放感のあるインテリアにした。　　　　　　　　　〈森　京介〉(86-07)

設計：森　京介建築事務所
協力：構造/大島コンサルタント
施工：建築/熊谷組横浜支店
　　　内装/横浜高島屋

上/1階・プロショップ
下/3階・ラケット　ボール　コート
Top/ The pro shop at the 1st floor.
Bottom/ The racket ball court at the 3rd floor.

Sweat

Based on the policy that this club should have an image intended for young people, its interior has been designed along that line.

In view of Japanese young people today, it was judged that a dignified and composed European atmosphere would be hardly accepted by them.

Generally, European clubs prefer an exclusive layout in which the reception and front are recognizable by the members alone, or rather hard to recognize by those who visit for the first time. As far as this club is concerned, however, since it may be visited by young people and non-members, by giving up the European exclusive image of a high class club, it employed a popular, open image for its interior.

Design: Kyosuke Mori

構　　造：ＳＲＣ造
規　　模：地上4階　塔屋1階
面　　積：敷地/3,871.01㎡　建築/1,910.24㎡　床/1階　1,746.57㎡　2階　1,247.04㎡　3階　1,168.12㎡　4階　820.97㎡　塔屋 49.82㎡　合計5,032.52㎡
工　　期：1985年5月7日～1986年1月31日

施設概要：開業/1986年2月1日　営業時間/午前10時～午後10時　定休日/毎月第3火曜日　施設/プール　ガーデンプール　子供プール　スキューバダイビングプール　ジャグジープール　テニスコート　ラケットボールコート　ゴルフクリニック　エステティックサロン　アスレチックジム　エアロビクススタジオ　ウェルネスラボラトリー　ヨーガ＆ベーシックスタジオ　会議室　料飲施設/レストラン　ティールーム　ピアノ＆バーラウンジ　和風割烹　ディスコ　その他/プロショップ　駐車場　システム/会員制　経営/㈱スウェット　従業員数/施設運営部門(インストラクターほか)20人　管理部門60人　合計80人

Structure : SRC
Scale : 4 stories above the ground, and 1 roof floor
Area : Site/3,871.01 m²; Building/1,910.24 m²; Floor/1st floor 1,746.57 m², 2nd floor 1,247.04 m², 3rd floor 1,168.12 m², 4th floor 820.97 m², roof floor 49.82 m², totaling 5,032.52 m²
Term of construction: May 7, 1985 to January 31, 1986
Facilities : Opening/February 1, 1986; Open time/10:00 a.m. to 10:00 p.m.; Closed regularly on/3rd Tuesday every month; Equipment/pool, garden pool, children's pool, scuba diving pool, Jacuzzi pool, tennis court, racket ball court, golf clinic, aesthetic salon, athletic gymnasium, aerobics studio, wellness laboratory, yoga & basic studio, conference room; Eating & drinking facilities/restaurant, tearoom, piano & bar lounge, Japanese cuisine restaurant, disco; Others/pro shop, parking lot; System/membership; Management/Sweat Co.; Number of employees/Facilities operation department (instructor, etc.) 20, administrative department 60, totaling 80

材料仕様
屋根/豆砂利コンクリート金鏝押さえ　テニスコート:ゴムチップ天圧t＝8着色及びライン　外壁/モルタル木鏝塗下地　磁器タイル貼り　ステンレス鏡面板t＝1.5貼り　正面玄関柱/樹脂成形疑石柱　外部床/屋外テラス:磁器タイル貼り200角
〈1階　ロビー〉床/テラゾブロック貼り600×t＝25　幅木/テラゾブロック貼りh＝200　壁/テラゾブロック貼り550角t＝25　ミラー貼りt＝5　モルタル金鏝押さえＶＰ　天井/ＰＢt＝9寒冷紗パテしごきＶＰ
〈1階　ティールーム〉床/テラゾブロック貼り　600×400 t＝25　幅木/テラゾブロック貼りh＝550　壁/モルタル金鏝押さえＶＰ　天井/ＰＢt＝9寒冷紗パテしごきＶＰ
〈1階　レストラン〉床/フェルトt＝10下地　カーペット貼り　幅木/堅木(黒)h＝100　合板堅羽目染色(黒)h＝900　1800　御影石貼りh＝900　1800　壁/プラスター下地　プラスター塗　モルタル金鏝押さえＡＥＰ　天井/ＰＢ寒冷紗パテしごきＶＰ
〈1階　プール〉床/プール用磁器質タイル貼り115×240　壁/モルタル金鏝押さえエポキシ系吹き付けタイル　天井/ＦＢt＝5耐質性パーライト吹き付き　柱/ステンレス鏡面仕上及びテラゾブロック貼り　柱頭/樹肥成形疑石
〈2階　ピアノ＆バーラウンジ〉床/フェルトt＝10下地　カーペット貼りt＝7　幅木/一部テラゾブロック　壁/砂岩小端積み　モルタル金鏝押さえダークミラーt＝5貼り　テラゾブロック貼り400角　天井/ＰＢt＝9寒冷紗パテしごきＶＰ
〈3階　エアロビクススタジオ〉床/合板t＝15下地　楢フローリングt＝18特殊貼りウレタン塗装　幅木/木製ＯＳＣＬ　h＝60　壁/モルタル金鏝押さえＶＰ　ＰＢt＝12　下地ＶＰ　天井/ＰＢt＝9下地　石綿吸音板貼りt＝12
〈3階　アスレチックジム〉床/モルタル金鏝押さえt＝30下地　体育用カーペットt＝20　じゅうたんt＝7二重貼り　幅木/ソフト幅木h＝60　木製/ＯＳＣＬ　h＝100　壁/モルタル金鏝押さえＶＰ　ＰＢt＝12下地　ＶＰ　天井/ＰＢt＝9下地　石綿吸音板貼りt＝12

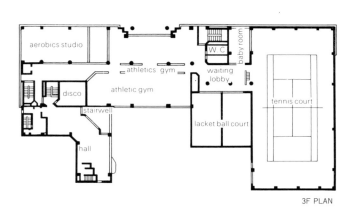

3F PLAN

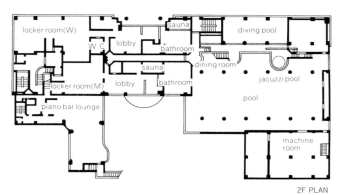

2F PLAN

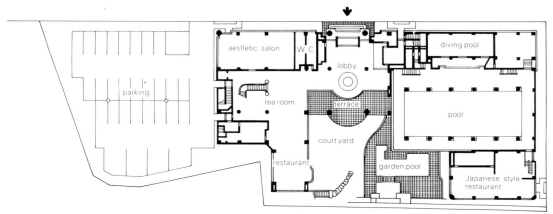

1F PLAN　S＝1:800

西側外観をみる

The west side appearance.

プロスパークラブサンダ

高松市木太町字東浜2702番1　Phone/0878-37-4666

撮影/高橋　章

Prosper Club Sanda
2702-1, Higashihama, Kida-cho, Takamatsu city, Kagawa, Japan
Phone/0878-37-4666

1階・喫茶　クラブ会員だけでなく　一般にも開放されている
The tea room at the 1st floor; opened not only to the members, but also
to ordinary guests.

101

入口ゲートを通して北側外観をみる

The north side appearance viewed across the entrance gate.

1階・25mプール全景

A whole view of 25 m pool.

2階・アスレチックルーム　The athletic room at the 2nd floor.

1階・ショップコーナー　The shop corner at the 1st floor.

プロスパークラブ サンダ

この施設は　スイミングスクールのみの施設ではなく　利用者にいくつかのスポーツを楽しんでもらう設備と環境を提供し　ヘルシーな時代のニーズに応じうる　総合的なスポーツクラブを目指し　スイミングスクール　エアロビクススタジオ　アスレチックジム　子供スポーツ教室喫茶等を併設し　香川県下では　初めての総合スポーツ施設である。
全体の色彩は　清潔で明るく　楽しさのある健康建築をイメージし　内外ともホワイトを基調として　プールサイドはブルー　その他のコーナーには赤　青　緑　黄とカラフルな色使いをポイントとした。

〈榎　秀生〉(86-07)

設計：エノキ建築事務所
協力：構造/森設備事務所
施工：大成建設四国支店

構　造：RC造
規　模：地上3階
面　積：敷地/2,594㎡　建築/1,349㎡　床/1階 1,331㎡　2階 420㎡
　　　　3階 234㎡　合計 1,985㎡
工　期：1985年11月25日～1986年4月25日

施設概要：開業/1986年4月26日　営業時間/午前6時～午後9時　定休日/なし　施設/温水プール　フィットネススタジオ　アスレチックジム　システム/会員制　経営/㈲プロスパーサンダ　小倉武雄　従業員数/インストラクター15人

Prosper Club Sanda

This club is aimed to offer not only swimming school facilities, but also equipment and environment for allowing users to enjoy a number of sports, and thereby serve as a general sports club that responds to the needs of the times for healthy life. Consisting of a swimming school, aerobics studio, athletic gymnasium, children's sports class, etc., and also having an adjacent tearoom, etc., "Prosper Club Sanda" is the first such general sports center in Kagawa Prefecture.
Generally, to present a clean, bright image of an amusing, pleasant building for health, both interior and exterior are finished with white as the basic tone, while the poolside uses blue, and the other corners uses red, blue, green and yellow, thus giving a colorful image.

Design: Hideo Enoki

Structure : RC
Scale　　: 3 stories above the ground
Area　　: Site/2,594 m²; Building/1,349 m²; Floor/1st floor 1,331 m², 2nd floor 420 m², 3rd floor 234 m², totaling 1,985 m²
Term of construction: November 25, 1985 to April 25, 1986
Facilities : Opening/April 26, 1986; Open time/6:00 a.m. to 9:00 p.m.; Fixed close/nil; Facilities/heated pool, fitness studio, athletic gymnasium; System/membership; Management/Takeo Ogura, Proper Sanda Co.; Number of employees/ instructor 15

材料仕様
屋根/アルミ亜鉛合金メッキ鋼板横貼り　外壁/塗装合板型枠コンクリート弾性吹き付けタイル　一部含浸性防汚材塗　外部床/モルタル鏝磨き　目地:タイル貼り　サイン/スチールOP　床/モルタル鏝磨き　ホモジニアスビニール床タイルカーペット貼り磁器質タイル貼り　楢フローリング貼りEP　壁/塗装合板型枠コンクリート弾性吹き付けタイル　一部含浸性汚材塗　天井/PBパテしごきAEP　コンクリートコンシール塗　プール/結露防止塗材　家具/木製フフラッシュOP

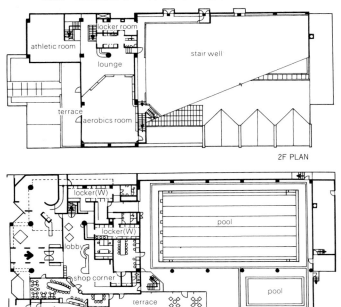

2F PLAN

1F PLAN

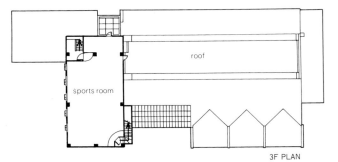

3F PLAN

1階・カフェテリアよりメインスタジオをみる

The main studio viewed from the cafeteria at the 1st floor.

ティップネス

東京都渋谷区宇田川町16-4　Phone/03-770-3531

撮影/飯嶋裕司

Tipness
16-4, Udagawa-cho, Shibuya-ku, Tokyo, Japan
Phone/03-770-3531

外観全景
The entire appearance.

2階リゾートフロアをみる　プール　ジェットバス　タンニングルーム（日焼室）の構成
The 2nd resort floor, consisting of a pool, jet bath and tanning room (sun-room).

上/1階のメインスタジオよりロビー方向をみる
下/3階のエクササイズフロアをみる
Top/ The lobby area viewed from the 1st floor main studio.
Bottom/ The 3rd exercise floor.

Tipness

The concept of "Tipness" is a club surrounded with nature and green. Mainly aimed to capture office ladies, white has been chosen as the basic tone to give a bright, healthy image, rather than a gorgeous image. The dynamic lines of the building represented by its three components – aerobics atudio, athletic gymnasium and pool – have been systematically combined with the locker rooms, and the rooms have been arranged according to the division between "dry" and "wet" dynamic lines. The aerobics studio at the 1st floor also incorporates the elements of an event hall so that it can be used as a stage with the staircase landing as a circle. Although the front road is narrow and there is a setback, this drawback has been rather utilized for the exterior design, and a window with curved surface has been formed in a semi-vaulted style. The skylight of two-stage in 1/4 circle and white outer wall are helping in creating an atmosphere worthy of bright fitness club. Opening the window, you can see the bright sky, and even forget that you are in the midst of a "sunless" street.

Design: Shoji Nishiwaki

Structure : SRC
Scale : 3 stories above the ground, and 1 roof floor
Area : Site/585.44 m²; Building/503.22 m²; Floor/1st floor 496.69 m², (including kitchen 9 m²), 2nd floor 491.45 m², 3rd floor 400.85 m², roof floor 15.84 m², totaling 1,404.83 m²
Term of construction: August 31, 1986 to March 10, 1987
Facilities : Opening/April 1, 1987; Open time/Monday to Friday – 7:00 a.m. to 10 p.m., Saturday – 9:30 a.m. to 10:00 p.m., Sunday – 9:30 a.m. to 7:00 p.m; Fixed close/nil; Equipment/various devices for fitness, main studio, sub studio, pool, jet bath; Others/cafeteria, sports goods shop; System/membership; Management/Tipness Co.; Number of employees/40

ティップネス

この施設のコンセプトは　自然と緑に囲まれた
クラブ。ターゲットはOLを主体とし　豪華さよ
り明るく健康的であるべく　色彩は白を基調と
した。建物の動線としてのエアロビクススタジ
オ　アスレチックジム　プールの3つの要素に
対してロッカー室を有機的に組合せドライ動線
とウェット動線との区分けから室の配列をきめ
た。1階のエアロビクススタジオはイベントホ
ールとしての要素も取り入れ　階段の踊り場を
円形としてステージにも利用できる。外部デザ
インの構成として　前面道路が狭いためセット
バックがあり　逆にそれを利用して半分のヴォ
ルト状に曲面窓を設けた。2階の¼円のスカイ
ライトと白いネオパリエの外壁が明るいフィッ
トネスクラブの雰囲気を造っている。窓を開け
ると空が見え明るく開放的で　ビルの谷間に居
ることを忘れさせてくれる。

　　　　　〈西脇昭二/リック一級建築士事務所〉(87-07)
設計：リック一級建築士事務所
協力：設備/雄建築設備設計事務所
施工：清水建設

構　　　造：SRC造
規　　　模：地上3階 塔屋1階
面　　　積：敷地/585.44㎡　建築/503.22㎡　床/
　　　　　1階 496.69㎡（内 厨房9㎡）2階
　　　　　491.45㎡　3階 400.85㎡　塔屋
　　　　　15.84㎡　合計 1,404.83㎡
工　　　期：1986年8月31日〜1987年3月10日

施設概要：開業/1987年4月1日　営業時間/月〜
　　　　　金曜日　午前7時〜午後10時　土曜日
　　　　　午前9時30分〜午後10時　日曜日　午
　　　　　前9時30分〜午後7時　定休日/なし
　　　　　施設/フィットネス用機器各種　メイ
　　　　　ンスタジオ　サブスタジオ　プール　ジ
　　　　　ェットバス　その他/カフェテリア
　　　　　スポーツグッズショップ　システム/
　　　　　会員制　経営/㈱ティップス　従業員
　　　　　数/40人

材料仕様
屋根/アスファルト防水の上　軽量コンクリート直押さえ
外壁/結晶化ガラス貼り　コンクリート打ち放し下地吹き付
けタイル仕上　サッシ/アルミ及びステンレス　外部床/御影
石貼りバーナー仕上　床/御影石貼り本磨き仕上＆バーナー
仕上　イタリア楓貼り　タイルカーペット貼り　幅木/ステ
ンレス鏡面仕上　樹脂幅木＆壁/外彩模様塗装　ビニールク
ロス貼り　吹き付けタイル貼り仕上　天井/PB下地　ネッ
ト天井　照明器具/ダウンライト　家具/塩路材生地仕上

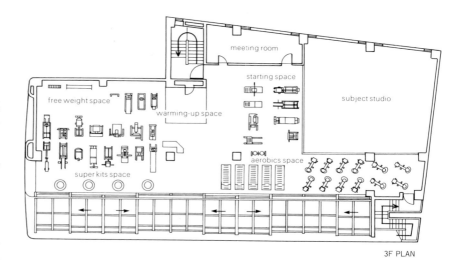

3F PLAN

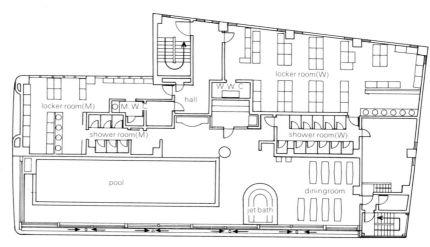

2F PLAN

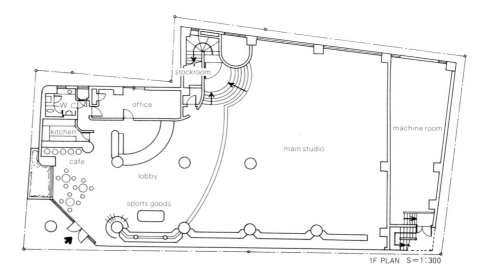

1F PLAN　S=1:300

全景をみる

A whole view.

クアハウス石和

山梨県東八代郡石和町八田330-5　Phone/0552-63-7071

撮影/飯嶋裕司

Kurhaus Isawa
Isawa-machi, Higashi-Yatsushiro-gun, Yamanashi, Japan
Phone/0552-63-7071

正面入口廻りをみる
The front entrance area.

1階バーデゾーン全景　運動浴を中心に全身　部分浴　圧注浴　ドゴール浴　気泡浴等が葡萄の房のイメージで構成されている
A whole view of the 1st floor Bade zone. With the exercise bath in the center, the whole/partial body bath, pressure-pouring bath, de Gaulle bath, bubble bath, etc. are arranged in an image of grapes cluster.

富士山形の窓がある1階ホール待合席
The waiting seat at the 1st floor hall with a window shaped like Mt. Fuji.

3階・ツイン客室
The twin guest room at the 3rd floor.

上／２階・体力測定管理室の入口廻り　左手に男子浴室　右手に女子浴室
下／女子浴室（裸バーデゾーン）　奥は露天風呂がある

Top/ The entrance area of the physical strength measurement/control room at the 2nd floor. The male bathroom at left and female bathroom at right.

Bottom/ The female bathroom (naked Bade zone); there is an open-air bath at an inner part.

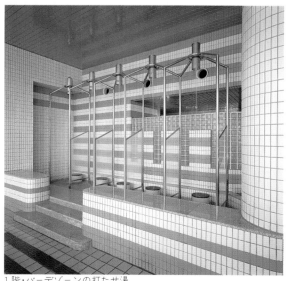

１階・バーデゾーンの打たせ湯
The shower bath in the 1st floor Bade zone.

１階・バーデゾーンの寝湯
The lie-down bath in the 1st floor Bade zone.

クアハウス石和

昭和38年に突如 温泉が湧出し その温泉を活用したリハビリテーション温泉病院「石和温泉病院」が開設されたが、この「クアハウス石和」は同病院が全国に先駆けて人間ドック併設型クアハウスとして建設したものである。

施設は 地域表現として山梨県の名産ブドウの青紫 赤紫を基調に ワイン(白 赤 ローゼ) 柿(だいだい) 桃(桃色) の色彩を 白をベースとした建物にあしらった。

また施設全体に自然光を取り入れ 明るく 開放的 健康的な空間構成を採り 精神の開放 ストレスの解消に適した快適空間を目指した。とくに バーデゾーン(浴槽ゾーン)はサイドライト トップライト を大きく採用した。

バーデゾーンは 水着スタイル(1階)と裸スタイル(2階)の混合方式の利用により 水着利用の欠点を取り除いた。

〈矢崎英夫/西尾建築設計事務所〉(88-12)

設計:西尾建築設計事務所
協力:構造/構設計事務所
　　　機械/ユニ設備設計
　　　電気/小野設備設計事務所
施工:建築/早野組
　　　内装/早野組 インテリアさの

構　造:RC造
規　模:地上3階 塔屋1階
面　積:敷地/14,855㎡ 建築/1,582㎡ 床/1階 1,501㎡ 2階 1,241
　　　　㎡ 3階 306㎡ 塔屋 18㎡ 合計 3,066㎡
工　期:1986年6月19日〜1987年5月5日

施設概要:開業/1987年6月15日 営業時間/平日 午前9時〜午後7時
　　　日曜日 午前10時〜午後5時 休館日/祝日 毎月第3月曜日及
　　　び年末年始 施設/宿泊客室 10(シングル6 ツイン4) 水着
　　　バーデゾーン(かぶり湯 歩行湯 寝湯 蒸気浴 うたせ湯 ソラリ
　　　ウム 箱蒸し 全身浴 部分浴 ドゴール浴 圧注浴 噴水気泡浴
　　　運動浴) 裸バーデゾーン(全身部分浴 サウナ 水風呂 噴出浴
　　　洗い場 露天風呂) 泉質はアルカリ性単純温泉 コースメニュ
　　　ー/宿泊人間ドック(1泊2日) 日帰り人間ドック(1日) 中間
　　　チェック 成人病検診 健康増進コース 経営/医療法人 石
　　　和温泉病院 天野 健 従業員数/医師1人 保健婦1人 ヘ
　　　ルスケアトレーナー3人 管理栄養士1人 メディカル スタ
　　　ッフ12人 合計18人

Kurhaus Isawa

In 1963 a hot spring gushed out suddenly, and "Isawa Onsen Byoin" (Isawa Hot Spring Hospital) was opened to utilize the hot spring for rehabilitation. "Kurhaus Isawa" was constructed by the hospital as a Kurhaus capable of complete physical check-up – the first such center in Japan.

To give a local presentation with color, the building has employed bluish purple and purplish red of grape – a staple of Yamanashi Prefecture – as the basic tone, accented with wine colors (white, red rose), persimmon (reddish yellow), and peach (pink) against the white background.

The entire facilities let in natural light to create a bright, open, healthy and pleasant space that is suitable for releasing the mind and getting rid of stress. The Bade (bath) zone, among others, comes with a larger sidelight and toplight.

The Bade zone allows both swimsuit style (1st floor) and naked style (2nd floor) to eliminate the conventional inconvenience.

Design: Hideo Yazaki

Structure : RC
Scale : 3 stories above the ground, and 1 roof floor
Area : Site/14,855 m²; Building/1,582 m²; Floor/1st floor 1,501 m², 2nd floor 1,241 m², 3rd floor 306 m², roof floor 18 m², totaling 3,066 m²
Term of construction: June 19, 1986 to May 15, 1987
Facilities : Opening/June 15, 1987; Open time/weekday – 9:00 a.m. to 7:00 p.m., Sunday – 10:00 a.m. to 5:00 p.m.; Closed/holiday, 3rd Monday every month and year-end to New Year's days; Equipment/hotel room 10 (single 6, twin 4), swimsuit Bade zone (consisting of various types of hot spring), naked Bade zone (consisting of various types of hot spring) – simple alkaline spring; Course menu/complete physical checkup (a night's stay), complete physical checkup (a day's trip), intermediate check-up, adult disease diagnosis, health improving course; Management/Ken Amano, Isawa Onsen Byoin (Isawa Hot Spring Hospital); Number of employees/doctor 1, health nurse 1, health care trainer 3, supervisory dietitian 1, medical staff 12, totaling 18

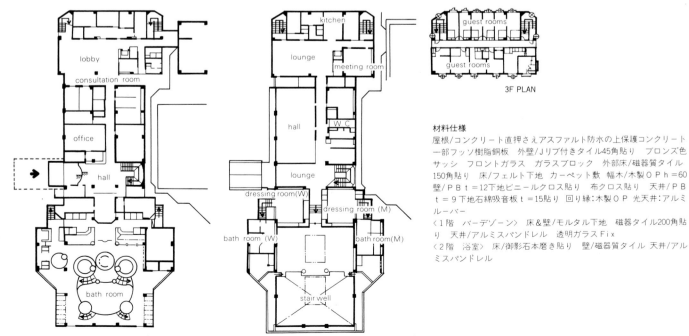

1F PLAN　　2F PLAN　　3F PLAN

材料仕様

屋根/コンクリート直押さえアスファルト防水の上保護コンクリート 一部フッソ樹脂銅板 外壁/Jリブ付きタイル45角貼り ブロンズ色サッシ フロントガラス ガラスブロック 外部床/磁器質タイル150角貼り 床/フェルト下地 カーペット敷 幅木/木製OP h=60 壁/PB t=12下地ビニールクロス貼り 布クロス貼り 天井/PB t=9下地石綿吸音板 t=15貼り 回り縁:木製OP 光天井:アルミルーバー

〈1階 バーデゾーン〉床&壁/モルタル下地 磁器タイル200角貼り 天井/アルミスパンドレル 透明ガラスFix

〈2階 浴室〉床/御影石本磨き貼り 壁/磁器質タイル 天井/アルミスパンドレル

1階・正面入口ホール前よりフロア中央に中庭を配したロビー廻りをみる
The lobby area with a courtyard in the floor center viewed from the 1st floor front entrance hall.

駐車場側より正面外観をみる
The front appearance viewed from the parking lot side.

プール側の外観をみる
The appearance in the pool side.

クアハウス九谷

石川県能美郡寺井町泉台東10番地　Phone/0761-58-5050

撮影/荒木義久

Kurhaus Kutani
Terai-cho, Nomi-gun, Ishikawa, Japan　Phone/0761-58-5050

上/1階・バーデゾーンの全身浴前より運動浴を中心にみる
下/1階・バーデゾーンのかぶり湯前より全景をみる

Top/ The exercise bath viewed from the whole body bath in the 1st floor Bade zone.
Bottom/ A whole scene of the 1st floor Bade zone viewed from the shower bath.

1階・プールゾーン全景みる　一般プール　子供プール　スパイラルスライダーの三つの施設て構成されている
A whole view of the 1st floor pool zone, consisting of an ordinary pool, children's pool and spiral slider.

1階・休憩コーナーをみる
The rest corner at the 1st floor.

1階・プールゾーンのホットタブ前より子供プールとスパイラルスライダー施設をみる
The children's pool and spiral slider viewed from the hot tub in the 1st floor pool zone.

クアハウス九谷

外観は"アクア(水)ヘルス 自然の緑"をテーマとし シンプルで かつ三世代の語らいが生まれる温かさを建物に表現し 玄関ロビー正面に配した中庭は テーマを融合したつくりとなっており 利用者を優しく迎えてくれる。

今回 地元の人々にクアハウスを身近に接してもらうために設けられた健康温泉ゾーンはクアゾーンの動線とは明快に分かれ 管理上の合理化が図られている。バーデゾーン(浴槽ゾーン)は水着着用混浴方式を採用し ゾーンの重複が避けられたことと 天井が柔らかな曲線でデザインされ プールともども天井高が適切であったため バーデゾーンおよびプールは空間にゆとりをもちながら合理的におさまった。

なお バーデゾーンは すべての浴槽から晴れた日には白山連峰が眺められるように配慮した。　〈山下憲三／エム・エー・シー建築研究所〉(88-12)

基本設計:塚設計・計画事務所
設計:設計管理／エム・エー・シー(MAC)研究所
協力:設備／マッハ設備設計研究所
施工:西松建設

構　造:RC造
規　模:地下1階 地上2階
面　積:敷地/38,506㎡ 建築/2,488㎡ 床/地下1階 374㎡ 1階 2,439㎡(内 厨房84㎡) 2階 941㎡ 合計 3,754㎡
工　期:1987年9月15日～1988年7月25日

施設概要:開業/1988年8月6日 営業時間/午前10時～午後10時 休館日/なし 施設概要/バーデゾーン(かぶり湯 うたせ湯 気泡湯 箱蒸し 渦巻きプール ミストサウナ 遠赤外線サウナ) 健康温泉ゾーン(トレーニングルーム レストルーム マッサージ室 健康相談室) 泉質はナトリウム－硫酸塩 塩化物泉(含食塩芒硝泉) 弱アルカリ性低張性高温泉 入館料/大人(中学生まで)1500 小学生800 子供400 会員制システムあり 経営/㈶寺井町余暇健康開発公社 従業員数/職員14人 ヘルスケアートレーナー2人 スポーツ指導員1人 看護婦1人 パート・アルバイト7人 テナント従業員(レストラン 売店)計10人 合計35人

Kurhaus Kutani

Having the appearance designed to represent the theme "Aqua(Water), Health and Green of Nature," the building expresses simplicity and warmth in which communications between three generations will be made naturally. The courtyard arranged in front of the porch lobby is also designed to embody the theme of "Kurhaus Kutani" and welcomes guests gently.

The health hot spring zone provided this time for community inhabitants to become acquainted with the Kurhaus, is clearly separated from the Kur zone for rationalized management. The Bade (bathroom) zone employs a mixed swimsuit bathing system to prevent the zone overlapping. Moreover, since the Bade zone's ceiling has been designed with gentle curves and the ceiling height was adequate, together with that of the pool, both the Bade zone and pool have been reasonably installed in a comfortable space.

Incidentally, on a fine day, the Hakusan range can be overlooked from all bathrooms in the Bade zone.

Design: Syozo Tsukamoto + Kenzo Yamashita

Structure : RC
Scale : 1 under and 2 stories above the ground
Area : Site/38,506 m²; Building/2,488 m²; Floor/1st basement 374 m², 1st floor 2,439 m² (including kitchen 84 m²) 2nd floor 941 m², totaling 3,754 m²
Term of construction: September 15, 1987 to July 25, 1988
Facilities : Opening/August 6, 1988; Open time/10:00 a.m. to 10:00 p.m; Fixed close/nil; Equipment/Bade zone – various types of hot spring, whirling pool, mist sauna, far-infrared ray sauna, Health hot spring zone – training room, rest room, massage room, health consulting room, Hot spring ingredients – sodium sulfate, chloride (containing sodium chloride and crude sodium sulfate), weak alkaline, hypotonic, high temperature spring; Management/Teraimachi Yoka Kenko Kaihatsu Kosha(Teraimachi Leisure & Health Development Corporation); Number of employees/staff 14, health care trainer 2, sports instructor 1, nurse 1, part-time 7, tenant (restaurant and selling shop) employee 10, totaling 35

材料仕様
屋根/コンクリート アスファルト防水 外壁/モルタル下地炻器二丁掛けタイル カーテンウォール 熱線反射ガラス 外部床/モルタル下地磁器質タイル貼り200角 床/モルタル下地じゅうたん敷 壁&天井/PB下地ビニールクロス貼り
〈バーデゾーン〉床/モルタル下地磁器質タイル貼り200角 壁/モルタル下地磁器質タイル貼り50×100 天井/ホワイトアルミスパンドル貼り

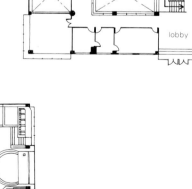

2F PLAN

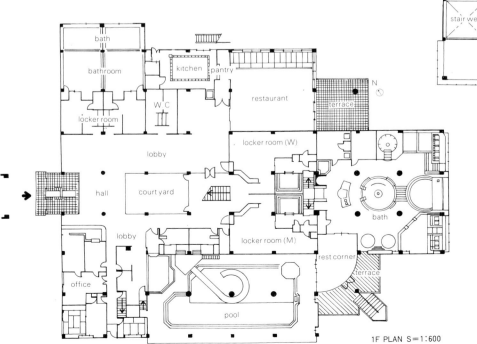

1F PLAN S=1:600

センターコートを通してクラブハウス棟をみる
The club house building viewed across the center court.

山中湖庭球倶楽部

山梨県南都留郡山中湖村山中352-1　Phone/0555-62-3390

撮影/鳴瀬　亨

Yamanakako Tennis Club
352-1, Yamanaka, Yamanakako-mura, Minami-Tsuru-gun, Yamanashi, Japan　Phone/0555-62-3390

ニュー山中湖ホテル（既存）前よりスーパーデッキエントランスをみる
The super deck entrance viewed from New Yamanakako Hotel (existing).

アウトドアコート群を巡るスーパーデッキをみる

The super deck passing by the outdoor courts.

クラブハウス棟　その後方がインドアコート棟
The club house building behind which stands the indoor court building

インドアコートをみる
The indoor court.

クラブハウス棟のラウンジをみる

The lounge in the club house building.

山中湖庭球倶楽部

この施設は　山中湖畔にほど近く　富士山に向かって延びる細長い敷地
に計画されたリゾートの会員制テニスクラブである。
細長い敷地には　延長550mにおよぶ枕木を敷並べた歩行デッキをつくり
各施設を結んでいる。
この"スーパーデッキ"は　単なる歩行デッキである以上に　人々が自由
に自己を演じる舞台装置となるように意図したもので　スポーツ　レジ
ャーを通じて自己実現をはかる　小さな旅の道筋でもある。
<北村昌三/スーパービジョン>(87-07)

企画:リゾートボックス
設計:スーパービジョン
施工:浅沼組

構　　造:クラブハウス/木造　インドアコート/S造
規　　模:クラブハウス/2階　インドアコート/平屋
面　　積:敷地/34,200㎡　建築/クラブハウス 253㎡　インドアコート
　　　　2,925㎡　床/クラブハウス 408㎡　インドアコート 2,925㎡
工　　期:1985年11月19日〜1986年5月20日

施設概要:開業/1986年5月24日　営業時間/午前10時〜午後9時　定休日
　　　　/なし　施設/宿泊客室 50　クラブハウス テニスコート 18
　　　　(インドア4　アウトドア14)　システム/会員制　ナイター設備
　　　　あり　経営/㈱リゾートボックス　長谷川茂　従業員数/40人

Yamanakako Tennis Club

Standing close by Lake Yamanaka, "Yamanakako Tennis Club" is a membership resort club planned at a narrow site extending towards Mt. Fuji.
The narrow site is covered with a walking deck of crossties 550 m in total length, connecting the facilities.
This "Super Deck" has been designed to serve as not a mere walking deck, but as a stage where people play themselves freely. In this sense, it also is a place passed by along a short trip for self-realization through sports and leisure.

Design: Super Vision

Structure : Club house building/wooden; Indoor court building/S
Scale : Club house/2 stories; Indoor court/1 story
Area : Site/34,200 m²; Building/club house 253 m², indoor court 2,925 m²; Floor/club house 408 m², indoor court 2,925 m²
Term of construction: November 19, 1985 to May 20, 1986
Facilities : Opening/May 24, 1986; Open time/10:00 a.m. to 9:00 p.m.; Fixed close/nil; Equipment/guest room 50, club house, tennis court 18 (indoor 4, outdoor 14), with lighting equipment for night play; System/membership; Management/Resort Box Co., Shigeru Hasegawa; Number of employees/40

材料仕様
〈クラブハウス〉　屋根/銅板一文字葺き　外壁/米松南京下見貼りOP　床/楢フローリングt＝15ワックス仕上　壁/米松本実貼りOS　天井/米松南京下見貼りOS
〈インドアコート〉　屋根/長尺板葺き　外壁/化粧石綿スレート板　床/アスファルトカラーペイント　壁/米松板貼り＆化粧石綿スレート板　天井/エチレン断熱シート貼り
〈スーパーデッキ〉　デッキ/ケンパス材

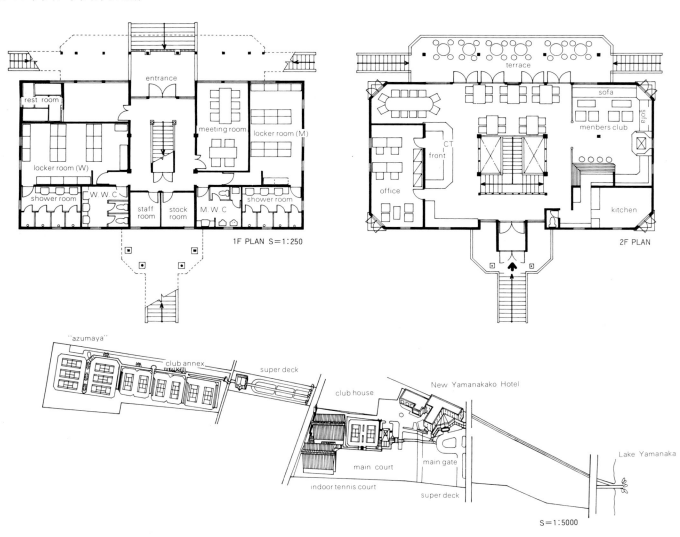

クラブハウス棟外観をみる

The appearance of the club house building.

南側外観をみる　ウッディなクラブハウス棟とテント造のインドアコート
The south side appearance. The woody club house building and tented indoor court.

シーサイド テニスクラブ 高松

高松市屋島西町2490　Phone/0878-41-6377

撮影/大竹静市郎

Seaside Tennis Club Takamatsu
2490, Yashima-Nishimachi, Takamatsu city, Kagawa, Japan　Phone/0878-41-6377

Ａコート前テラスよりクラブハウス棟をみる

The club house building viewed from the terrace in front of court A.

上/テラスを通してＡコートをみる
下/クラブハウスのサンルーム
Top/ Court A viewed across the terrace.
Bottom/ The sun-room in the club house.

クラブハウス１階のラウンジスペース
The lounge space at the 1st floor club house.

鉄骨造りテント張り構造の軽快なインドアコート
The bright indoor court in the tented steel frame structure.

シーサイド テニスクラブ 高松

このクラブは 屋島の塩田跡地に建設された。設計計画としては雨天
夜間の利用に対応できる装備として 2面収容のインドアコートと屋外
コート6面にも すべてナイター照明を設置した。
クラブハウスは 木造平屋建 ラウンジスペースは 特に木造としての
テクスチュアを生かすことを考え 床 壁 天井ともフローリング貼りとし
サッシも木製建具を使用した。インドアコートは鉄骨トラス造りで 壁
面は天気の状態で自由に開閉できるカーテン式になっているので 屋内
コートにありがちな閉鎖的な空間ではなく 屋外につながった空間とし
て プレーが楽しめるようにした。　〈丹澤 裕/集建築設計〉(87-07)
企画:日本プロテニスエンタープライズ
設計:集建築設計
施工:鹿島建設四国支店

構　　造:クラブハウス棟/木造　インドアコート/S造
規　　模:クラブハウス棟/平屋　インドアコート/平屋
面　　積:敷地/5,664.63㎡　建築/クラブハウス棟 289㎡ インドアコー
　　　　ト棟 1,365㎡　床/クラブハウス棟 277.9㎡　インドアコート
　　　　棟 1,365㎡)
工　　期:1984年11月15日～1985年7月1日

施設概要:開業/1985年7月6日　営業時間/午前9時～午後9時 定休日
　　　　/なし 施設/クラブハウス テニス コート8(インドア2
　　　　アウトドア6) システム/会員制 経営/㈲ウエノ 従業員数/
　　　　コーチ3人 オフィス4人 パート アルバイト4人 合計11人

Seaside Tennis Club Takamatsu

This club was constructed on the site of an old salt field in Yashima. In order to allow players to enjoy tennis at night or even when it is raining, all of two indoor courts and six outdoor courts are equipped with lighting for night game.

The club house is a wooden one-storied building, and the lounge space is finished with flooring on all of its floor, wall and ceiling, in order to utilize the wooden texture. The sashes are also of wooden make. The indoor courts are of steel-framed trass construction, and the wall surface is designed as a curtain system that can be opened/closed at will according to the weather condition. Thus, differing from indoor courts placed in a closed space, these indoor courts are placed in a space openly connected to the outdoors, so that players can enjoy tennis in a bright atmosphere.

Design: Yutaka Tanzawa

Structure : Club house building/wooden; Indoor court building/S
Scale : Club house/1 story; Indoor court/1 story
Area : Site/5,664.63 m²; Building/club house building 289 m², indoor court building 1,365 m²; Floor/club house building 277.9 m², indoor court building 1,365 m²
Term of construction: November 15, 1984 to July 1, 1985
Facilities : Opening/July 6, 1985; Open time/9:00 a.m. to 9:00 p.m.; Fixed close/nil; Equipment/club house, tennis court 8 (indoor 2, outdoor 6); System/membership; Management/Ueno Co.; Number of employees/coach 3, office staff 4, part-time 4, totaling 11

材料仕様
〈クラブハウス棟〉 屋根/アスファルトシングル葺き　外壁/杉羽目板 t=15横貼りOS　外部床/タイル&インターロッキングブロッキング貼り　サイン/木彫刻　床/木材縮処理床材 t=22&塩ビ系長尺床材　壁&天井/杉板OS　一部クロス貼り
〈インドアコート棟〉 屋根&外壁/テント貼り　床/ウレタン系塗床材

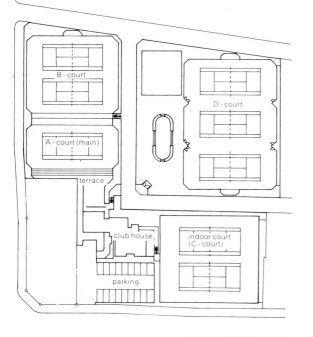

SITE PLAN S=1:1500

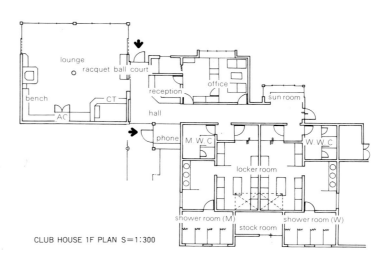

CLUB HOUSE 1F PLAN S=1:300

雁行した大屋根でダイナミックに構成されたアプローチ側正面外観をみる
The approach side front appearance dynamically accented with the big ranging roof.

コース側より北面外観をみる
The north side front appearance viewed from the course side.

水海道ゴルフクラブ

茨城県水海道市坂手町貝置5213　Phone/02972-7-1061

Mitsukaido Golf Club
Sakata-machi, Mitsukaido city, Ibaragi, Japan　　Phone/02972-7-1061

撮影/マキフォトグラフィック（外観）
　　わたなべスタジオ（インテリア）

池に面した南面外観をみる　1階のラウンジと2階のレストランがこの環境に面して配されている
The south side front appearance facing the pond. The 1st floor lounge and 2nd floor restaurant are open to the pond.

2階・レストラン

The 2nd floor restaurant.

1階・玄関ホールのフロント横よりトップライトを持つラウンジ方向をみる
The lounge area under a toplight viewed from the reception side of the 1st floor entrance hall.

水海道ゴルフクラブ

このゴルフクラブは 常磐自動車道 谷部原ICから車で10分 関東屈指の名門パブリックゴルフ場として親しまれてきたが 新しく法人会員専用のメンバー制ゴルフ場として生まれ変わった。

新生水海道ゴルフクラブのメンバーは 一部上々クラスの企業 400社の役員が中心となり "緑の社交場" 造りをテーマとした。

トップライトをもつ大空間と池に向かって大きく開かれたラウンジ 食堂をはじめ 和室とVIPルームを含んだ8つのゲストルームは ホテルオークラと業務提携により きめ細かい運営がなされている。

新クラブハウスは "水" をテーマに滝 溜り 流れをもつ池を新設しこの池を中心に配した各部屋との有機的つながりに特徴をもたせるように計画した。 〈神田 孜＋内海幸男／竹中工務店〉(88-06)

企画：三菱商事国内建設部
設計・施工：竹中工務店

構　　造：RC造　一部S造（屋根）
規　　模：地上2階
面　　積：敷地／83,000㎡　建築／3,056㎡　床／1階 2,996㎡　2階 1,083㎡（内 厨房150㎡）　合計 4,079㎡
工　　期：1987年3月15日～10月31日

施設概要：開業／1987年11月6日　営業時間／午前7時25分～午後6時　定休日／毎月15日 30日　システム／会員制　経営／㈱水海道ゴルフクラブ 従業員数／オフィス24人　キャディ71人　食堂14人 厨房13人　合計122人

Mitsukaido Golf Club

Located at a place 10 minutes by car from Yabehara IC, Joban Highway, "Mitsukaido Golf Club" is one of the distinguished public golf links in Kanto District that has been patronized by many golfers. Recently, it has been renewed into a membership golf club exclusive for corporate members.

Centering around the officers of some 400 companies listed on the 1st Section of Tokyo Stock Exchange, the members of the new-born Mitsukaido Golf Club wished to create a "social club rich with green." A large hall under a toplight, lounge widely opened towards a pond, dining hall, and eight guest rooms, including Japanese and VIP rooms, are attentively operated under a business tieup with the Hotel Okura. Pursuing "water" as its theme, the new club house has been newly provided with a pond having a waterfall, reservoir and flow, so that the rooms are organically associated with this pond.

Design: Takenaka-Komuten

Structure : RC; S in part (roof)
Scale : 2 stories above the ground
Area : Site/83,000 m²;　Building/3,056 m²;　Floor/1st floor 2,996 m², 2nd floor 1,083 m² (including kitchen 150 m²), totaling 4,079 m²
Term of construction: March 15 to October 31, 1987
Facilities : Opening/November 6, 1987;　Open time/7:25 a.m. to 6:00 p.m.;　Closed regularly on/15 and 30 of every month;　System/membership;　Management/Mitsukaido Golf Club Co.;　Number of employees/office staff 24, caddie 71, dining room 14, kitchen 13, totaling 122

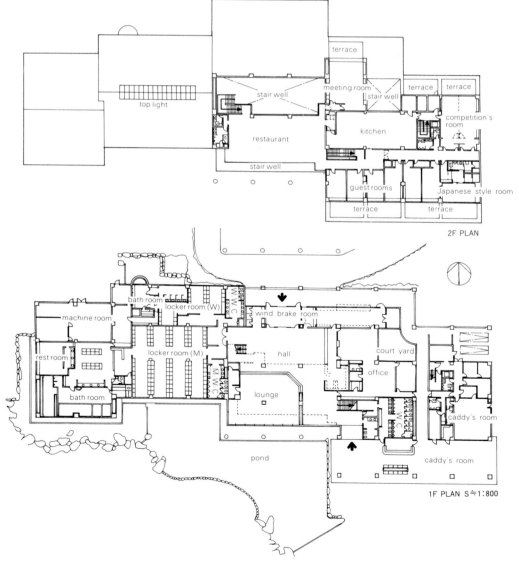

材料仕様
屋根／鉄骨　ALC板下地瓦葺き　外壁／コンクリート下地炻器質タイル貼り 外部床／アスファルト舗装 ゴムチップ舗装
〈レストラン〉 床／スパイク用 カーペット 幅木／ホワイトオーク h＝150 壁／ホワイトオーク練り付け石綿ボード貼り 樹脂プラスター塗装 天井／樹脂プラスター塗装 照明器具／シャンデリア＆ブラケット スチール金メッキ仕上 テーブル＆椅子／橅ウレタンクリア塗装

2F PLAN

1F PLAN S≒1:800

コース側よりみたクラブハウス全景

A whole scene of the club house viewed from the course side.

Fuji-Country Dejima Club
Dejima-mura, Niihari-gun, Ibaragi, Japan   Phone/0298-96-1011

集成材による木造りトラス架構のレストランフロア

The restaurant floor of wooden trass structure using aggregate materials.

撮影/門馬金昭

富士カントリー出島倶楽部

茨城県新治郡出島村下軽部881 Phone/0298-96-1011

トップライトを見上げる

The toplight looked up at from the floor.

材料仕様
屋根/南アフリカ産天然厚形スレート　外壁/議院錆石正層乱積み　二丁掛け割肌風タイル貼り
〈レストラン部分内装〉　床/タイルカーペット　床/スタッコ仕上　天井/木松野地板 t＝38　シャンデリア　デザイン/空間工場　小玉慎憲　製作:山田照明

富士カントリー出島倶楽部

このクラブハウスは　霞ヶ浦の持つ緑豊かな自然に溶け込む素朴で　重厚さのある欧風のカウントリーハウスを目指し　すべてにゆったりと寛げる落ち着いた雰囲気を提供するという基本コンセプトの中で　大きな空間を表現した。

ゴルフを通して人びととの触れ合いの場として最高の演出をするダイニングルームは　八角形の広々としたスペース(340㎡)で　窓越しには遠く筑波山系の山々やコース全体が見渡せるゆったりとした空間とした。(天井高14m)

内部の色調は木のあたたかさと自然のぬくもりに接し　欧州より直接調達した家具と調和し　高級感を持ちながらハデさを押えさ　落ち着いてゆったりでき　雰囲気のでる色合いで全体をまとめてみた。

〈長谷昇／日建設計〉(88-11)

設計:日建設計
施工:建築/東海興業
　　　内装/三越

構　　造:ＲＣ造　一部木造架構
規　　模:地上2階
面　　積:敷地/20,000㎡　建築/4,211.6㎡　床/1階 3,308.7㎡　2階
　　　　 3,234.8㎡　合計 6,543.5㎡
工　　期:1987年4月～1988年6月4日

施設概要:開業/1988年9月28日　営業時間/午前8時～午後6時 定休日
　　　　 /毎週月曜日　経営/富士カントリー㈱

Fuji-Country Dejima Club

Imaging a simple but dignified European country house that hermonizes with Kasumigaura's nature full of green, this club house intends to offer a composed atmosphere in which guests can relax themselves in spacious facilities.

Specially arranged for cordial communications through golf, the dining room is a spacious octagonal place (340 m²) with the ceiling height at 14 m, it allows guests to overlook the entire course and mountains in the Tsukuba Range through the windows.

The interior is finished with colors that agree in tone with the warmth of wood, add to gentleness of nature, and harmonize with furniture directly secured from Europe – gorgeous but less showy so that guests can relax themselves in a composed atmosphere.

Design: Noboru Hase

Structure : RC; Wooden building in part
Scale　　 : 2 stories above the ground
Area　　　: Site/20,000 m²;　Building/4,211.6 m²;　Floor/1st floor
　　　　　　 3,308.7 m², 2nd floor 3,234.8 m², totaling 6,543.5 m²
Term of construction: April, 1987 to June 4, 1988
Facilities : Opening/September 28, 1988;　Open time/8:00 a.m. to
　　　　　　 6:00 p.m.;　Fixed close/every Monday;　Management/
　　　　　　 Fuji-Country Co.

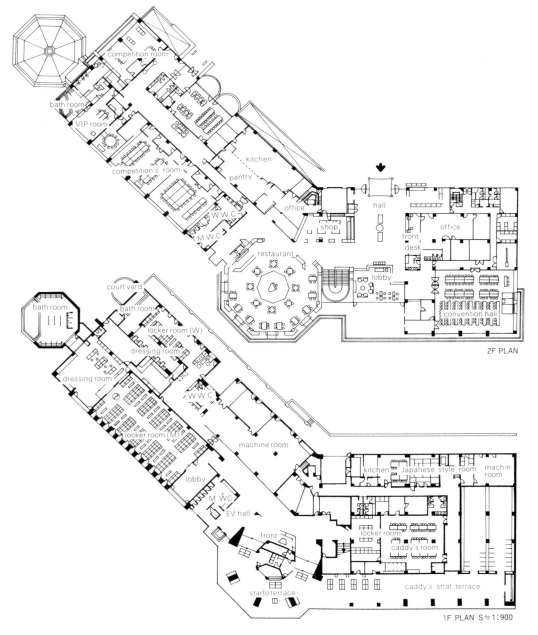

2F PLAN

1F PLAN S≒1:900

ランドマーク的"いばった屋根"のファイブハーフの外観 The appearance of "Five-Half" with the "proud" roof that looks like a landmark.

ファイブハーフ＆ザ コースバー

静岡県伊東市吉田1006　サザンクロスカントリークラブ　Phone/0577-45-1234

撮影/原　栄三郎

Five-Half & The Course Bar
1006, Yoshida, Ito city, Shizuoka, Japan　Phone/0577-45-1234

材料仕様
〈ファイブハーフ〉　屋根/鋼板一文字葺き　寒水掻き落とし　柱&梁/米松構造用集成材
床/木煉瓦　幅木/米松　h＝150　壁/寒水掻き落とし　天井/寒水掻き落とし
〈ザ コースバー〉　屋根/コンパネ t＝12下地シート防水　芝生植え込み　外壁/土壁左官
仕上　柱&梁/米松構造用集成材　床/木煉瓦　壁/土壁左官仕上　天井/米松板貼り染色

ファイブハーフのカウンターをみる
The counter of "Five-Half."

"目覚めた大地"を表現し　大地に埋め込まれたザ コースバー

"The Course Bar" buried under the ground expressing the "awakened land."

ファイブハーフ＆ザ コースバー

〈イン／いばった屋根〉

起伏の少ない平地に位置し　ラウンドする客の視点が　かなり上から見下ろすことになるので　屋根にポイントを置いた。

大きく張りだした屋根がランドスケープと相対し　小さいながらも己の存在を誇示する形をとった。

〈アウト／目覚めた大地〉

女性を　うつ伏せにしたような　柔らかなグリーンの起伏との一体感を狙い　建物を土の中に埋めた。埋まったこの建物が　建物としてではなく　大地が起き上がってきた様を表現してみた。

双方の建物とも潮風をもろに受けるため　鉄骨やコンクリートは避け集成材による構造仕上しとした。

〈吉尾浩次／インテリアデザインオフィス ノブ〉(88-11)

設計：インテリアデザインオフィス ノブ

協力：構造／鈴木　基

施工：斎藤木材工業

構　　造：木造
規　　模：平屋
面　　積：敷地／825,000㎡　建築／ファイブハーフ 96.00㎡　ザ コースバー 87.48㎡　床／ファイブハーフ 43.74㎡（内 厨房5.5㎡）ザ コースバー 58.32㎡（内 厨房9㎡）
工　　期：1988年3月1日〜4月28日

施設概要：開業／1988年5月17日　営業時間／午前8時30分〜午後4時30分　定休日／なし　客席数／各16席　客単価／400円　客回転数／10回　メニュー／フルーツ ジュース400　お茶300　果実酒400　生ビール400　カクテル450　経営／㈱サザンクロス 北村重憲 従業員数／4人

Five-Half & The Course Bar

[IN/Proud Roof]

Standing on a plain field having less ups and downs, this shop is looked down upon from golfers who are taking a round. So, the design emphasis was placed on the roof.

The widely projected roof stands against the landscape, asserting itself, although it is small in size.

[OUT/Awakened land]

Aimed to make the building unite with the ups and downs of gentle green that make us imagine a woman lying on her face, the building was buried in the ground. The entire image expressed, however, is the land that is just going to rise up from under the ground.

Since both buildings are directly exposed to a sea breeze, they have been structurally finished with aggregate materials, avoiding the use of steel frame or concrete.

Design: Hiroji Yoshio

Structure : Wooden building
Scale : 1 story above the ground
Area : Site/825,000 m²;　Building/Five-Half 96 m², The Course Bar 87.48 m²;　Floor/Five-Half 43.74 m² (including kitchen 5.5 m²), The Course Bar 58.32 m² (including kitchen 9 m²)
Term of construction: March 1 to April 28, 1988
Facilities : opening/May 17, 1988;　Open time/8:30 a.m. to 4:30 p.m.; Fixed close/nil; Number of guest seats/16 each; Unit price per guest/400 yen;　Turnover of guests/10 times; Menu/fruits juice, tea, fruit liquor, draft beer, cocktail, etc.;　Management/Sazan cloth Co., Shigenori Kitamura; Number of employees/4

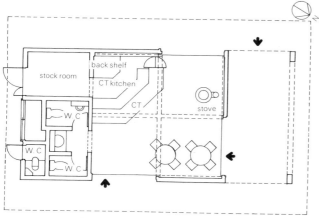

FIVE-HALF PLAN S=1:150

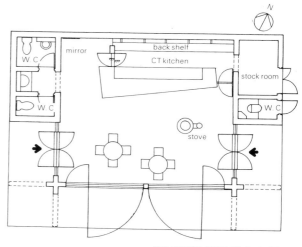

THE COURSE BAR PLAN S=1:150

正面ゲート（東南側外観）をみる

The front gate (the southeast side appearance).

東京ドーム ビッグエッグ

東京都文京区後楽丨丁目3-6丨　Phone/03-811-2111

撮影/本木誠一

Tokyo Dome Big Egg
1-3-61, Koraku, Bunkyo-ku, Tokyo, Japan　　Phone/03-811-2111

北東側外観をみる　手前は後楽園第3遊園地

The northeast side appearance; visible in your side is the 3rd Amusement Park of Korakuen.

正面ゲート（人工地盤2階）をみる　ドーム外周の半分をめぐる大庇はサンバイ
ザーと名づけられている

The front gate (artificial foundation at the 2nd floor); the large eaves extending over half the entire dome circumference are named "Sun Visor."

東京ドーム　ビッグ　エッグ

50年の歴史を刻んだ旧後楽園球場が姿を消して　その隣接地に　わが国初の大規模空気膜構造による多目的スタジアムである「東京ドーム"ビッグ エッグ"」が誕生した。

エアドームの内部には　各階のコンコースに　飲食ショップが機能的に配置されている。

4階のスタンドバー「トップ オブ ザ ビッグ エッグ」からは　窓外の景観も楽しめ　3階のレストラン「スイート クラブ」では　ゆったりと落ち着いた雰囲気にひたることができる。数々のハイテク技術を駆使したエアドームにあっても　観客をもてなすサービス空間の充実に心がくばられている。　　　　　　　　　　　　　　　〈日建設計・竹中工務店〉（88-05）

設計・監理：日建設計東京本社
　　　　　　竹中工務店 東京一級建築士事務所
施工：竹中工務店

構　　　造：SRC造 一部RC造　低ライズケーブル空気膜構造（屋根）
規　　　模：地下2階 地上6階
面　　　積：敷地/111,371.97㎡　建築/46,755.48㎡　客席/1階席 13,700
　　　　　　㎡　バルコニー席 2,100㎡　2階席 6,700㎡　グランド/
　　　　　　13,000㎡　人工地盤/15,700㎡　屋根/28,592㎡
高　　　さ：最高/地上 56.19m　グランドから61.69m　軒高/15.90～
　　　　　　35.90m
工　　　期：1985年5月16日～1988年3月17日

施設概要：開業/1988年3月17日　定休日/なし　店舗/飲食店　ファスト
　　　　　　フード　スーベニールなど10店　その他/収容数 2階席1万
　　　　　　6000人　バルコニー席2700人　バルコニー席（スイート）300人
　　　　　　1階席（内野）2万7000人　1階席（外野）1万人　合計5万6000
　　　　　　人　ゲート数/14　駐車数/559台収容
　　　　　　経営/㈱後楽園スタジアム

Tokyo Dome Big Egg

When the old Korakuen Stadium disappeared after 50 years of history, "Tokyo Dome Big Egg" came into being adjacent to the old stadium. It is Japan's first multi-purpose stadium of large scale air membrane structure.

The eating & drinking shops are functionally arranged at each floor's concourses inside the air dome. From the stand bar "Top of the Big Egg" at the 4th floor, guests can enjoy scenery outside the window. In the restaurant "Suite Club" at the 3rd floor, guests can relax themselves in a composed atmosphere. Thus, even in the air dome built by fully utilizing a variety of high technologies, considerations are given to creation of hospitable guest service space.

Design: Nikken-Sekkei Tokyo,
　　　　Takenaka-Komuten Tokyo

Structure : SRC (RC in part). low rise cable air membrane structure (roof)
Scale　　 : 2 under and 6 stories above the ground
Area　　　: Site/111,371.97 m²;　Building/46,755.48 m²;　Guest seats/1st floor seat 13,700 m², balcony seat 2,100 m², 2nd floor seat 6,700 m²;　Ground/13,000 m²;　Artificial foundation/15,700 m²;　Roof/28,592 m²
Height　 : Maximum/56.19 m above the ground;　Height from the game ground/61.69 m;　Eaves/15.90 to 35.90 m
Term of construction: May 16, 1985 to March 17, 1988
Facilities : Opening/March 17, 1988;　Fixed close/nil;　Shop/restaurant, fast food, souvenir and others 10;　Accommodation/2nd floor seats 16,000 persons, balcony seats 2,700 persons, balcony seats (suite) 300 persons, 1st floor seats (infield) 27,000 persons, 1st floor seats (outfield) 10,000 persons, totaling 56,000 persons;　Number of gates/14; Parking lot accommodation/559 cars;　Management/Korakuen Stadium Co.

左上/2階・ハンバーガーテーブル席中央のディスプレイをみる
左下/3階・レストランをみる

Left, top/ The display in the center of the table seat area of the 2nd floor hamburger restaurant.
Left, bottom/ The restaurant at the 3rd floor.

2階・スタンド最上部よりみた56,000人を収容するドーム内全景　グランドから天井頂部まで61.69m²

A whole scene of the dome capable of accommodating 56,000 people, as viewed from the highest level of the stand at the 2nd floor. 61.69 m from the game ground to the ceiling top.

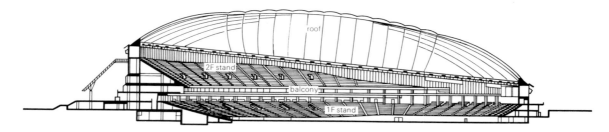

SECTION

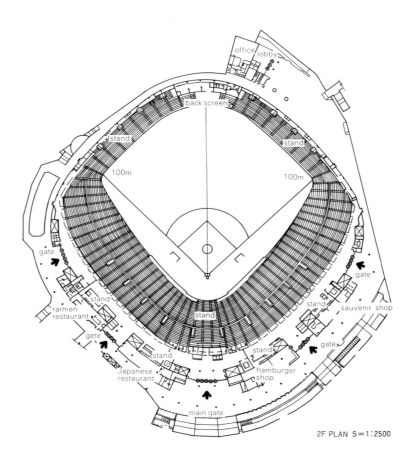

2F PLAN S=1:2500

材料仕様
膜屋根／4フッ化エチレン樹脂コーティングガラス繊維布　コンプレッションリング部屋根／フッ素樹脂焼き付け塗装アルミパネル　サンバイザー／斜め屋根：アルミカーテンウォール　透明
網入りガラス　平屋根：アルミ折り板葺き　外壁／プレキャストコンクリート樹脂系塗装吹き付け　人口地盤／床：磁器タイル貼り　階段／擬石ブロック敷　客席／床：プレキャストコンクリート
椅子：高密度ポリエチレンブロー成形　手摺／ステンレスパイプ　グラウンド／アスファルトコンクリート下地アンダーパッド付き人口芝敷　フェンス：ラバーフェンス防球ネットフェンス

熱供給源てある長野市清掃工場の屋上みた外観
The appearance viewed from the roof of Nagano Municipal Refuse Disposal Plant whose waste heat is utilized for "Sun Marine Nagano."

正面入口をみる　　　　　　　　　　　　　　The front entrance.

西側よりみた外観　　　　　The appearance viewed from the west side.

サンマリーンながの

長野市大字大豆島字川端向8585-65　Phone/0262-21-5535

Sun Marine Nagano
8585-65, Mamejima, Nagano city, Nagano, Japan
Phone/0262-21-5535

撮影/本木誠一

139

140

上/中央燈台の上よりギャラリー方向をみる　イースター島のモアイ像　ナスカ高原の地上絵などの演出がなされている
左頁/　プール全景をみる　清掃工場内で発生する高圧蒸気を利用し　熱交換器により工場内で約80℃の高温水を発生させこの高温水を「サンマリーンながの」内に熱交
　　　換器　放熱器　その他により　プール　浴室　給湯　シャワー　冷・暖房などに利用する

Top/ The gallery area viewed from atop the lighthouse in the center. The moais of Easter Island, accented with ground pictures drawn Naska Highland.
Left page/ The entire pool scene.　By utilizing high pressure steam generated in a refuse disposal plant, about 80°C of high temperature water is produced within the plant by means of a heat exchanger, and the hot water is used through a heat exchanger, radiator, etc. within "Sun Marine Nagano" to supply hot water for pools and shower, as well as for cooling/heating.

構　　造：管理棟/RC造　プール棟/S造
規　　模：管理棟/地下1階　地上2階　プール棟/S造　平屋一部3階
面　　積：敷地/17,928㎡　建築/6,358㎡　床/管理棟 2,923㎡　プール棟
　　　　　5,772㎡　合計 8,695㎡
工　　期：1984年6月22日～1985年10月9日

施設概要：開業/1985年10月23日　営業時間/管理棟　平日　午前9時～午後
　　　　　8時　日曜・祭日　午前9時～午後6時　プール棟　平日　午後
　　　　　1時～午後8時　日曜・祭日　午前9時～午後6時　定休日/な
　　　　　し　毎年9月16日～10月14日　12月29日～12月31日は休館　施
　　　　　設/管理棟　1階　玄関　エントランスホール　受付　事務室　更衣
　　　　　室　浴室（男女別　各30人　同時使用可）　採暖室　監視員控室　2
　　　　　階　大広間（舞台付 200人収容）
　　　　　和室4（28畳　16畳2　8畳）　飲食コーナー　放送室　3階
　　　　　機械室　プール棟　1階　造波プール（長さ40m　幅4～19m
　　　　　水深0～1.2m　波長15～30m　波高20～60cm）　流水プール（一
　　　　　周170m　幅4m　水深1m）　スライダープール（2連　長さ30m
　　　　　50m）　競泳プール（25×11.4m　水深1.15～1.35m）　飛込プー
　　　　　ル（6.5×5m　水深3.5m　飛び板1m）　2階　ギャラリー（プー
　　　　　ル利用者の飲食スペース）　3階　沐浴スペースと屋上広場（プー
　　　　　ルサイドの延長）　クア　コーナー（サウナ　気泡浴など）　ラウ
　　　　　ンジ　屋上広場
　　　　　料金/入館料　一般500（管理棟のみの場合は200）　小・中学生
　　　　　200　経営/（社）長野市開発公社　従業員数/23人（内　プール担
　　　　　当12人　日曜・祭日はアルバイト10人増）

Structure : Administrative building/RC; Pool building/S
Scale : Administrative building/1 under and 2 stories above the ground; Pool building/S, part of one-storied building has 3 stories.
Area : Site/17,928 m²; Building/6,358 m²; Floor/administrative building 2,923 m², pool building 5,772 m², totaling 8,695 m²
Term of construction: June 22, 1984 to October 9, 1985
Facilities : Opening/October 23, 1985; Open time/administrative building—9:00 a.m. to 8:00 p.m. on weekdays, 9:00 a.m. to 6:00 p.m. on Sunday and holiday; Pool building—1:00 p.m. to 8:00 p.m. on weekdays, 9:00 a.m. to 6:00 p.m. on Sunday and holiday; Fixed close/nil, closed from September 16 to October 14, and December 29 to 31 every year; Equipment/administrative building—1st floor—porch, entrance hall, reception, office, locker room, bathroom (separately for male and female, accommodating 30 each, two bathrooms can be used simultaneously), warming room, guard waiting room, 2nd floor—grand hall (with stage, accommodating 200 guests), Japanese room 4 (28 mats, 16 mats × 2, 8 mats), eating & drinking corner, broadcasting studio, 3rd floor—machine room, Pool building—1st floor—wave-making pool (40 m in length, 4 to 19 m in width, 0 to 1.2 m water depth, 15 to 30 m in wavelength, 20 to 60 cm in crest), water flowing pool (170 m/round, 4 m in width, 1 m in water depth), slider pool (× 2, 30 m and 50 m in length), swimming race pool (25 × 11.4 m, 1.15 to 1.35 m in water depth), diving pool (6.5 × 5 m, 3.5 m in water depth, diving board 1 m), 2nd floor—gallery (eating & drinking space for pool users), 3rd floor—bathing space and roof square (extension of poolside), Kur corner (sauna, bubble bath, etc.), lounge, roof square; Management/Nagano-shi Kaihatsu Kosha (Nagano City Development Corporation); Number of employees/23 (including 12 staffs taking charge of pools, 10 part-timers added on Sunday and holiday)

サンマリーンながの

企画の出発点は現代社会に欠落しており　今後大切なものは何か？——
それは“やさしさと心くばり”であり　その根底は自治体として　何によって　市民に貢献するかであった。
今後数十年　高齢者人口の増加は避けることができない　今何をなすべきかという基本コンセプト作りよりこの計画は始まった。
“海浜への夢　長野に海を”からテーマである“トロピカルポート”を設定し　港の見える丘が生まれた。亜熱帯植物と共に帆船　灯台　モアイの像の造形　及び流水造波スライダーの各プール　スコールは　動きとスリルと音があり躍動的である。どれも基本コンセプトの具体化であり環境作りの演出であった。大広間　レストランはプール棟内を眺望できる位置にあり　管理棟と一体感を増し　特に平日は高齢者の利用が多く　なごやかな場となっている。
〈小沢和弘/大建設計名古屋事務所〉(86-07)

企画：長野市
設計：大建設計名古屋事務所
施工：前田建設工業　北信土建　J.V.

Sun Marine Nagano

The starting point of planning "Sun Marine Nagano" was to find out what the modern society is lacking, and what is important to us from now on. The reply was "gentleness and care." This inquiry originated from the local government in pursuing what contribution they should make to citizens. For scores of years to come, the aged population will increase inevitably. What should they do now in preparation for it? This was the basic question to be solved when making the basic concept.

In view of "Let's create a sea in Nagano to satisfy people's longing for a beach," the theme "Tropical Port" was set, and a hill commanding a view of port was brought into being. Accented with subtropical plants, a sailing boat, lighthouse and moais, the flowing wave-making slider pools and squalls are dynamic with full of motion and thrill. All these have been arranged to materialize the basic concept and create an environment suitable for it. The large hall and restaurant are situated at a place from which guests can overlook the pool facilities. In harmony with the administrative building, these facilities are frequented by old people especially on weekdays in a homely atmosphere.

Design: Kazuhiro Ozawa

材料仕様
屋根/カラー合金メッキ鋼板　t＝0.5角波葺き　FRP t＝1.2角波板　一部アスファルト防水豆砂利コンクリート t＝60押さえ伸縮目地切り　外壁/合板型枠コンクリート化粧打ち放しアクリル系吹き付けタイル化粧目地切り西側妻面/FRP t＝1.2角波葺き
〈玄関ポーチ〉庇/屋根：カラーステンレス防水 t＝0.4　見付・軒天：ホーロー鋼板パネル t＝1.6　床/床用磁器質タイル貼り150角
〈プール〉床&幅木/モルタル金鏝下地　エポキシ樹脂系塗床　壁/合板型枠コンクリート化粧打ち放しアクリル系吹き付け　天井/屋根材あらわしのまま

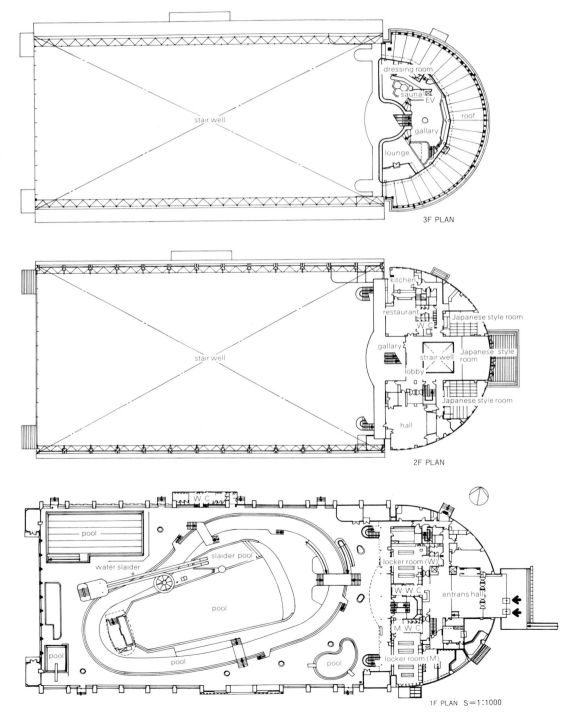

3F PLAN

2F PLAN

1F PLAN　S=1:1000

上/北側メインアプローチのスロープからみたウォーターガーデン棟
下/北陸自動車道からみた西側外観全景

Top/ The water garden building viewed from the slope of the main north side approach.
Bottom/ The entire west side appearance viewed from Hokuriku Motor Road.

ルネスかなざわ

金沢市高柳町一字70-1　Phone/0762-51-7000

撮影/三輪晃久写真事務所

Renais Kanazawa
70-1, Takayanagi-cho, Kanazawa city, Ishikawa, Japan
Phone/0762-51-7000

２階・グルメガーデンの和風座敷より屋外ガーデンプールをみる
The outdoor garden pool viewed from Japanese style seat area of the 2nd floor gourmet garden.

プールサイドレストランよりウォーターガーデン方向をみる
The water garden area viewed from the poolside restaurant.

ウォーターガーデン中央のウェイブプール

The wave pool in the center of the water garden.

ヨーロピアン リゾートスタイルを取り入れた１階大浴場　The big bathroom at the 1st floor designed in an European resort style.

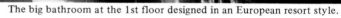

上/アクアラウンジ上部のトップライトを持つ吹抜け
左下/アプローチに配された入口ドーム
Top/ The stairwell having a toplight above the aqua lounge.
Left, bottom/ The entrance dome arranged at the approach.

ルネス かなざわ

「ルネス かなざわ」はＪＲ金沢駅から わずか５分という恵まれた立地に本格的なアクティブリゾート施設として誕生した。

北陸特有のどんよりとした気候の中にあって 南欧のすがすがしさを求め 遊・食・美・憩をメインファクターとし 水・光・緑によるアメニティ空間の創造を基本コンセプトとした。

設計に当り よりスムーズな動線確保のため プランに回避性を持たせエンターテイメントとして 施設中央にアトリウムを設けた。また 直径60ｍのドームの中には 従来の温水プールの常識を破った数々の水体験ができる遊泳空間（ウォーターガーデン）を創った。

素材及び色彩は よりナチュラルな素材で軽やかな落ち着きを演出し照明はランニングコストを軽減するために できるだけ放電管を採用した。

〈高田 保/創和〉(88-06)

企画：金沢レジャー企画
設計：一級建築士事務所 創和
協力：造園/地球号 構造/鹿島建設設計部
施工：鹿島建設北陸支社

構　　造：Ｓ造　ＲＣ造
規　　模：地下１階 地上３階
面　　積：敷地/45,462.41㎡ 建築/10,008.48㎡ 床/地下１階 3,512.96㎡ １階 8,886.00㎡ ２階 4,887.69㎡ ３階 1,762.98㎡ 塔屋 279.26㎡ 合計 19,328.89㎡
工　　期：1987年３月18日〜1987年12月18日

施設概要：開業/1987年12月19日 営業時間/24時間 定休日/なし 施設/ウォーターガーデン（アクアスライダー ウェイブ プール ストリーム プール ガーデン プール シンクロ プール チャイルド プール サウナ ジャグジー 寝台ジャグジー 屋外ジャグジー） スパガーデン（男女大浴場 サンルーム サウナ シャワー） アミューズスペース（男女レストルーム 日光浴コーナー 映画館 ゲームコーナー 娯楽室）料飲施設/レストラン１(268席) 和風座敷１(178席) 宴会場１(390席) ラウンジ１ 料金/入館料 大人2800 中人1400 小人900 （３時間コース）大人1800 中人700 経営/高山物産㈱ 高山正一 従業員数/サービス150人 厨房50人 パート アルバイト80人 合計280人

Renais Kanazawa

Favorably situated, i.e. only 5 minutes from JR Kanazawa Station, "Renais Kanazawa" came into being as full-scale, active resort facilities.

In a dull weather local to Hokuriku (Northern) district, "Renais Kanazawa" has been designed to create an amenity space of water, light and green, pursuing a refreshing air of South Europe by combining play, eating, beauty and rest as the main factors.

In designing "Renais Kanazawa," more smooth dymanic lines have been secured by planning it with a circuital feature, as materialized by an entertaining atrium in the center. In the dome 60 m in diameter, a unique swimming space ("Water Garden") has been provided where a vareity of swimming experiences can be enjoyed, going beyond the conventional image of a heated pool. More natural materials and colors have been employed to present an airy, but composed atmosphere. As for lighting, in order to reduce the cost, many glow lamps have been employed.

Design: Kenji Umemoto

Structure : S; RC
Scale　　 : 1 under and 3 stories above the ground
Area　　 : Site/45,462.41 m²;　Building/10,008.48 m²;　Floor/1st basement 3,512.96 m², 1st floor 8,886.00 m², 2nd floor 4,887.69 m², 3rd floor 1,762.98 m², roof floor 279.26 m², totaling 19,328.89 m²
Term of construction: March 18 to December 18, 1987
Facilities : Opening/December 19, 1987; Open time/24 hours; Fixed close/nil;　Equipment/Water Garden (aqua slider, wave pool, stream pool, garden pool, synchronized swimming pool, child pool, sauna, Jacuzzi, sleeping Jacuzzi, outdoor Jacuzzi), Spa Garden (big baths for males and females, sunroom, sauna, shower), Amusement Space (rest rooms for males and females, sunbathing corner, movie theater, game corner, amusement room);　Eating & drinking facilities/restaurant 1 (268 seats), Japanese style room 1 (178 seats), banquet hall 1 (390 seats), lounge 1; Management/ Shoichi Takayama, Takayama Bussan Co.;　Number of employees/Service 150, kitchen 50, part-time 80, totaling 280

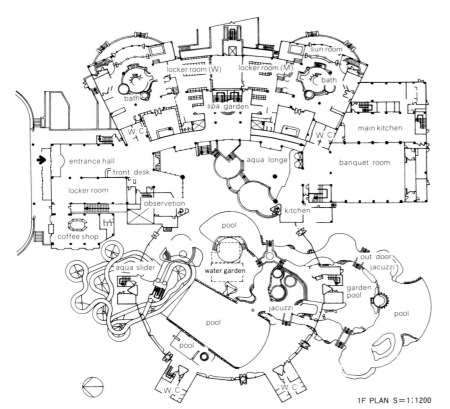

1F PLAN S=1:1200

材料仕様

屋根/コンクリート下地折り板屋根 洋瓦葺き アスファルト断熱防水下地コンクリート金鏝仕上 外壁/コンクリート打ち放し下地弾性アクリルタイル吹き付け 外部床/アスファルト インターロッキングブロックタイル
〈パブリック部分内装〉床/コンクリート金鏝下地特注じゅうたん 長尺床材 幅木/塩ビ幅木 壁/コンクリート金鏝下地クロス貼り 繊維薄塗材 天井/コンクリート＋ボード下地クロス貼り 繊維薄塗材 石綿吸音板 ビニールクロス貼り

南側正面入口廻りをみる　右上に空中自転車「ピーターパン」の軌道がみえる　高さ10ｍの二人乗り　自転車で　一周約320ｍ
The south side front entrance area. Visible at the upper right part is the track of the aerial bicycle "Peter Pan." A two-man bicycle running along about 320 m track that is 10 m high above the ground.

カーニバルショーケース

兵庫県多紀郡篠山町矢代　Phone/0795-52-5222

撮影/福本正明

Carnival Showcase
Yashiro Sasayama-cho, Taki-gun, Hyogo, Japan　Phone/0795-52-5222

アプローチ階段よりみる
The entire appearance viewed from the approach staircase.

上/「ピーターパン」
下/２階バルコニーよりジャグジー タワーをみる
Top/ "Peter Pan."
Bottom/ The Jacuzzi tower viewed from the 2nd floor balcony.

2階より1階カフェと池を見下す

The 1st floor cafe and pond looked down upon from the 2nd floor.

東南アジア オーストラリア ポリネシアなどの熱帯花木が楽しめる「トロピカル ルーム」
The "Tropical Room" where you can enjoy Southeast Asian, Australian, Polynesian and other tropical flowering plants.

2階プールをみる　　　　　　　　　　　　　The 2nd floor pool.

1階レストランをみる　　　　　　　　　　　The 1st floor restaurant.

カーニバルショーケース

丹波篠山に計画されたこの施設は 既存のキャンプ場 宿泊施設 運動施設 研究施設 フィールドアスレチック 魚つり場などに付加され冬季 雨天時 そして夜間の誘客装置として機能する。

斜面に位置する施設群は 植物展示を中心に 劇場 温水プール 露天風呂 レストラン カフェ アイスクリームショップ スーベニールショップなどで 川の流れる街路や塔の見える 細路地や坂道 階段 橋などとともに中世的な街並みを形成している。この"街"全体は大きなガラスケースで覆われ 天候 季節に影響されない外部空間の内部化が図られている。

この施設には 多くの消費を刺激する仕掛けや機能が組み込まれている。そしてなによりも そうした仕掛けや機能が複合された"街"という 楽しみに満ちた空間と快適な時間を消費させる装置である。

〈栗生 明/栗生総合計画事務所〉(88-12)

総合プロデュース：エー・エー・ピー
設計：栗生総合計画事務所
施工：竹中工務店 三井建設共同企業体

Carnival Showcase

Installed in Sasayama, Tanba, "Carnival Showcase" has been added to the existing camping ground, hotel facilities, sport facilities, research facilities, field athletic ground, fishing spots, etc., aimed to serve as a place for attracting guests in winter, on rainy days, and at night.

A group of facilities are installed on the slope, including a theater, heated pool, open-air bath, restaurant, cafe, ice cream shop and souvenir shop. Together with a street with a side stream, lanes from which a tower is visible, inclines, staircases, bridges, etc., a town reminding us of European medieval scenes is formed. This "town" is covered with huge glass to secure an enclosed space not affected by weather or season.

"Carnival Showcase" has a variety of built-in settings and functions that stimulate consumption. Among others, it serves as a place where visitors can consume joyful space and comfortable time in a "townish" atmosphere.

Design: A. Kuryu Architect & Associates

構　　造：RC造＋S造
規　　模：地下1階 地上2階 塔屋1階
面　　積：敷地/148,208.00㎡　建築/2,502.76㎡　床/地下1階 79.39㎡
　　　　　1階 2,168.01㎡　2階 1,225.85㎡　塔屋 41.04㎡　合計
　　　　　3,514.29㎡
工　　期：1988年2月〜10月

施設概要：開業/1988年10月15日　定休日/なし　施設/ユニトピア　ささ
　　　　　山　入園料 600　プランツ ミュージアム（砂漠 熱帯 高山の
　　　　　体験）午前10時〜午後6時　トロピカルルーム（熱帯花木室）
　　　　　午前10時〜午後6時　シンデレラ ホール（花の円舞場）　午前
　　　　　10時〜午後6時　レストラン　カモミール/30席　午前11時〜
　　　　　午後2時30分　午後5時〜9時30分　カフェ リンデンバウム
　　　　　50席　午前10時〜午後9時30分　スパハウス（プール＆ジャグ
　　　　　ジー）午前10時〜午後9時　入場料1200　ピーターパン（空中
　　　　　自転車）300　けやき小劇場（AVホール）204席　運営/松下電気
　　　　　産業労働組合

Structure : RC + S
Scale : 1 under and 2 stories above the ground, and 1 roof floor
Area : Site/148,208.00 m²;　Building/2,502.76 m²;　Floor/1st
basement 79.39 m²,　1st floor 2,168.01 m²,　2nd floor
1,225.85 m²,　roof floor 41.04 m², totaling 3,514.29 m²
Term of construction: February to October 1988
Facilities : Opening/October 15, 1988; Fixed close/nil; Equipment/
Unitopia Sasayama, Plants Museum (where you can enjoy
desert, tropical and highland experiences), Tropical Room
(with tropical flowering plants), Cinderella Hall (round
flowery dance hall), Restaurant Chamomile (30 seats –
11:00 a.m. to 2:30 p.m., 5:00 p.m. to 9:30 p.m.),
Cafe Lindenbaum (50 seats – 10:00 a.m. to 9:30 p.m.),
Spa House (pool & Jacuzzi), Peter Pan (aerial bicycle),
Keyaki Sho Gekijo (small AV hall – 204 seats);　Manage-
ment/Labor Union of Matsushita Electric Industrial Co.

材料仕様
屋根/網入りガラス t＝12　一部アスファルト防水　外壁/アルミサッシ　透明フロートガラス t＝5　コンクリート打ち放し撥水剤塗り付け　大谷石貼り（中庭）外部床/インターロッキ
ングブロック　グラニットタイル（中庭）
〈展示通路〉床/グラニットタイル貼り　一部玉砂利洗い出し　壁/コンクリート打ち放し　一部リブ折り　天井/PBEF
〈レストラン「カモミール」〉床/パーケットフロアOP拭き取りUC　タモ練り付けOP拭き取りUC　壁＆天井/OP寒冷紗FE
〈カフェ「リンデンバウム」〉床/玉砂利洗い出し　壁/アルミサッシ　透明ガラス t＝5　天井/網入りガラス t＝6.8
〈スパハウス〉床/ジュートカーペット　壁/ビニールクロス貼り　天井/石綿吸音貼り
〈プール〉床/磁器タイル貼り　腰/ポリコンモザイクタイル貼り　壁/コンクリート打ち放し　天井/コンクリート打ち放し　天井/トップライク　一部室内プール用石綿吸音板貼り
〈AVホール客席〉床/タイルカーペット貼り　壁/コンクリート打ち放し　一部グラスウールの上サランネット貼り　天井/スチールφ＝6　ピッチ100　メッシュ錆止めOP

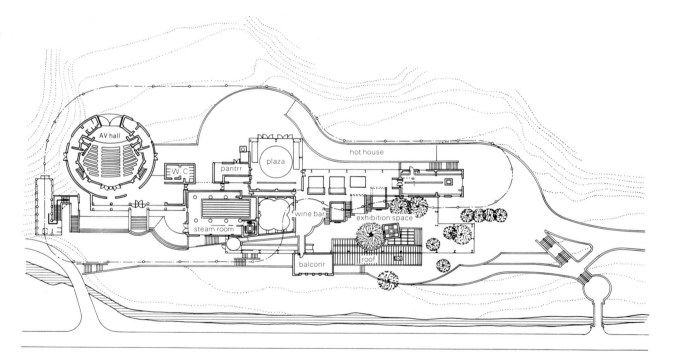

2F PLAN

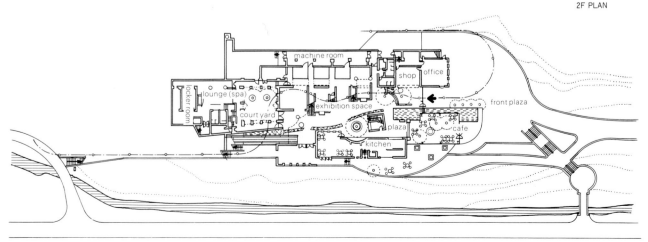

1F PLAN S=1:1000

「ユー アー ザ キャプテン」（大迷路）を空中歩廊より見下す「You are the Captain" (big maze) looked down upon from the aerial corridor.

撮影/鳴瀬 亨

大迷路のブリッジ「スペース ゴルフ」と「ムーン カート レーサー」のコーナーを見下す"Space Golf" and "Moon Cart Racer" corners looked down upon from the big maze's bridge.

アメージング スクエア

東京都足立区千住関屋町19-1　Phone/03-882-8011

Amazing Square
19-1, Senjusekiya-cho, Adachi-ku, Tokyo, Japan
Phone/03-882-8011

正面入口ゲートをみる

The front entrance gate.

ヒット21の内部 迷路の各所には光センサーが設置されており さまざまな
仕掛けで入場者を簡単には抜け出させない

The inside of "Hit 21." Photo sensors are arranged here and there
along the maze, and together with various tricks, prevent the entrants
from getting out of it easily.

カウンターをみる

The counter.

この施設は 製鉄会社が新規事業開発の一環として 工場跡地利用を兼ねスポーツ レジャー事業へ進出した第一号である。

1600坪の大迷路と世界初のハイテク ゲーム迷路(1200坪)の2大迷路 TVゲームの主人公体験ができるスペース アドベンチャーのほか カフェテリアレストランを有し これまでの遊園地イメージを一掃する宇宙感覚で全施設を演出した。迷路だけではなく 複合化したアミューズメント施設を目指したわけである。

また来客は日曜と祭日がメインで平日とのギャップが大きいが 夜でも遊べる迷路を開発し売りものにしている。　　　〈依田 渡〉(88-06)

総合プロデュース:協同宣伝
企画・デザイン:依田 渡
ディレクター:依田 渡 服部達郎
設計・施工:建築/清水建設
　　　　　内装/丹青社(レストラン)村山(ビーム・チェイサー)

構　　造:S造
規　　模:平屋
面　　積:敷地/33,939.36㎡　建築/1,985.05㎡　床/レストラン 535.35㎡(内 厨房80.06㎡) ビーム チェイサー/859.20㎡ その他/642.48㎡ 合計 2,037.03㎡ 迷路/ヒット21(ハイテク ゲーム迷路)3,960㎡ ユー アー ザ キャプテン(大迷路)5,280㎡
工　　期:1987年7月6日〜10月10日
施設概要:開業/1987年10月10日 営業時間/冬期 午前10時〜午後7時 夏期 午前10時〜午後9時 定休日/なし 入場料/大人500 小人300 設備&使用料/ユー アー ザ キャプテン(大迷路)500 ヒット21(ハイテク ゲーム迷路)600 ビームチェイサー(スペース アドベンチャー)800 スペース ゴルフ ガーデン300 ムーン カート レーサー300 料飲施設/レストラン(カフェテリア形式)180席 経営/アメージング㈱ 従業員数/20人 パート アルバイト280人 合計300人

Amazing Square

"Amazing Square" is the first such attempt at participation in a sports & leisure field made by a steel company, as part of its new development project by utilizing its old factory site.

It has a gigantic maze (5,184 m²) and the world's first high tech game maze (3,888 m²) side by side with space adventure facilities where you can enjoy an experience of a TV game hero. Coupled with a cafeteria restaurant, "Amazing Square" sweeps the conventional amusement park image, by offering not merely mazes, but also composite amusement facilities.

Visitors mainly come on Sunday and holiday, and less visitors on weekdays. To attract more guests, the mazes are designed to be enjoyed even at night.

Design: Wataru Yoda

Structure : S
Scale : 1 story building
Area : Site/33,939.36 m²; Building/1,985.05 m²; Floor/restaurant 535.35 m² (including kitchen 80.06 m²); Beam chaser/859.20 m²; Others/642.48 m², totaling 2,037.03 m²; Maze space/hit 21 (high tech game maze) 3,960 m², You are the Captain (big maze) 5,280 m²
Term of construction: July 6 to October 10, 1987
Facilities : Opening/October 10, 1987; Open time/winter season — 10:00 a.m. to 7:00 p.m., summer season – 10:00 a.m. to 9:00 p.m.; Fixed close/nil; Equipment/You are the Captain (big maze), Hit 21 (high tech game maze), Beam Chaser (space adventure), Space Golf Garden, Moon Cart Racer; Eating & drinking facilities/restaurant (cafeteria style) 180 seats; Management/Amazing Co.; Number of employees/staff 20, part-time 280, totaling 300

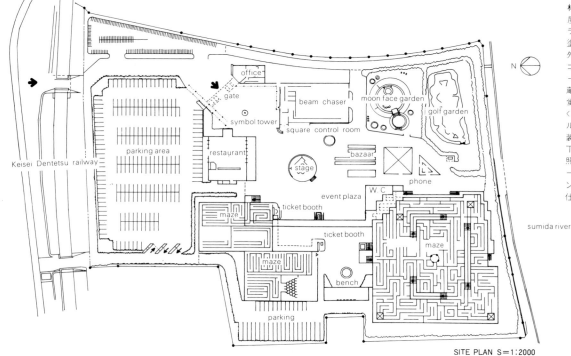

SITE PLAN S=1:2000

材料仕様

屋根/ルーフデッキ山高37 t =0.6 レストラン屋根一部亜鉛鉄板メラミン焼き付け塗装 外壁/カラー角波鉄板 t =0.4貼り 外部床/コンクリート打ち放し ゲート/コルゲイトパイプOP塗装 サイン/スチールチャンネル文字 アクリル(ネオン内蔵) 迷路/桙材ラッカー吹き付け 一部蛍光塗料
〈レストラン〉塩ビタイル貼り 幅木/アルミ型押材 壁/PB下地クラッキング塗装 一部ビニールクロス貼り 天井/PB下地ビニールクロス貼り アルミ型押材 照明具/ダウンライト ブラケッド ポール スタンド テーブル/楢染色ウレタン塗装 什器/楢板目木地クリアラッカー仕上

外観全景をみる

The entire appearance.

小諸 よろこびの街

長野県小諸市三和１丁目3023-１　Phone/0267-22-3501

撮影/鳴瀬　亨

Yorokobino-machi Komoro
1-3023-1, Miwa, Komoro city, Nagano, Japan　Phone/0267-22-3501

天井を見上げる　大架構大空間を生かすためすべて吊りシステム

上/ファサード150×700の大断面集成材の力強い曲線
下/ディスプレイを通してみる
Top/ Facade. The powerful curves of large 150 × 700 sectional aggregate members.
Bottom/ An inside scene viewed from behind the display stove.

The ceiling looked up at. In order to effectively utilize the large space
with the huge framing, all lighting equipment is suspended.

小諸 よろこびの街
米松構造用集成材(150×700)のアーチ形の大断面材7本からつくられた
空間は いままでにない 力強く柔らかな大空間である。最高高さ8.42
mのドーム空間である。従来 パチンコ店の天井は 照明をはじめ遊技台
の関連機器で覆われているのが普通だが ここ「小諸 よろこびの街」で
は 天吊形照明のみで 大架構の特長を十二分に生かしている。18個の
トップライトからの陽光は 柔らかい空間を一層引き立てている。遊技
台間隔が狭く 天井も低く 閉鎖的空間が多い他店に比して 「小諸 よ
ろこびの街」はまさに明るく健康的なパチンコ店である。 〈編集部〉(88-11)
設計:環建築アトリエ
施工:丸子建設

構　　造:木造
規　　模:平屋
面　　積:敷地/4,268.80㎡　建築/721.38㎡　床/594.18㎡
工　　期:1988年6月16日～8月25日

施設概要:開店/1988年9月9日　営業時間/午前10時～午後11時 定休日
　　　　　/なし　施設/遊技台　280台(パチンコ　スロットマシン) 経営/
　　　　　㈲東亜実業　従業員数/30人

Yorokobino-machi Komoro

This 'pachinko' shop is open in an unusually powerful and soft dome
space formed with seven huge arched sectional members made of
American pipe aggregate (150 × 700), 8.42 m in max. height.
In the case of conventional pachinko shops, the ceiling is usually
covered with lighting and play related equipment. Here in "Yorokobino-machi Komoro," the ceiling is covered only with the ceiling-suspended lighting to fully utilize the huge framing. The sunlight from
18 toplights makes the soft space even more comfortable. Differing
from other shops where pachinko play boards are installed at narrow
intervals in a closed space whose ceiling is low, "Yorokobino-machi
Komoro," just as the shop name (Town of Joy, Komoro) suggests, is
a bright, healthy pachinko shop.

Design: Yutaka Gonda

Structure : Wooden building
Scale　　 : 1 story building
Area　　 : Site/4,268.80 m²; Building/721.38 m²; Floor/594.18 m²
Term of construction: June 16 to August 25, 1988
Facilities : Opening/September 9, 1988;　　Open time/10:00 a.m. to
　　　　　 11:00 p.m.　Fixed close/nil;　Equipment/playing boards
　　　　　 280 (pachinko, slot machine);　Management/Toa Jitsugyo
　　　　　 Co.;　Number of employees/30

材料仕様
屋根/長尺カラー鉄板 t=2.8瓦棒葺き　アーチ梁/米松構造用集成材　外壁/米松 w=70
防腐保護塗装　床/テラゾタイル貼り　大理石　壁&天井/米松 w=70貼り　難燃小幅板
t=12貼り　網入り透明ガラス t=6.8

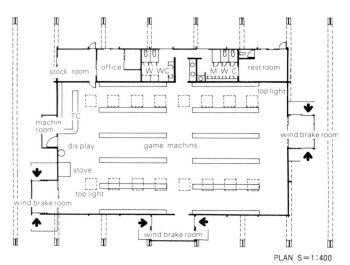

PLAN S=1:400

ライブディスコ＆プールバー/ *Live Disco & Pool Bar*

全景と周囲のロケーション　右手にウォーターフロントが拡がり　背後に首都高速・羽田線新山下ランプ

The entire scene and surrounding location. Visible in the right side is the waterfront, and behind this club building lies Shin Yamashita Ramp of Metropolitan Speedway Haneda Line.

水路越しに外観をみる

The appearance viewed across a waterway.

撮影/本木誠一

横浜ベイサイドクラブ

横浜市中区新山下 3 丁目7-9
Phone/ライブディスコ:045-623-5100
　　　プールバー　:045-623-5300

Yokohama Bay Side Club
3-7-9, Shinyamashita, Naka-ku, Yokohama city, Japan
Phone/Live Disco: 045-623-5100　　Pool Bar: 045-623-5300

横浜ベイサイドクラブ

行き着くところまで　いってしまった感のあるディスコテック。照明器
具の落下で死者まで出してしまった背景には　エスカレートしなければ
客が驚かなくなってしまったことも一つの原因のようである。今回の計
画では　日本人の現在の遊びの始まりであった20数年前のヨコハマ　遊
びが東京より先行していた時代にたち戻ってみた。
われわれの年代には懐かしく　現代の若者には新鮮に　そんな素朴な発
想がこの店のアイデアの出発点である。米軍　横田基地の中にあった「エ
アメンズクラブ」。ソウルミュージックに合わせてベトナム帰りの黒人兵
が踊っていた光景を見て感動し　新宿のジャズ喫茶の夜だけをディスコ
に変えてしまったことがある。そんな経験が「横浜ベイサイドクラブ」を
つくらせた。
　　　　　　　　　　　　　　　　　　　〈林　宏海／スタジオ208〉(88-03)

企画：林　宏海＋スタジオ208
設計：スタジオ・ギア
施工：トライ

構　　造：S造
規　　模：地上2階
面　　積：床／1階 626.6m²　2階 393.0m²(内 厨房 34m²)
　　　　　合計1,019.6m²
工　　期：1987年10月1日～12月9日

施設概要：開店／1987年12月16日　営業時間／ライブディスコ　午後6時～
　　　　　午前1時　プールバー　午後2時～午前4時　定休日／なし
　　　　　客席数／ライブディスコ 350席　プールバー 64席(ビリヤード
　　　　　15台)　客単価／ライブディスコ 4500円　プールバー 2500円
　　　　　客回転数／ライブディスコ 1.5回　プールバー 6回　システム／
　　　　　チケット制　料金／ライブ ディスコ：チャージ料　男3500　女
　　　　　3000　プールバーゲーム料／午後6時まで　1時間 800　10時
　　　　　以降　1時間 1000　メニュー／コーヒー　ビール　水割り　各500
　　　　　ソフトドリンク　各種500　カクテル類500～　バーボン スコッ
　　　　　チ S750　コニャック S1500　スパゲティ　カレー　ひめさ
　　　　　ざえの洋風焼 750　ビーフシチュー1250　サーロインステーキ
　　　　　3000　経営／㈲横浜ベイサイドクラブ　従業員数／サービス 45
　　　　　人　厨房6人　パート・アルバイト30人　合計81人

材料仕様

外壁／コルテン鋼カーテンウォール　フォールディングドア　外部床／コンクリート打ち
〈プールバー内装〉床／モルタル下地米松材OSワックス仕上　幅木／タモ材OSCL
壁／リブ付きブロック積み　既存躯体壁VP塗装　天井／既存躯体小屋裏VP塗装　照明
器具／スポットライト　ペンダント
〈ライブディスコ内装〉床／モルタル下地エポキシ樹脂系塗床材　壁／リブ付きブロック
化粧積みVP塗装　モルタル下地スタッコ塗装　天井／鉄骨床組あらわし　LGS組PB
下地合成樹脂系吹き付け塗材　照明器具／スポットライト

Structure : S
Scale : 2 stories above the ground
Area : Floor/1st floor 626.6 m², 2nd floor 393 m² (including kitchen 34 m²), totaling 1,019.6 m²
Term of construction: October 1 to December 9, 1987
Facilities : Opening/December 16, 1987; Open time/live disco 6:00 p.m. to 1:00 a.m., pool bar 2:00 p.m. to 4:00 a.m.; Fixed close/nil; Number of guest seats/live disco 350, pool bar 64 (billiard table 15); Unit price per guest/live disco 4,500 yen, pool bar 2,500 yen; Turnover of guests/live disco 1.5 times, pool bar 6 times; System/ticket system; Menu/coffee, beer, whisky, cocktails, soft drinks, cognac, spaghetti, beef stew, beefsteak, etc.; Management/Yokohama Bay Side Club Co.; Number of employees/service 45, kitchen 6, part-time 30, totaling 81

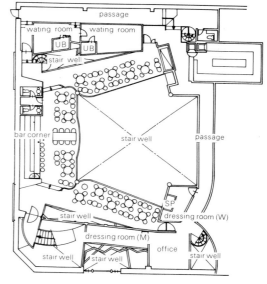

2F PLAN S=1:400

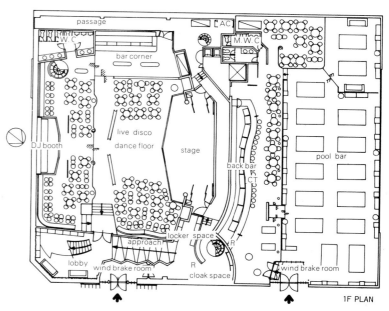

1F PLAN

Yokohama Bay Side Club

Discotheques that seem to have developed as far as they could, even
to a point where a guest was squeezed to death by the dropping lighting equipment. Behind such accident lies a fact that guests are no
longer amazed at ordinary setting – they are greedy for more exciting
scenes. In designing this disco, the producer returned to the days 20
odd years ago when playing in Yokohama, the birth-place of play of
modern Japanese young, had gone ahead of playing in Tokyo.
Dear to our generation, and fresh to today's young – this simple idea
is the starting point of this disco club. Deeply moved once by viewing
the black soldiers, who returned from Vietnam, dancing with soul
music at the "Airmen's Club" that was within the Yokota base of
American forces, the producer changed the night operation of a tea
house with jazz in Shinjuku into a disco. Such experience has moti-
vated the producer to design "Yokohama Bay Side Club."

Produce: Hiromi Hayashi

上/ライブディスコのステージからダンスフロアを通して 1・2階客席方向をみる　正面奥部はDJブース
下/ライブディスコの2階入口側から1階ステージ方向をみる
Top/ The 1st and 2nd floors guest seat areas viewed from the live disco stage through the dance floor. DJ booth is visible at the inner front part.
Bottom/ The 1st stage area viewed from the live disco's 2nd floor entrance side.

ネオンオブジェがきらめくプールバー上部の吹抜け空間

The stairwell space at the upper part of the pool bar with glistening neon objets.

プールバー入口風除室上部のネオンサイン

The neon sign above the windbreaking room beside the pool bar's entrance.

プールバーの奥より入口方向をみる　ヤジロベー スタイルの照明柱が客席と
ビリヤード スペースを分割する

The entrance area viewed from the inner part of the pool bar. The lighting pillars like balancing toys ('yajirobei') separate the guest seat area and billiards space.

ディスコ＆レストランバー／*Disco & Restrant Bar*

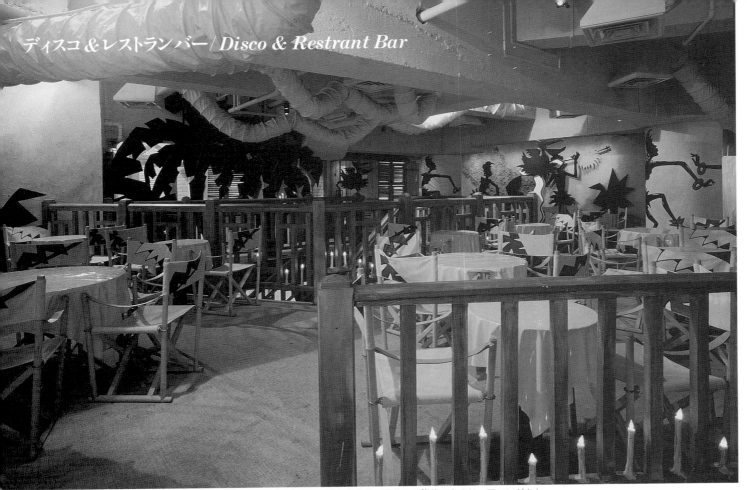

中地下１階のバーカウンター席側から階段吹抜け越しにレジカウンター方向をみる　天井の蛇腹状のものはエアコンダクト
The register counter area viewed from the bar counter seat side at the semibasement, across the stairwell. The member like bellows on the ceiling is an air duct.

撮影／鳴瀬　亨

中地下１階のレジカウンター脇より地下１階への階段吹抜け部をみる
The stairwell along the staircase leading to the 1st basement, viewed from the register counter at the semibasement.

ジャバ ジャイブ

東京都港区六本木３丁目10-3　六本木スクエアビル中地下１階　地下１階
Phone／03-478-0087

Java-Jive
3-10-3, Roppongi, Minato-ku, Tokyo, Japan　　Phone／03-478-0087

162

ジャバ ジャイブ

"ジャバ ジャイブ"とは ニューヨークの俗語(スラング)でコーヒーダンサーを意味している。六本木の しかもディスコの集中するスクエアビルの中で 典型的なディスコとなることを避け あえてレストラン ライブミュージック ダンスフロアを核とした新業態を創出した。制約された立地条件の中で 単に綺麗さや目新しさではなく スペースを蘇生し 商業的に成功することにプライオリティを置いている。

プロジェクトメンバーは サム ロパタ ケンビリントンINC サーペンタイン スタジオらのニューヨーカー スタッフを迎え メニュー開発をヘレン マックアーキレーンに依頼し 本格的なカリブ家庭料理を提供している。　　　　　　　　　　　　〈武藤重遠／カザテック〉(88-10)

トータルデザイン コンサルティング：カザテック
設計：サム ロパタ
協力：ライティング コンサルタント／ケンビリントンINC
　　　インテリア ペイント ワーク／サーペンタイン スタジオ
　　　フード コンサルタント／ヘレン マックアーキレーン
施工：平林デザイン　ローザ工芸

面　　積：床／中地下1階 300㎡　地下1階 360㎡　合計 660㎡(内 厨房
　　　　45㎡)
工　　期：1988年4月8日～5月30日

施設概要：開店／1988年6月1日　営業時間／午後6時～深夜　定休日／なし　客席数／230席　客単価／5000円　システム／チケット制　料金／入場料 男4000 女3000 メニュー／カニのグラタンカリブ風1500　アボガドとジンジャーのスープ900　レンズ豆のサラダ900　カリブ風カレー1500　ジャバジャイブ ラム カクテル1200　ピナ コラーダ1200　コロナエキストラビール900　経営／エープロジェクト㈱　従業員数／32人

Java-Jive

"Java-Jive" is a New Yorker's slung meaning a coffee dancer. Avoiding a stereotyped course – i.e. becoming another disco in a square building that is crowded with discos – a new-type operation has been created by combining a restaurant, live music and dance floor. In utilizing the limited space, a priority has been given to a commercial success to be achieved by renewing the space, rather than to decorative beauty or novelty.

As project members, New Yorkers, including Sam Lopata, Ken Billington Inc. and Serpentine Studio staffs, were invited, while the menu was undertaken by Helen McArlane to offer the orthodox Caribbean home dishes.

Design: Sam Lopata

Area　　　: Floor/semibasement 300 m², 1st basement 360 m², totaling 660 m² (including kitchen 45 m²)
Term of construction: April 8 to May 30, 1988
Facilities : Opening/June 1, 1988; Open time/6:00 p.m. to midnight; Fixed close/nil;　Number of guest seats/230;　Unit price per guest/5,000 yen; System/ticket system; Menu/dishes imaging Carib as theme, beer and other drinks;　Management/A Project Co.;　Number of employees/32

材料仕様
〈中地下1階客席〉 床／鉄骨組デッキプレート軽量コンクリート下地サイザル麻カーペット敷　壁／コンクリートブロック組積みPB t＝12＋ラスボード t＝7下地エージング塗装　天井／軽量鉄骨組PB t＝12下地VP吹き付け塗装
〈地下1階客席〉 床／簡易防水処理の上白砂敷込み t＝30～50　ダンスフロア：メープル材板目 t＝40ワックス仕上　壁／コンクリートブロック組積み PB t＝12＋ラスボード t＝12下地エージング塗装及び古材化粧仕上　天井／軽量鉄骨組PB t＝12下地VP吹き付け塗装　一部鉄骨組デッキプレートOP艶消し仕上　家具／テーブル＆椅子デザイン：サムロパタ　製作：カッシーナジャパン

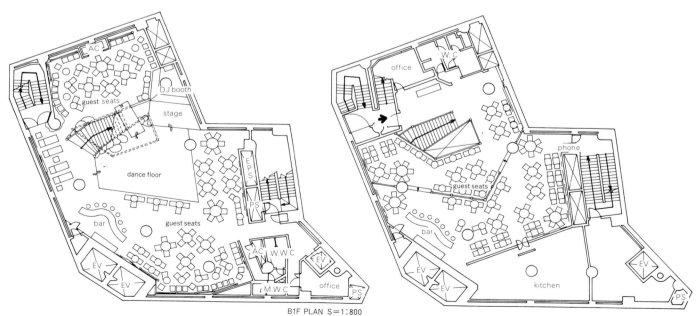

B1F PLAN S＝1:800

MB1F PLAN

163

上/地下１階ダンスフロアからみたバー　カウンター席とテーブル席　カリブのビーチをイメージさせるため客席の床は白砂敷
下/中地下１階のバー　カウンター席廻り

Top/ The bar counter seat and table seat areas viewed from the dance floor at the 1st basement. In order to give an image of the Caribbean beach,
the guest seat floor is covered with white sand.
Bottom/ The bar counter seat area at the semibasement.

上/地下１階壁面の切り絵オブジェ　合板を切り抜いたコーヒーダンサーのシルエットはモーターによりユックリと動く
下/地下１階ＤＪブース脇の壁面オブジェ　シャワーブースにはペリカンとコーヒーダンサーがいる
Top/ The cutout paper pattern objets on the wall of the 1st basement. The coffee dancer's silhouette cut out from plywood is moved slowly by a motor.
Bottom/ The wall objets beside the DJ booth at the 1st basement. There are pelican and coffee dancer at the shower booth.

シティリゾート ファシリティ/*City Resort Facilities*

雁行する壁面とアール面の対比によるファサード　　　　The facade featuring the walls in a row contrasting with the radiused wall.

ジャスマックプラザ

札幌市中央区南7条西3丁目　Phone/011-513-7777

Jasmac Plaza
Nishi 3-chome, Minami 7-jo, Chuo-ku, Sapporo city, Japan
Phone/011-513-7777

撮影/安達　治（※はジャスマック）

ジャスマック プラザ

この施設のある敷地は　札幌の南7条通りから鴨々川に及ぶ長大なもの
で　しかも角地。われわれの計画の狙いは　この条件を最大に生かすこ
とであった。100mを越える圧倒的な長さを強調する外壁タイルのパター
ン　雁行する壁面とR面のコントラスト　シンボリックな列柱によって
この街区にワクワクするような環境の創出をはかったつもりである。
また吹抜け大空間のセントラルコートは　屋外空間の如く仕立てられ
周囲には路傍店舗のように開放的な空間が展開する。北国の街並には珍
しい新鮮な光景が出現したと思う。
ホテルの客室は　敷地の特性から変形S字形プランを採用し　充分なプ
ライバシーと眺望を確保した。　　　　　　　〈金子　満/弾設計〉(89-01)
設計:建築/弾設計
　　　内装/テトラ エム ディー
協力:構造/坪井善隆研究室　設備/マグマ　内装/櫓下設計事務所
施工:建築/辰村組・不二建設共同企業体
　　　内装/ボックス プランニング　河原木建築設計

構　　造:SRC造
規　　模:地下2階 地上11階　塔屋2階
面　　積:敷地/3,094.49㎡　建築/2,558.43㎡　床/地下2階 347.20㎡
　　　地下1階 2,183.67㎡　　1階 1,874.18㎡　　2階 1,537.73㎡
　　　3階 1,863.97㎡　4階 2,094.08㎡　5階 1,822.58㎡　　6階
　　　1,211.73㎡　　7階 1,136.24㎡　　8階 1,148.01㎡　　9階
　　　1,120.78㎡　10階 1,089.76㎡　11階 983.55㎡　塔屋1階
　　　85.73㎡　塔屋2階 33.16㎡　駐車場 1,662.75㎡
　　　合計 20,195.12㎡
工　　期:1986年8月下旬～1988年9月30日

施設概要:開業/1988年10月13日　営業時間/午前11時～午後11時 定休日
　　　/なし　システム/宿泊宴会パック(宿泊料 入浴料 朝食代を含
　　　む) 1万2000 1万5000 1万7000　ゲストルール プラン(10
　　　人以上2時間単位) 3000～5000　各種 料理コース 宴会コー
　　　スあり　経営/㈱ジャスマック　従業員数/サービス300人　厨
　　　房200人　合計500人

Jasmac Plaza

The site on which "Jasmac Plaza" stands is extensive, ranging from Minami 7-jo Street in Sapporo City to River Kamogamo, and occupies a corner lot. The planner tried to fully utilize this condition. The pattern on the tiled outer wall stressing the overwhelming length (more than 100 m), walls arranged in a row contrasting with the radiused wall, and symbolic colonnade – with these elements, the planner has tried to create an exciting environment in this area.

The central court in the huge stairwell space is finished as if it lies in an outdoor space, surrounded again with an open space just like a roadside shop. Thus, it is believed that a scene very rare and fresh for a street in a northern district has been brought into being.

In view of the peculiar site location, a deformed S-shape plan has been employed for the hotel's guest rooms, with due considerations given to privacy and view.

Design: Mitsuru Kaneko

Structure : SRC
Scale　　 : 2 under and 11 stories above the ground, and 2 roof floors
Area　　 : Site/3,094.49 m²; Building/2,558.43 m²; Floor/2nd basement 347.20 m², 1st basement 2,183.67 m², 1st floor 1,874.18 m², 2nd floor 1,537.73 m², 3rd floor 1,863.97 m², 4th floor 2,094.08 m², 5th floor 1,822.58 m², 6th floor 1,211.73 m², 7th floor 1,136.24 m², 8th floor 1,148.01 m², 9th floor 1,120.78 m², 10th floor 1,089.76 m², 11th floor 983.55 m², 1st roof floor 85.73 m², 2nd roof floor 33.16 m², parking lot 1,662.75 m², totaling 20,195.12 m²
Term of construction: late in August, 1986 to September 30, 1988
Facilities : Opening/October 13, 1988; Open time/11:00 a.m. to 11:00 p.m.; Fixed close/nil; System/hotel & banquet in package (including hotel, bath and breakfast charges) available in three types – guest room plan (for rent in unit of 2 hours by more than 10 persons), various dish courses and banquet courses available; Management/Jasmac Plaza Co.; Number of employees/service 300, kitchen 200, totaling 500

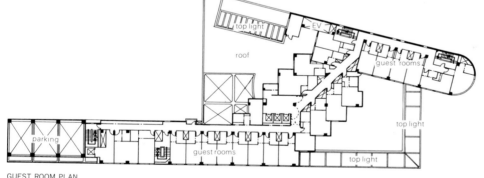

GUEST ROOM PLAN

材料仕様
屋根/アスファルト防水 軽量コンクリート押さえ
外壁/御影石貼り　磁器質タイル貼り　開口部/カ
ラーアルミサッシ ステンレスサッシ
〈3階　大浴場〉床/御影石バーナー仕上　壁/御
影石本磨き　天井/ステンレスリブ材焼き付け塗装
〈5階　ザナドゥ〉床/楢材染色フローリング貼り
壁/グラスウール布団貼り　丸柱/真鍮板腐食加工
一部サンダー加工仕上　天井/布貼りスライディン
グパネル トップライト/スチール製パンチングメ
タルカバー取付メラミン焼き付け塗装

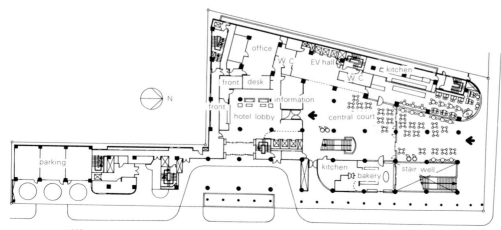

1F PLAN S＝1:800

1階アプローチのセントラルコート※

The central court at the 1st floor approach.

正面アプローチ　パニックドアの採用により外部と内部が一体化した構成
The front approach. By means of a panic door, the inside and outside are integrated.

「ジャスマックプラザホテル」の1階フロント
The 1st floor front area of "Jasmac Plaza Hotel."

３階 「鴨々川温泉・湯香郷」奥の男性用露天風呂 隣りに女性用がある※
The open-air bath for males at an inner part of "Kamogamo-gawa Onsen Toukagou" (3rd floor). Adjacent to it is a bath for females.

5階 "フェスティバルシアター"

"Festival Theater" at the 5th floor.

上/6階のエレベーターホール廻り
下/2階 "ビューティスタジオ"のカット＆セットブース
Top/ The elevator hall area at the 6th floor.
Bottom/ The cut & set booth of "Beauty Studio" at the 2nd floor.

上/地下1階 「四季の味・花遊膳」のビッグカウンター
下/「花遊膳」 最奥の和室宴会場
Top/ The big counter of "Shikino-aji Hana-yuzen" at the 1st basement.
Bottom/ The innermost Japanese style banquet hall of "Hana-yuzen."

レストラン/*Restaurant*

東南側外観をみる　　　　　　　　　　　　　　　The south side appearance.

ヘミングウェイ

大阪市此花区常吉2-20　Phone/06-466-3522

撮影/村瀬武男

ヨットハーバーよりみる　　　　The appearance viewed from the yacht harbor.

Hemingway
2-20, Tsuneyoshi, Konohana-ku, Osaka city, Japan　　Phone/06-466-3522

天井を見上げる　柱　梁によるプリミティブなグリット構成　　　　The ceiling looked up at. The primitive grid configuration of pillars and beams.

開口部側のテーブル席をみる

The table seat area in the opening side.

ヘミングウェイ

このレストランのある北港及び安治川周辺は 大阪のウォーターフロント地区として最近注目されてきているところである。
インテリアはニューヨークのソーホー地区にあるロフト文化のようなプリミティブで豊かな空間をめざした。空間を分節するために鉄骨の柱梁のビルディングエレメントによるグリット構成と垂直方向へと視線を誘導するアイキャッチャーとしての廻り階段という 必要最少限度の舞台装置により 変化のあるインテリアを形づくった。ここでは人間と周りの環境が主体であり あらゆるインテリアエレメントは すべてニュートラルな背景となっている。〈藤本被王/ピー アイ エー〉(88-11)

設計:建築/昭和設計
　　　　内装/ピー アイ エー
協力:サイン/ストロイエ
施工:福井組

構　造:S造
規　模:地上3階
面　積:敷地/110,546.02㎡　建築/404.59㎡　床/1階 336.41㎡(内
　　　　厨房60.17㎡) 2階 296.21㎡　3階 44.33㎡　合計 676.95㎡
工　期:1988年4月21日〜6月20日

施設概要:開店/1988年7月2日　営業時間/午前10時〜午後11時 定休日
　　　　/なし 客席数/90席　テラス席 30席　合計 120席　客単価/
　　　　1000円 客回転数/3〜5回 メニュー/車海老のアメリカンソース煮1500　シーフード スパゲッティ900　シーフード ピラフ800　コース料理5000 7000　コーヒー350 ジュース500　経営/マリーナ観光㈱ 従業員数/サービス6人　厨房7人 パートアルバイト9人　合計22人

Hemingway

The area in the vicinity of Port Kita and River Aji is drawing attention as a waterfront zone in Osaka. This restaurant is open in this area. Imaging a "loft" culture in SoHo, New York, the interior of "Hemingway" has been designed to create a primitive and rich space. In order to segment the space and give a variety to the interior with a minimum of stage setting elements, the grid composition of steel skeleton pillars and beams has been combined with the spiral staircase as an eye-catcher that guides your sight vertically. Here, guests and the surrounding environment are the subject, and all interior elements serve as the neutral background.

Design: Showa Sekkei, P.I.A. Inc.

Structure : S
Scale : 3 stories above the ground
Area : Site/110,546.02 m²; Building/404.59 m²; Floor/1st floor 336.41 m² (including kitchen 60.17 m²), 2nd floor 296.21 m², 3rd floor 44.33 m², totaling 676.95 m²
Term of construction: April 21 to June 20, 1988
Facilities : Opening/July 2, 1988; Open time/10:00 a.m. to 11:00 p.m.; Fixed close/nil; Nunber of guest seats/90, terrace 30, totaling 120; Unit price per guest/1,000 yen; Turn-over of guests/3 to 5 times; Menu/light meals and course dishes centering around seafoods, coffee, juice, etc.; Management/Marina Kanko Co.; Number of employees/ service 6, kitchen 7, part-time 9, totaling 22

材料仕様
屋根/フッ素樹脂焼き付け塗装鋼板 t =0.4横葺き 外壁/石綿セメント押し出し成形板 t =60 磁器質小口タイル貼り サッシ/アルミ合金製電解着色 外部床/アスファルト防水の上磁器質タイル貼り150角 床/天然木化粧複合フローリング t =11貼り 壁/PBt =12ビニールエナメル塗装 柱&梁/SOP 天井/PBt =9ビニールエナメル塗装 カウンター/赤松SOP拭き取りの上ラッカー

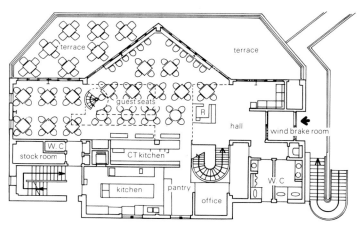

PLAN　S=1:300

帆を連想させるアルミパンチング板の壁面スクリーン

The punched aluminum plate wall screen that reminds us of a sail.

撮影／藤原　弘

正面外観をみる

The front appearance.

カフェ ドゥ クレセント

滋賀県大津市南志賀1丁目字外山田808-2　ハイツ志賀岡本ビル2階
Phone／0775-21-0864

Café de Crescent
1-chome, Minami-shiga, Otsu city, Shiga, Japan
Phone／0775-21-0864

上/周囲の景観　風　光　緑を取り込む大きな開口部
下/中央テーブル席を通して入口方向をみる

Top/ The large opening designed to incorporate the surrounding scenery, wind, light and green.
Bottom/ The entrance area viewed across the central table seat.

風をきって進む舳先（へさき）　The stem going ahead breaking the wind.

Café de Crescent

Facing the brilliantly white Lake Biwa and green Omi Shrine, "Café de Crescent" is open in facilities that consist of shops, including a café, and collective housing units.

The café is lifted by the air flowing from the lake, and the lake gives an image of sea. Under the intense sunlight, modern architecture's keyword, "ship," is associated with. The paved site reminds us of a deck. The quadrangular pyramid glass toplight, meandering membranous outer wall, widely opened transparent wall surface, open grating staircase leading to the 2nd floor of the bright deck where the wind is blowing through, punched aluminum plate wall that stands upright and reminds us of a sail, two metal pillars just like masts – all these make up a "hull."

Design: Hideaki Imai

Structure : S
Scale   : 2 stories above the ground
Area   : Site/378.71 m²; Building/163.40 m²; Floor/(shop) 48.08 m² (including kitchen 7.58 m²)
Term of construction: June 20 to December 29, 1987
Facilities : Opening/March 1, 1988;   Open time/7:00 a.m. to 11:00 p.m.;   Fixed close/nil;   Number of guest seats/27;   Unit price per guest/550 yen;   Menu/spaghetti, sandwich, coffee, tea, soft drinks, beer, etc.;   Management/Tohru Sugada;   Number of employees/kitchen 1, part-time 2, totaling 3

カフェ ドゥ クレセント

白く輝く琵琶湖と近江神宮の緑に臨むこの施設は　カフェを主体とした店舗と集合住宅で構成されている。カフェは湖から流れる大気に持ち上げられ　また湖が海のイメージを与え　強い日差しの中　近代建築のキーワード "船" が連想される。甲板を想い起こさせるペーブされた敷地。四角錐のガラスのトップライト　外壁のうねる皮膜　大きく開放された透明ガラスの壁面　風が吹き抜け光が満ちるデッキ　2階へ上がる開放されたグレーチングの階段　帆を連想させる垂直に立つアルミパンチング板の壁面　マストが如き2本の金属柱　それらが "船体" を形づくる。

〈今井秀明／今井建築設計事務所〉(88-05)

設計：今井建築設計事務所
協力：構造／ワイエックス構造デザイン事務所
　　　設備／洛陽設計事務所
施工：駒音建設

構　　造：S造
規　　模：地上2階
面　　積：敷地／378.71㎡　建築／163.40㎡　床／(店舗)48.08㎡(内 厨房7.58㎡)
工　　期：1987年6月20日〜12月29日

施設概要：開店／1988年3月1日　営業時間／午前7時〜午後11時 定休日／なし　客席数／27席　客単価／550円　メニュー／スパゲティ500〜600　サンドイッチ500〜600　コーヒー280〜450　紅茶280〜350　ソフトドリンク280〜500　ビール500　経営／菅田徹　従業員数／厨房1人　パート アルバイト2人　合計3人

材料仕様
屋根／アルミ亜鉛合金メッキ鋼板　外壁／アルミパンチング板 t＝2　金属長尺成形板 t＝2　外部床／玉砂利コンクリート洗い出し　床／モルタル下地樹脂系タイル　壁／アルミ平板加工　横目ガラスタイル貼り　一部大理石貼り　天井／PBt＝12寒冷紗貼りEP　テーブル／甲板：橅集成材ウレタンクリア塗装　脚：スチール(黒)焼き付け塗装

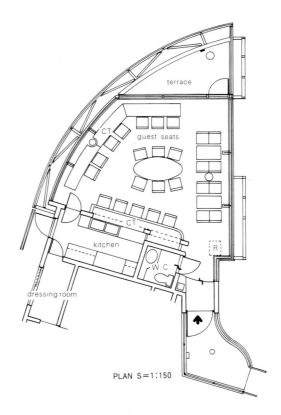

PLAN S=1:150

西側よりみた高さ22mの巨大な魚のモニュメント　鯉の跳ねるフォルムをイメージしたもので　表面はチェーンリングメッシュのウロコで覆われている
The huge monument of fish 22 m high, viewed from the west side. Imaging a form of huge jumping carp, the surface is covered with scales of chain ring mesh.

フィッシュダンス

神戸市中央区波止場町　メリケンパーク内
Phone/078-333-8000

撮影/松村芳治

北側からのロケーション　海上を横断する高速道路越しにポートアイランドの荷揚げ埠頭がみえる
The location viewed from the north side.　Port Island's loading wharf visible acros
the speedway　that is crossing over the sea.

Fish Dance
Hatoba-cho, Chuo-ku, Kobe city, Japan　Phone/078-333-8000

西側正面よりみた魚のモニュメントとスパイラル タワー　右端はテイクアウトコーナーの入口
The fish monument and spiral tower viewed from the western front side.　In the right side is the entrance to the takeout corner.

1階レストラン左奥コーナーより客席を通してレジ及び2階の鉄板焼コーナーをみる
The register and 2nd floor hot plate corner viewed from the 1st floor restaurant inner left side corner, across the guest seat area.

2階のスパイラル タワー側より鉄板焼コーナーと1階レジ コーナー方向をみる
The hot plate corner and 1st floor register corner viewed from the spiral tower at the 2nd floor.

海岸側東面の大きなガラス開口部より店内をみる
The inside viewed from the large glass opening in the east side facing the sea.

フィッシュダンス

私は数年前から魚の形というものを　ポストモダニズムに対する反動としてとらえてきた。その後　このプロジェクトが進行するなかで　その魚を置いてみたいという話があり　勇気を出して　魚のモニュメントを導入した。魚に鯉を選んだのは　子供の頃から馴染みの深い魚であったということと　北斎の鯉の絵に魅かれたということである。

もう一つ　このレストランで試みたことは　建築そのものと周辺の環境をどうすれば一体化することができるかであった。レストランの内部に入ると　高速道路や税関の建物　後ろの古い神戸の街並み　そして魚のモニュメントが見え　外部との一体感が感じられるようになっている。

〈フランク・O・ゲーリー/文責編集部〉(87-07)

設計：フランク・O・ゲーリー
実施設計：神戸港振興協会　環境開発研究所
施工：竹中工務店

構　　造：S造
規　　模：地上2階　塔屋1階
面　　積：敷地/3,272.67㎡　建築/624.09㎡　床/1階 624.09㎡　2階 293.33㎡　塔屋 24.35㎡　合計 941.77㎡(内 厨房145.4㎡)
工　　期：1986年11月8日〜1987年4月20日

施設概要：開店/1987年4月29日　営業時間/午前11時〜午後11時　定休日/なし　客席数/190席　客単価/1500円　客回転数/4.2回　メニュー/フィッシュダンスピザ1000　海の幸オムレツ900　明太子とバジリコのスパゲティ900　鉄板焼サーロイン1500　魚介類のお好み焼1500　カクテル600〜500　串カツ(15本)2000　スパイシードッグ(テイクアウト)250　経営 事業主体/神戸市港湾局　(社)神戸港振興協会　委託経営運営/(株)ワールド　(株)ルモンテグルメ　従業員数/サービス10人　厨房13人　パート アルバイト20人　合計43人

Fish Dance

Since a few years ago, I have recognized the shape of fish as a reaction to postmodernism. Then, in the course of this project underway, there arose a plan for placing a fish objet. Hence, I introduce a monument of fish. I have chosen carp because I have been very familiar with it, and have also been attracted by the paintings of carp by Hokusai, a master painter of Edo Era.

Another attempt I have made with this restaurant has been to find a way for harmonizing the building itself with the surrounding environment. Entering the restaurant, you see a speedway, customs building, old streets in Kobe, and monument of fish, harmoniously continuing from the outside to the inside.

Design: Frank O. Gehry

Structure : S
Scale : 2 stories above the ground, and 1 roof floor
Area : Site/3,272.67 m²; Building/624.09 m²; Floor/1st floor 624.09 m², 2nd floor 293.33 m², roof floor 24.35 m², totaling 941.77 m² (including kitchen 145.4 m²)
Term of construction: November 8, 1986 to April 20, 1987
Facilities : Opening/April 29, 1987; Open time/11:00 a.m. to 11:00 p.m.; Fixed close/nil; Number of guest seats/190; Unit price per guest/1,500 yen; Turnover of guests/4.2 times; Menu/pizza, omelet, spaghetti, steak, hot plate seafood, spitted cutlet, cocktails, and spicy hot dog takeout; Management/Kobe Municipal Port & Harbor Bureau and Kobe-ko Shinko Kyokai (Port Kobe Promotion Association), entrusted to World Co. and L'Monte Gourmet Co.; Number of employees/service 10, kitchen 13, part-time 20, totaling 43

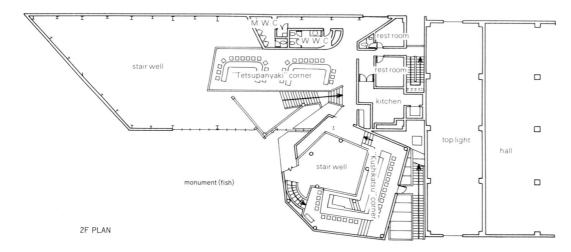

2F PLAN

材料仕様
屋根　外壁/レストラン棟：亜鉛引き波型鉄板 t＝0.6 フッ素樹脂塗装　スパイラル棟：銅板 t＝0.4一文字葺き250×400　サイン スチール亜鉛メッキ　床/モルタル鏝押さえ　一部フローリング目地切り仕上に防塵塗料　直貼り楢材フローリング t＝15　幅木/モルタル鏝押さえ h＝100　ビニールペイント塗分け　壁/石膏ボード　エマルジョンペイント　天井/硬質木片セメント板 t＝40エマルジョンペイント吹き付け　EP吹き付け石膏ボード t＝9エマルジョンペイント　カウンター/トップ：楢集成材

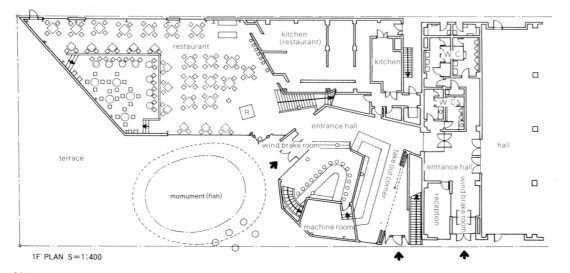

1F PLAN S=1:400

川ごしにみる建物全景

The entire appearance of "Jion Shoji Ajigawa Delivery Center" viewed across the river.

ルーポール

大阪市西区安治川Ⅰ丁目Ⅰ-17　ホワイトベースⅠ階
Phone/06-584-3122

撮影/福本正明

Loophole

1-1-17, Ajikawa, Nishi-ku, Osaka city, Japan　　Phone/06-584-3122

ルーポール

「ルーポール」はファッションメーカーの物流センター内にあり　大阪港に注ぐ安治川を河口から約4km逆上った倉庫街に位置する。この地区の再開発計画の最初の施設であるこの建物は　できるだけシンボリックにまた従来の倉庫建築を越えた表現力をもったものになるようデザインした。

国道側の1～2階の一画にある「ルーポール」は　この地区の活性化の一つとして計画された。木とモルタル搔落し　石といった材質感のある材料で構成されたモノトーンの空間は　従来のカフェバー等に飽きた人々に新鮮な印象を与えるものと考えている。

〈北野俊二/永田・北野建築研究所〉(88-08)

設計:永田・北野建築研究所
施工:建築/清水建設
　　　内装/東亜製作所

構　　造:SRC造
規　　模:地下1階 地上5階 塔屋1階
面　　積:敷地/1,468.12㎡　建築/1,001.45㎡　床(レストランのみ)/1階 155.00㎡(内 厨房41.5㎡)　2階 107.80㎡　合計 262.80㎡
工　　期:1988年4月1日～5月31日

施設概要:開店/1988年6月10日　営業時間/フリータイム 午前11時30分～午後4時　メンバーズタイム 午後5時～午前3時(日曜 祭日は午後11時まで)　定休日/なし　客席数/1階 38席 2階 39席　合計 77席　客単価/フリータイム1000円 メンバーズタイム4500円　メニュー/多国籍料理 56種 500～1500　樽入り スコッチウィスキー(S)700～　ビール500～　カクテル800～　ソフトドリンク500～700　経営/㈱マテリアル 従業員数/サービス4人　厨房4人　パート アルバイト5人　合計13人

Loophole

"Loophole" is open within a physical distribution center of a fashion goods manufacturer, situated in a warehouses quarter about 4 km upstream the mouth of River Aji that is flowing into the Osaka Port. This quarter is currently under the redevelopment program, and this building is the first such building constructed under the program. Thus, with a view to making it far more expressive than conventional warehouse buildings, it has been designed as symbolically as possible. "Loophole" occupying part of the 1st and 2nd floors facing the highway, has been installed to activate this quarter. The monotonous space composed of simple quality materials, such as wood, scraped mortar and stone, will give a fresh impression to those who are fed up with conventional cafe bars, etc.

Design: Shunji Kitano

Structure : SRC
Scale 　: 1 under and 5 stories above the ground, and 1 roof floor
Area 　: Site/1,468.12 m²; Building/1,001.45 m²; Floor (restaurant only)/1st floor 155.00 m² (including kitchen 41.50 m², 2nd floor 107.80 m², totaling 262.80 m² (including kitchen 41.50 m²)
Term of construction: April 1 to May 31, 1988
Facilities : Opening/June 10, 1988; Open time/free time 11:30 a.m. to 4:00 p.m., members time 5:00 p.m. to 3:00 a.m. (by 11:00 p.m. on Sunday and holiday); Fixed close/nil; Number of guest seats/1st floor 38, 2nd floor 39, totaling 77; Unit price per guest/free time 1,000 yen, members time 4,500 yen; Menu/multinational dishes (56 types), casked Scotch whisky, beer, cocktails, soft drinks; Management/Material Co.; Number of employees/service 4, kitchen 4, part-time 5, totaling 13

南側の正面外観をみる

The south side front appearance.

上/2階への階段途中より店内全景をみる
右上/1階より見返す
右下/吹抜け横の2階通路　右側に個室が並ぶ

Top/ The entire inside scene viewed from somewhere along the staircase leading to the 2nd floor.
Right, top/ A scene looked back upon from the 1st floor.
Right, bottom/ The 2nd floor aisle beside the stairwell. Visible in the right side are private rooms.

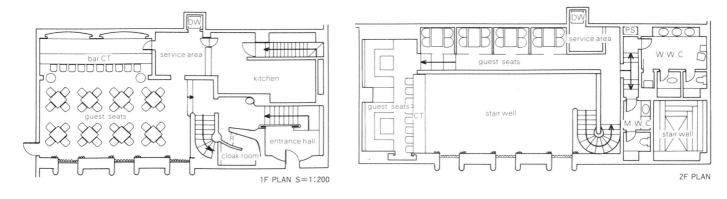

1F PLAN S=1:200

2F PLAN

材料仕様
屋根/コンクリート下地シート防水　外壁/コンクリート下地モザイクタイル貼り45角　開口部/アルミサッシ　ジュラクロン焼き付け仕上　外部床/コンクリート下地磁器質タイル貼り100
角　床/モルタル鏝押さえ下地大理石　ゴムタイル t＝5　タイルカーペット敷500角　幅木/モルタル鏝押さえ下地楢CL　h＝90　壁/コンクリート下地　モルタルリシン掻き落とし
一部御影石　2階ボックス席パーティション:特殊強化ガラス　天井/PB下地寒冷紗LEP仕上　1階カウンター席前柱/コンクリート鉄板巻加工VP塗装

入口階段中ほどより外観をみる　右手に"海"をイメージしたプールにヨットを浮べている
The appearance viewed from midway along the entrance staircase. Visible at right is the yacht floating on the pool imaging the "sea."

撮影/飯嶋裕司

歩道よりプールを通してみる　　　　　　　　　A night scene viewed from the pavement across the pool.

東京都世田谷区駒沢 4 丁目11-9　Phone/03-487-4465

Ing Komazawa
4-11-9, Komazawa, Setagaya-ku, Tokyo, Japan　　Phone/03-487-4465

イング駒沢

駒沢公園通りを挟んで駒沢公園の向かい 高級住宅が建ち並ぶ中に この建物は立地している。

このプロジェクトの目的は "市街地の真っ只中に 海を持ってくる" を基本コンセプトとし 駒沢公園を舞台にくり広げられるスポーツ 遊びの拠点になる場を提供することであった。設計のポイントは 外装は海のイメージがあまりにも写実的にならないよう また反面 非現実的にならないように努めた。

店内は装飾品でごまかさないことを意図に "海" の持つイメージのブルーを基調とし 他は素材の持つ色調をそのまま表現し 高い天井 大きな窓からくる開放感を重視し 飲食店に必要な清潔な空間づくりを心掛けた。

〈木本 淳／アーバン工房〉(88-11)

設計：アーバン工房
施工：新建築

構　　造：S造
規　　模：地上2階
面　　積：敷地／975.82m² 建築／432.81m² 床／1階 360.00m² 2階 383.31m²（内 厨房52.80m²）合計 743.31m²
工　　期：1987年12月16日〜1988年5月20日

施設概要：開店／1988年5月25日 営業時間／午前11時30分〜午前2時 定休日／なし 客席数／カウンター18席 ホール116席 テラス28席 合計162席 客単価／1800円 客回転数／4.5回 メニュー／ニース風サラダ700 ソールのフライ地中海風1200 海老と野菜のスペイン風1400 ノルウェイ産サーモン酸味ソース1700 ヒナ鳥のコンフィー1900 コーヒー300 ビール500〜700 経営／㈱ピーエーフーズ 羽生田健介 従業員数／サービス10人 厨房12人 パート アルバイト11人 合計33人

Ing Komazawa

This building stands in the midst of a row of select residences across Komazawa Park.

Keeping in mind the basic concept "Bring the sea into the midst of a street," this project was aimed to offer a place for those who come to Komazawa Park to enjoy sports. Design considerations were given so that the exterior does not give too realistic nor too unrealistic an image of sea.

In order not to dazzle guests with showy ornaments, the blue image of "sea" has been stressed as the basic tone, accented with natural colors of materials used, while giving an open sense through high ceiling and wide windows, thus creating a clean space essential to the restaurant.

Design: Jun Kimoto

Structure : S
Scale : 2 stories above the ground
Area : Site/975.82 m²; Building/432.81 m²; Floor/1st floor 360.00 m², 2nd floor 383.31 m² (including kitchen 52.80 m²), totaling 743.31 m² (including kitchen 52.80 m²)
Term of construction: December 16, 1987 to May 20, 1988
Facilities : Opening/May 25, 1988; Open time/11:30 a.m. to 2:00 a.m.; Fixed close/nil; Number of guest seats/counter 18, hall 116, terrace 28, totaling 162; Unit price per guest/ 1,800 yen; Turnover of guests/4.5 times; Menu/European dishes, coffee, beer, etc.; Management/B. A. Foods Co., Kensuke Hanyuda; Number of employees/service 10, kitchen 12, part-time 11, totaling 33

材料仕様

屋根／鉄骨下地石綿波型スレート葺きOP 外壁／鉄骨下地石綿波型スレート貼り OP ステンレス鏡面仕上 アルミサッシ（ブラック） 外部床／磁器質タイル貼り100角 インターロッキング アスファルト舗装 床／粘板岩貼り400角 フローリング貼り 壁／石綿波型スレートあらわし 二丁掛けタイル貼り メラミン化粧板アルミ見切りスリット 天井／木毛 セメント板貼り 照明器具／コードペン スポットライト 白熱燈 家具／楢材練り付け黒目ハジキ塗装

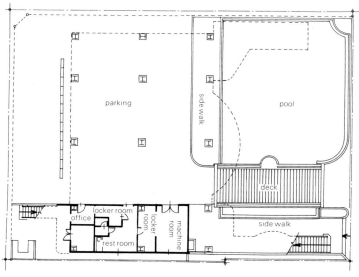

1F PLAN S=1:400

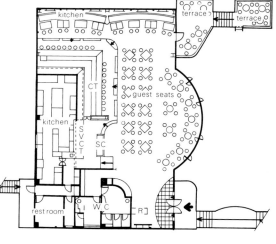

2F PLAN

2階レジカウンター前より店内奥をみる
Looking into the inner part from the 2nd floor register counter.

R形のテーブル席よりバーカウンター方向をみる
The bar counter area viewed from the R-shaped table seats.

右上/店内奥のパーティ専用のテーブル席
右下/バーカウンター席
Right, top/ The inner table seat area exclusive for party.
Right, bottom/ The bar counter seats.

駐車場スペースからみた外観　枕木をイメージさせる米松積みの外壁が重厚感の中にも柔らかい印象を与える
The appearance viewed from the parking space. The outer wall of piled American pine logs reminding us of crossties gives a dignified but gentle impression.

伊　助

兵庫県三田市対中町1439
Phone/0795-63-5375

撮影/福本正明

Isuke

1439, Tainaka-cho, Sanda city, Hyogo, Japan
Phone/0795-63-5375

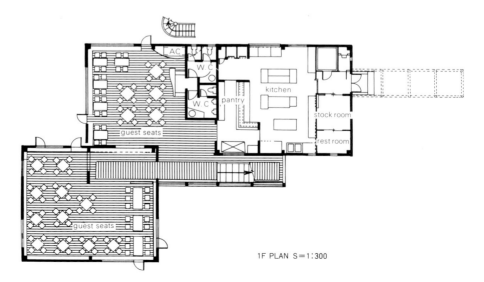

1F PLAN S=1:300

裏の田んぼからみた外観　道路と2階フロアが同じレベル
The appearance viewed from the paddy field at the back of the building. The road and 2nd floor lie at the same level.

国道より駐車スペース越しに外観をみる
The appearance viewed from the highway across the parking space.

伊助

高層ビルの生活に慣らされ　遠近感の無い不安定さを余儀なくされてきた都会人　その都会人たちの気持ちを踏まえた　居心地の良い豊かな空間を提供することが　今回の店づくりの主題である。

「伊助」は　大阪から福知山へ通じる国道176号沿いの　三田市郊外に位置している。

建物自体は　四方からの見え掛けを意識し　重量感のある2つのコアを軽快なガラスのドームで結んだ　単純でシンメトリックな手法で仕上げた。段差により分離された駐車場と建物は　ブリッジを架けることで店内導入の明確化を図った。

鉄骨による構造で装飾性は一切排除し　木材とモルタル小石洗い出しが主素材の　素直でナチュラルな味を表現してみた。

〈吉尾浩次/インテリアデザインオフィス ノブ〉(88-11)

設計：インテリアデザインオフィス ノブ
施工：建築/トヨクニ工務店
　　　内装/タクト

構　造：S造
規　模：地上2階
面　積：敷地/1,780.20㎡　建築/339.54㎡　床/1階 332.54㎡　2階 248.48㎡　合計 581.02㎡(内 厨房97.20㎡)
工　期：1988年4月1日〜8月12日

施設概要：開店/1988年8月13日　営業時間/午前11時30分〜午後10時　定休日/なし　客席数/140席　客単価/6000円　メニュー/ランチミニコース(2種)3000　伊勢海老のテルミドール2000　伊勢海老のオイル焼き3000　ディナー スペシャルコース5000　ロイヤルコース8000　インペリアルコース1万　ビール500　ハウスワイン グラス400　ハーフボトル1200　フルボトル1800　経営/㈱トヨクニ工務店　古河正義　従業員数/サービス5人　厨房7人　パート アルバイト5人　合計17人

Isuke

City inhabitants have been compelled to live in high-rise buildings unstably without perspective. In view of such urban mentality, the main theme of the current shop making has been set at offering a rich space comfortable to stay in.

"Isuke" is situated in the suburbs of Sanda City, along the highway #176 that leads from Osaka to Fukuchiyama.

Conscious of the appearance from four sides, the building itself has been finished in a simple and symmetrical manner by linking the weighty cores with a buoyant glass dome. The parking lot and building separated from each other, are bridged to secure a definite approach to the restaurant.

Constructed of steel frames, all decoration has been eliminated, and by mainly using wood and mortar with pebbles washed out, a simple and natural atmosphere has been created.

Design: Hiroji Yoshio

Structure : S
Scale　　 : 2 stories above the ground
Area　　　: Site/1,780.20 m²; Building/339.54 m²; Floor/1st floor 332.54 m², 2nd floor 248.48 m², totaling 581.02 m² (including kitchen 97.20 m²)
Term of construction: April 1 to August 12, 1988
Facilities : Opening/August 13, 1988;　　Open time/11:30 a.m. to 10:00 p,m.;　Fixed close/nil;　Number of guest seats/140; Unit price per guest/6,000 yen; Menu/fresh lobster dishes (from single items to course dishes), beer, house wine;　Management/Toyokuni Kohmuten Co., Masayoshi Furukawa;　　Number of employees/service 5, kitchen 7, part-time 5, totaling 17

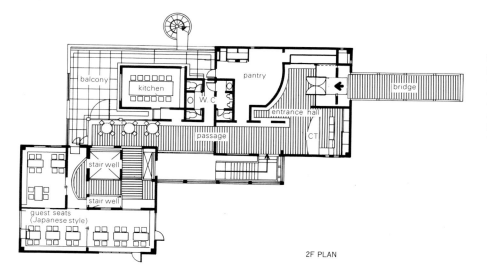

2F PLAN

材料仕様
屋根/デッキプレート下地アスファルトルーフィング砂利敷込み　外壁/米松150×230積みステイン仕上及びモルタル小石洗い出し　外部床/モルタル小石洗い出し　サイン/スチールの上アクリル切り文字貼りFL内蔵　床/米松板t＝40オイル仕上及びモルタル小石洗い出し　1階:米松150×230積み及びモルタル小石洗い出し　天井/YNプラスター鏝押さえ　照明器具/ダウンライト埋め込み　什器/米松OS拭き取りCL仕上

1階へおりる階段より見た青空の見えるドーム状天井
The domed ceiling through which the blue sky is visible, as viewed from the staircase leading down to the 1st floor.

190

アプローチのためのブリッジ入口方向を見る

The entrance area viewed from the approach bridge.

2階レジ前より入口方向
The entrance area viewed from the 2nd floor register.

上/1階右側の椅子席をみる
下/2階左奥の板貼り座敷席をみる
Top/ The chair seats in the right side of the 1st floor.
Bottom/ Boarded Japanese style seat area in the inner left part
of the 2nd floor.

191

焼肉 レストラン/Yakiniku Restaurant

ファサード 小さな丸窓の連続が軽快さを演出している
The facade. The small round windows in a row present a buoyant atmosphere.

大蔵谷牧場

神戸市西区伊川谷有瀬617
Phone/078-975-2006

撮影/山田誠良

外部テラス席をみる 左側にコンテナ棟が見える
The open-air terrace seat area. The container building is visible in the left side.

Okuradani-Bokujo
Ikawadani-Arise, Nishi-ku, Kobe city, Japan   Phone/078-975-2006

テラス席をみる 閉鎖的ファサードとは対象的に開放感がある演出
The terrace seat area. In sharp contrast to the closed facade, this area gives an open sense.

ファサード詳細　The round table seats.　円形テーブル席をみる　The facade details.

大蔵谷牧場

この焼肉レストランは　神戸市が開発している西神地区にあって　大蔵谷ICを出た東側に位置している。

計画は　系列店で以前使用していたコンテナをリニューアルすることでローコスト化を狙った。また従来の焼肉店ではなく英文字YAKINIKUとネーミング　イラスト及びロゴタイプで　新しいファッショナブルフーズのイメージを強調した。

店舗ゾーンは　コンテナ部分と　アウトドア的な天井の高いデッキ部分とに分けて開放感を演出するとともに　インテリアは　木質を多様して暖かみと普段着的気軽さを出した。ファサードは木組による多様的な面白さ　視覚的効果を意図した。　〈丸山雅美/山口デザイン事務所〉(88-11)

設計：山口デザイン事務所

施工：建築/セントラル
　　　内装/竹内工務店

構　　造：S造
規　　模：平屋　一部コンテナ
面　　積：敷地/2,770.95㎡　建築/449.85㎡　床/448.87㎡(内 厨房60.85㎡)
工　　期：1988年2月20日～4月20日

施設概要：開店/1988年4月27日　営業時間/午前11時～午後11時　定休日/なし　客席数/236席　客回転数/1回　メニュー/上ロース1300　ロース950　バラ800　上ミノ900　わかめスープ300　テールスープ700　サラダ350 400　ペアセット(2人分)3900　ファミリーセット(4～5人分)4800　ビール430 500　経営/㈱フジタニカンパニー　従業員数/サービス3人　厨房3人　パートアルバイト6人　合計12人

Okuradani-Bokujo

This yakiniku (barbecue) restaurant is situated in the east side of Okuradani Interchange in the west area of Kobe that is being developed by Kobe City.

In order to achieve low cost construction, the containers used previously by a chain restaurant have been renewed. In order to differentiate from conventional barbecue restaurants, this restaurant has employed the English naming "YAKINIKU" illustration and logotype to stress an image of new-type fashionable food service.

The shop zone is divided into the container segment and high-ceiling deck segment with an outdoor touch, thereby creating an open atmosphere. Meanwhile, by using wooden materials varying in quality, the interior is finished to give a warm, casual atmosphere. The facade has been designed to give a visual effect with pleasant woodwork varying in pattern.

Design: Masami Maruyama

Structure : S
Scale : 1 story building (container in part)
Area : Site/2,770.95 m²; Building/449.85 m²; Floor/448.87 m² (including kitchen 60.85 m²)
Term of construction: February 20 to April 20, 1988
Facilities : Opening/April 27, 1988; Open time/11:00 a.m. to 11:00 p.m.; Fixed close/nil; Number of guest seats/236; Turnover of guests/1; Menu/Korean barbecue dishes, soup, salad, set menu, beer, etc.; Management/Fujitani Company; Number of employees/service 3, kitchen 3, part-time 6, totaling 12

材料仕様

屋根/折り板亜鉛引きカラー鉄板　一部テント張り　外壁/コルゲートパネル　タモ材板貼り　外部床/アスファルト舗装　レンガタイル　サイン/ボンテ鋼板ネオンサイン　一部アクリル行灯　床/根太組コンパネ下地米松フローリング貼り　幅木/米松　h＝100　壁/合板貼り　天井/PB寒冷紗OP

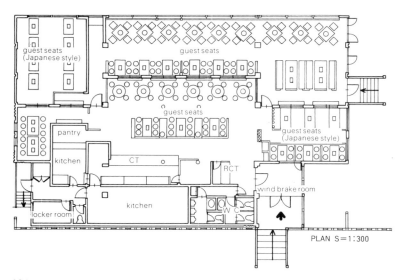

guest seats (Japanese style) / guest seats / guest seats / guest seats (Japanese style) / pantry / kitchen / CT / RCT / wind brake room / kitchen / WC / locker room

PLAN S=1:300

外観をみる

羅阿麺館

北海道苫小牧市有明2丁目7　Phone/0144-72-1192

撮影/安達　治

羅阿麺舘

この店は苫小牧市の郊外にある。今までのラーメン店の店構えをすっかり変身させ　もう少し豊かで　しかも親しみのある空間を提供するのが狙いである。

この「羅阿麺館」に使われた木は　すべて道産のものより選んだ。外壁の下見板は道南の杉　窓のフレームは朱利桜　内装に貼られた板や構造に使われた柱や梁　建具等はえぞ松　とど松　カウンター類はタモの集成材　小上りの床は楢のフローリング　玄関の天井にはセンの突板　テーブル　椅子等に使われた集成材は楢　そして館の内部にそびえ立つ3本の大柱は松前より切り出した杉である。

〈伊藤颯彩/あとりえ ふろむぜろ〉(88-05)

設計：あとりえ ふろむぜろ
施工：藤建設工業

構　　造：木造
規　　模：平屋
面　　積：敷地/947.03m²　建築/170.73m²　床/154.55m²(内 厨房 21.44 m²)
工　　期：1987年9月15日〜12月30日

施設概要：開店/1988年1月2日　営業時間/午前11時〜午後11時　定休日/なし　客席数/75席　客単価/450円　客回転数/13回　メニュー/ラーメン450　塩ラーメン450　味噌ラーメン450　ビール(ジョッキ)350　アイスクリーム100　ジュース100　経営/㈱竹山　竹山 健　従業員数/サービス3人　厨房5人　合計8人

Rarmen-kan

2-7, Ariake-cho, Tomakomai city, Hokkaido, Japan
Phone/0144-72-1192

Rarmen-kan

"Rarmen-kan" is open in the suburbs of Tomakomai City. In designing this shop, it was intended to change the conventional rarmen (Chinese noodle) shop image, and offer a little richer and familiar space.
All wooden materials used for "Rarmen-kan" have been selected from those genuinely produced in Hokkaido — Japan cedar (sugi) from the southern district for weatherboarding on the outer wall, Shuri cherry tree for window framing and interior, Yezo spruce/abies for pillars, beams and furniture, 'tamo' aggregate for counters, Japanese oak flooring for Japanese style seat area, 'sen' for porch's ceiling, Japanese oak aggregate for tables, chairs, etc., and Japan cedar brought from Matsumae for three huge pillars towering inside the shop.

Design: Sousei Ito

Structure : Wooden building
Scale　　 : 1 story above the ground
Area　　　: Site/947.03 m²; Building/170.73 m²; Floor/154.55 m² (including kitchen 21.44 m²)
Term of construction: September 15 to December 30, 1987
Facilities : Opening/January 2, 1988;　Open time/11:00 a.m. to 11:00 p.m.; Fixed close/nil; Number of guest seats/75; Unit price per guest/450 yen;　Turnover of guests/13 times;　Menu/various types of rarmen, beer, ice cream, juice, etc.; Management/Takeyama Co., Ken Takeyama; Number of employees/service 3, kitchen 5, totaling 8

小上り席をみる

Japanese style board seat area.

カウンター席をみる　窓側のベンチは待合 | The counter seat area. The window side bench is used for waiting guests.

材料仕様
屋根/塩ビ加工長尺カラー鉄板葺き　外壁/道南杉下見貼りステイン仕上　外部床/モルタル金鏝目地切り
床/磁器質タイル貼り100角　幅木/磁器質タイル貼り　壁/松貼り　柱:道南杉及びコンクリート　天井/
セン柾目板化粧合板貼り

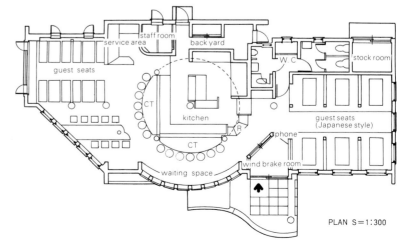

PLAN S=1:300

焼肉 レストラン & ディスコ/*Yakiniku Restaurant & Disco*

前面道路よりみる　手前がディスコ「ジェイ トリップ バー」で　三角形のトップライトの建物が焼肉レストラン「サージェント ヘッパーズ」
The appearance viewed from the front road. Visible in your side is the disco "J Trip Bar," and the triangular toplighted building is the barbecue restaurant "Sergeant Peppers."

スキー場の中に建つ施設　　　　The facilities standing in the skiing ground.

サージェント ペッパーズ＆ジェイ トリップ バー

新潟県南魚沼郡湯沢町三国字下ヨリエ181-1　Phone/0257-89-2789

Sergeant Peppers & J Trip Bar
181-1, Mikuni, Yuzawa-machi, Minami-Uonuma-gun, Niigata, Japan　　Phone/0257-89-2789

サージェント ペッパーズ＆ジェイトリップ バー

この施設は 新潟県 苗場スキー場のゲレンデを前面に望む雄大な自然環境の中に位置する。自然の形づくる曲線的な形態に対し 人工的な幾何学形態との対比が 純粋な形で実現できた。レストランは可視的立方体フレームの枠の中で 外から内が見え 内から外を望む透明な状態を表現し ディスコは外に対して閉じた箱を用意した。両者を不連続に配置し 挟まれた空間が広場として レストランのバーガーショップとディスコの出口 窓 また歩道との接点となり アクティビティを支えている。

〈川村正士〉(87-04)

設計:川村正士建築設計事務所
協力:オブジェ/日比野克彦
施工:建築/井川建設
　　　内装/鈴権商店

構　　造:サージェント ペッパーズ/RC造 ジェイ トリップ バー/RC造
規　　模:サージェント ペッパーズ/地上3階 ジェイ トリップ バー/地上2階
面　　積:敷地/845.84㎡ 建築/サージェント ペッパーズ 227.77㎡ ジェイ トリップ バー 191.96㎡ 床/サージェント ペッパーズ 1階 204.04㎡ 2階 180.73㎡ 3階 178.48㎡ 合計 563.25㎡(内 厨房58.9㎡) ジェイ トリップ バー 1階 183.49㎡ 2階 71.80㎡ 合計 255.29㎡(内 厨房9.9㎡)
工　　期:1986年7月24日～12月15日

施設概要:開店/1986年12月18日 営業期間/12月1日～5月5日 営業時間/サージェント ペッパーズ 午前11時～午前2時 ジェイ トリップ バー 午後5時～11時45分 定休日/なし 客席数/サージェント ペッパーズ 180席 ジェイ トリップ バー 150席 メニュー/サージェント ペッパーズ ビビンバ700 ロース900 カルビ1000 ランチ(2時まで)1000～ 生ビール(小) ビール(中)各700 日本酒600 グラスワイン(赤 白)各500 カクテル各種700～ ジェイ トリップ バー (フリードリンク制) 男3000 女2000 サージェント バーガー 280 ダブルバーガー380 焼肉弁当(カルビ ロース)各1000 コーヒー180 オレンジ ジュース160 経営/㈱三倶 従業員数/(両店合わせて) サービス20人 厨房7人 パート アルバイト20人 合計47人

Sergeant Peppers & J Trip Bar

These facilities are situated in a grand natural environment overlooking a slope of Naeba Skiing Ground, Niigata Prefecture. The artificial geometrical shapes could be genuinely contrasted with the curvilinear shapes created by nature. Covered with visible cubic framing, the restaurant expresses a transparent space from which the outside is visible, while the inside is visible from the outside. The disco has been designed as a box closed against the outside. These two are installed discountinuously, and the space sandwiched by them serves as a plaza linking the restaurant's burger shop, disco exit, window and pavement, thereby supporting the overall activities.

Design: Masashi Kawamura

Structure : Sergeant Peppers/RC, J Trip Bar/RC
Scale　　: Sergeant Peppers/3 stories above the ground, J Trip Bar/ 2 stories above the ground
Area　　 : Site/845.84 m²; Building/Sergeant Peppers 227.77 m², J Trip Bar 191.96 m²; Floor/Sergeant Peppers – 1st floor 204.04 m², 2nd floor 180.73 m², 3rd floor 178.48 m², totaling 563.25 m² (including kitchen 58.9 m²), J Trip Bar – 1st floor 183.49 m², 2nd floor 71.80 m², totaling 255.29 m² (including kitchen 9.9 m²)
Term of construction: July 24 to December 15, 1986
Facilities : Opening/December 18, 1986; Open period/December 1 to May 5; Open time/Sergeant Peppers – 11:00 a.m. to 2:00 a.m. J Trip Bar – 5:00 p.m. to 11:45 p.m.; Fixed close/nil; Number of guest seats/Sergeant Peppers 180, J Trip Bar 150; Menu/Sergeant Peppers – Korean dishes, beer, Japanese sake, wine, cocktails, J Trip Bar – free drink system, Sergeant Burger – hamburger, roast meat lunch box, coffee, orange juice, etc.; Management/ Sangu Co.; Number of employees/(total for two shops) service 20, kitchen 7, part-time 20, totaling 47

材料仕様

屋根/アスファルト防水3層の上軽量コンクリート打ち t =60 外壁/コンクリート打ち放し サッシ:アルミ及びステンレス 入口廻り/煉瓦積み 外部床/コンクリート金鏝仕上
〈サージェント ペッパーズ〉 床/カーペット敷 壁&天井/コンクリート打ち放し カウンタートップ/メラミン化粧合板 バーコーナーカウンターバック棚/ステンレス角棒及びステンレスパンチング
〈ジョイ トリップ バー〉 床/灰炭入りモルタル金鏝仕上 ダンスフロア/御影石本磨き 入口回り/ゴムシート貼り 壁&天井/コンクリート打ち放し カウンタートップ/メラミン化粧合板

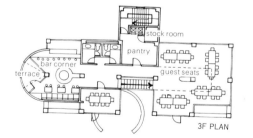

3F PLAN

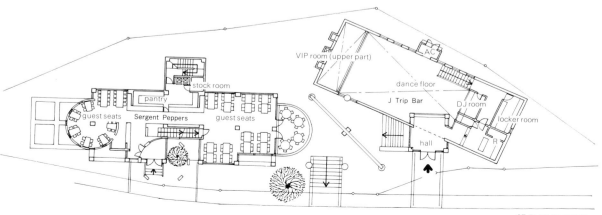

2F PLAN S=1:400

ディスコ「ジェイ トリップ バー」

The disco "J Trip Bar."

焼肉レストラン「サージェント ヘッパーズ」

The barbecue restaurant "Sergeant Peppers."

正面入口よりみた外観

The appearance viewed from the front entrance.

シュミットハウス

神奈川県足柄下郡箱根町箱根167　Phone/0460-3-7511

撮影/鳴瀬　亨

Schmidt House

167, Hakone, Hakone-machi, Ashigarashimo-gun,
Kanagawa, Japan　Phone/0460-3-7511

湖側よりみた夕景の店内
An inside scene in the evening viewed from the lake side.

サービスステーションをみる　段状の下がり天井　ダクトを兼ねた巨大な内柱と呼応するデザイン
The service station with the stairlike ceiling, designed to correspond to the huge pillar that also serves as a duct.

店内より湖をみる　富士山を中心にした景色の額縁になるように外のアーチをデザイン
The lake viewed from the inside. The exterior arch was designed so that it serves as a frame for scenery centering around Mt. Fuji.

店内全景をみる
The entire inside scene.

シュミットハウス

このレストランは箱根・芦ノ湖畔というわが国を代表するリゾート地に計画された。湖畔側と国道側の二面で道路と接していることから　両側を繋ぐ道空間を設営することがプログラムの根幹を成している。この道空間に沿って　幼い頃どこかで見た原風景の数々を重層させながら　記憶の中の都市を構築ないしは解体しようという　いうならば超文脈上の建築パフォーマンスを策定している。

断片化された建築の部分をいたずらに集積するといったブリコラージュ的手法に依拠したやり方は都市を記号で表記する行為ではあるが　むしろ都市生活者にあえて都市的事実の場を与え　このレストランを囲む自然風景との対立図式の中に　彼らなりのリゾートを見つけてもらおうという目論見があるといってよい。〈堀池秀人/堀池秀人都市建築研究所〉(87-03)

設計:堀池秀人都市建築事務所
協力:構造/織本匠構造設計事務所
　　　設備/建築設備設計研究所
施工:日本電建　箱根建設

構　　造:S造
規　　模:平屋
面　　積:敷地/995.33㎡　建築/385.02㎡　床/385.02㎡(内 厨房83㎡)
工　　期:1986年5月1日～10月1日

施設概要:開店/1986年10月12日　営業時間/午前11時～午後8時 定休日/なし　客席数/104席　客単価/1300円　客回転数/1.5回 メニュー/わかさぎとブラックバスのフライ1600　塩漬バラ肉とホワイトビーンズ煮込1600　ハンガリー風ビーフの煮込み1600　ドイツ風手造りソーセージの盛り合わせ600　イタリアンサバヤードポテト600　特製アイスクリーム400　経営/富士屋ホテル㈱　従業員数/サービス4人　厨房4人　合計8人

Schmidt House

This restaurant was planned at Ashinoko-han (by Lake Ashinoko), Hakone, one of the representative resort locations in Japan. Since it faces the road in the lake side and also the highway, the main purpose of the program has been to create an inter-road space connecting both sides. Along the inter-road space, a variety of scenes we once saw somewhere in our childhood, are arranged so that we can construct or deconstruct a city in our memory – thus, a "super-contextual architectural performance" has been pursued.

The fragmented architectural parts have been collaged to express a city in terms of symbols to provide city inhabitants with urban elements, and allow them to find their own resort in an urban atmosphere that forms a striking contrast with the natural scenery surrounding this restaurant.

Design: Hideto Horiike

Structure : S
Scale : 1 story above the ground
Area : Site/995.33 m²; Building/385.02 m²; Floor/385.02 m² (including kitchen 83 m²)
Term of construction: May 1 to October 1, 1986
Facilities : Opening/October 12, 1986; Open time/11:00 a.m. to 8:00 p.m.; Fixed close/nil; Number of guest seats/104; Unit price per guest/1,300 yen; Turnover of guests/1.5 times; Menu/fried fish, stewed meat, assorted sausage, special ice cream, etc.; Management/Fujiya Hotel Co.; Number of employees/service 4, kitchen 4, totaling 8

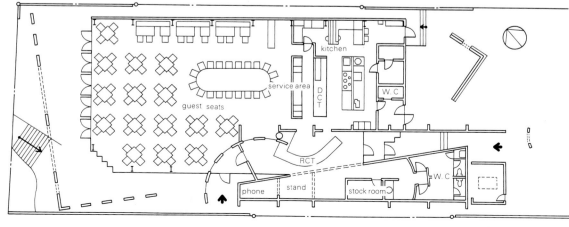

材料仕様
屋根/亜鉛合金板棒葺き t=0.5　外壁/コンクリート打ち放しウレタンクリア　一部アクリルリシン吹き付けコルテン鋼貼り t=2.3　外部床/舗石ブロック　床/玄関ホール:御影石貼り t=25磨き仕上　一部バーナー仕上　食堂/楢フローリング貼り t=15オイル拭き取り仕上　壁/玄関ホール:コンクリート打ち放しアクリルクリア　食堂/PB t=12寒冷紗EP　玄関ホール:漆喰塗　食堂/椴合板有孔ボード目透かし貼り

PLAN S=1:300

ファサードを見上げる　アルミ板　スレート　亜鉛鉄板　スチールワイヤーが演出する無国籍的調和
The facade looked up at. Nationality-free harmony presented by aluminum plate, slate, galvanized iron and steel wire.

スンダ

東京都渋谷区神山町5-15　Phone/03-465-8858

撮影/本木誠一

Sunda
5-15, Kamiyama-cho, Shibuya-ku, Tokyo, Japan
Phone/03-465-8858

ファサード
The facade

2階テーブル席をみる "無国籍" を表徴する壁画には本物の蝶がとめられている
The 2nd floor table seat area. Real butterflies are put on the wall painting that symbolizes a "nationality-free" state.

吹抜けを見下す　手摺はエントランスホールの "池" から上がってくる "大蛇" を表している
The stairwell looked down at. The handrail expresses a "huge serpent" crawling up from the "pond" of the entrance hall.

1階客席をアプローチよりみる
The 1st floor guest seat area viewed from the approach.

スンダ

今や ヤングピープルで構成され このゼネレーションによって多くの流行が生まれ あらゆる情報の発信地として 現在注目を浴びている "渋谷"…。

「スンダ」は このフィールドからちょっと離れた "神山町" に位置しこの地名は その昔 "神の住む山" と言い伝えられたそうで 私は この場所に神妙なテレパシーを感じ クライアントの協力を得て 以前から持ちつづけたコンセプト "自然と未来の時間的空間" をプランニングした。この店のイメージテーマは "マテリアルビューティ" でそれにストーリー性を持たせた。店内は原始人の住居であり 生活感や「衣食住」家をとりまく 自然界における生物などをデコラティブに表現した。外装に関しては 崩れかけた壁とローザストーンで自然の時の経過を表し 人工的なスンバ模様の木の彫刻とバリ島のテンプル(門)で やや原始宗教っぽい感性で "ヒューマンマインド" の表現を意図した。

料理は アジアを中心にした 無国籍料理で無添加 無農薬の素材で主に薬草 香草をできるだけ多くとり入れた調理方法を研究している。

〈鈴木修司/サイプランニング〉(88-08)

設計:サイプランニング
協力:1階壁画/平野敬子 2階壁画/ブレーブ荒井 フラワーオブジェ/鈴木淳子
施工:ニシオ企画

構　造:木造
規　模:地上2階
面　積:敷地/151.58㎡　建築/105.60㎡　床/1階 100.65㎡(内 厨房23.56㎡) 2階 100.65㎡ 合計 201.30㎡(内 厨房23.56㎡)
工　期:1987年10月2日～12月8日

施設概要:開店/1987年12月10日　営業時間/午後6時～午後11時 定休日/毎週日曜日　客席数/1階 24席　2階 46席　合計 70席 客単価/5000円 客回転数/1回　メニュー/トムヤンクン(海老スープ)1200 アサリ炒めタイランド800 サテ2000 蟹のスパイシーソース1500 チキンのココナッツミルク煮1000 インドネシアビール(ビンター)800 タイビール(シンハー)800 ウイスキー700 経営/裕和興産㈱ 飯澤 武 従業員数/サービス2人 厨房3人 パート アルバイト5人 合計10人

Sunda

Occupied by young people who have created a variety of fashions, "Shibuya" is currently drawing hot attention as a center for despatching every type of information.

"Sunda" is situated in Kamiyama-cho, a little away from the bustling center, this area was once said to have a "mountain where gods reside." Feeling a strange telepathy with this place, and in cooperation with the client, I have planned the long-cherished concept "natural space extending from past to future." The image theme of this shop is "material beauty," provided with story-telling elements. The inside shows a house of primitive people, decoratively expressing the lively primitive atmosphere of "eating, clothing and shelter" and living things in nature. The exterior, with the crumbling wall and rosa stone, expresses the lapse of time in nature, while expressing the "human mind" in a little primitive religious sense with wooden Sumba patterned wooden soulpture and Bali Island's temple.

Dishes served here are "nationality-free" dishes, centering around Asian dishes, cooked by using additive- and chemical-free materials with ample herb and fragrant plants.

Design: Shuji Suzuki

Structure : Wooden building
Scale : 2 stories above the ground
Area : Site/151.58 m²; Building/105.60 m²; Floor/1st floor 100.65 m² (including kitchen 23.56 m²), 2nd floor 100.65 m², totaling 201.30 m² (including kitchen 23.56 m²)
Term of construction: October 2 to December 8, 1987
Facilities : Opening/December 10, 1987; Open time/6:00 p.m. to 11:00 p.m.; Fixed close/every Sunday; Number of guest seats/1st floor 24, 2nd floor 46, totaling 70; Unit price per guest/5,000 yen; Turnover of guests/1 time; Menu/nationality-free dishes, centering around Asian dishes, beer, whisky, etc.; Management/Yuwa Kosan Co., Takeshi Iizawa; Number of employees/service 2, kitchen 3, part-time 5, totaling 10

材料仕様
屋根/カラー亜鉛鉄板貼り 外壁/アルミ板 スレート 亜鉛鉄板 H型鋼 外部床/石くずれ積み カラーモルタル掻き落とし 床/1階:石造り モザイクタイル貼り カラーモルタル 2階/じゅうたん敷 壁/1階:インド砂岩乱貼り モルタルたたき仕上 2階:石貼りモルタルたたき仕上 鉄腐食仕上 銅板 亜鉛板貼り 天井/PBVPアート処理 スチール梁/グラインダー仕上

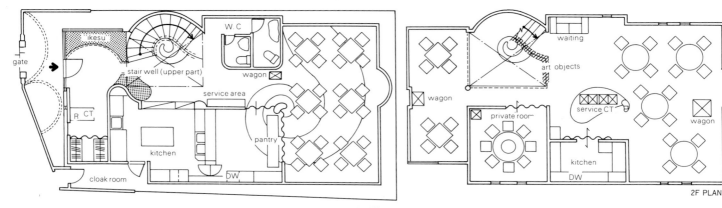

1F PLAN S≒170

2F PLAN

スキップアップした客席よりカウンター席方向をみる
The counter seat area viewed from the guest seats skipped up.

フラッグス 星屑食堂

東京都武蔵野市吉祥寺本町１丁目7-8　三峰ビル地下１階
Phone/0422-22-8443

撮影/本木誠一

Flags Hoshikuzu-Shokudo
1-7-8, Kichijoji-honcho, Musashino city, Tokyo, Japan
Phone/0422-22-8443

アプローチをみる
The approach.

うねる漆喰の階段　星空と　それを支えるかのようにオブジェ柱　無国籍あるいは多国籍空間
The meandering mortar staircase. The starlit sky and objet pillars standing as if supporting the sky. A nationality-free or multi-national space.

スキップアップしたテーブル席をみる　南国の植民地　露店食堂　スペイン　フランス　中国　インド……さまざまなデザインの調和
The table seats skipped up. The open-air restaurant at the southern colony; Spanish, French, Chinese, Indian and various other national elements are designed harmoniously.

カウンター席をみる　ここはインドか香港か　星空の下の屋台食堂
The counter seats. Where am I? India or Hong Kong? The open-air restaurant under the starlit sky.

フラッグス 星屑食堂

星。地球上どこでも見えるはずの星。そして　悲しいかな　都市ではほとんど見えない星。単なる星　しかし何億光年もの彼方からのメッセージ。

南国。古今東西を問わず　人々は南海の楽園を夢にみる。色とりどりの花々　鳥　そして果物　のんびりした時間。

都市にはない二大要素。彼女と　あるいは友だちと気楽に　のんびりと過ごせる　そして気取らずに。本来の自分の姿が出せる場所。そこでお互いに　または自分自身　こんな自分もあったのかと……。

磨き上げた黒御影石　真鍮　鉄にステンレス。16ビートのシンセドラム　赤いマニキュアにハイヒール　そんなハイ テックな空間はもうごめんです。

今　都会にほしいものは　もっともっとナイーブなもの　そう"君の笑顔"ではないでしょうか。都市が四角く高く　堅くなっていく中で　人びとは　その反対のもっとやさしく　リラックスできる　本当の意味の"いいかげん"を求めています。南国の元植民地の露店食堂　そこにはスペイン　フランス　そして中国　インド　色々な国の文化　人　料理がミックスされ　良いものだけが出て来ます。

"あいの子美人"に"屋台の料理"。そうそう　だから1930年代の画家や作家や金持ちは　みんな憧れ　南海の楽園に行きました。

そんなイメージでつくった「星屑食堂」です。　　　〈原　尚〉(88-08)

企画：フラッグス プランニング
設計：原　尚建築設計事務所
協力：壁画/本村元造
施工：滝新

材料仕様
床/モルタル　目地部分OP　壁/モルタル下地模様吹き付け塗材　漆喰塗　一部既存壁　天井/モルタル下地ジョリパット　星/日本画用金箔　家具/ランバーコア材OP

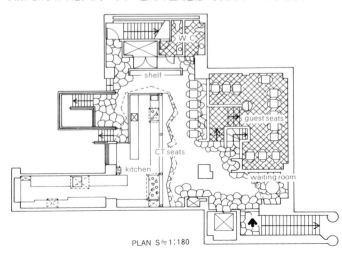

PLAN S≒1:180

面　　積：床/192.00㎡(内 厨房44.63㎡)
工　　期：1988年1月15日～3月3日

施設概要：開店/1988年5月8日　営業時間/正午～午後2時30分　午後5時30分～10時30分　定休日/毎週水曜日　客席数/50席　客単価/2000～3000円　メニュー/前菜盛り合わせ1500　パエリア3600　デカンタワイン(白900　赤1000)　ビール(中)500　輸入ビール600　経営/(有)フラッグス　恩海　光　従業員数/サービス4人　厨房5人　パート アルバイト4人　合計13人

Flags Hoshikuzu-Shokudo

Stars which should naturally be visible from any part of the earth, but, alas, can hardly be seen in cities. Though the stars are so common to us, starlight is a message from several hundred millions of light-years away.

Southern countries. For all ages and in all places, people have dreamed of a paradise in the southern sea, rich with flowers varying in color, numerous birds and fruits, and time passes leisurely.

Two major elements not experienced in cities. You can enjoy with your girl or other friends at ease, leisurely, and unaffectedly. You can find your innate self, almost amazing to you and your friends. The polished black granite, brass, iron and stainless steel. We no longer wish a high tech space noisy with a 16-beat synthesizing drum, accented with red manicure and high-heeled shoes!

What is needed now in cities might be something more naive – "your smile," yes! Against the tendency of cities to be increasingly crowded with square, lofty and hard buildings, people are asking for the opposite, i.e. more gentle, relaxed and "casual" atmosphere in the true sense of the word. A street stall in the former southern colony where only the essence of culture, people and dishes from Spain, France, China, India and other countries is mixed.

A "beauty of mixed blood" and "street stall dishes." So, fine artists, writers, rich men, etc. in the 1930's – all went to the southern paradise, a longed-for place.

Keeping these ideas in view, "Flags Hoshikuzu-Shokudo" was brought into being.

Design: Hisashi Hara

Area   : Floor/192.00 m² (including kitchen 44.63 m²)
Term of construction: January 15 to March 3, 1988
Facilities : Opening/May 8, 1988;   Open time/noon to 2:00 p.m., 5:30 p.m. to 10:30 p.m.;   Closed regularly on/every Wednesday;   Number of guest seats/50;   Unit price per guest/2,000 to 3,000 yen;   Menu/mainly South European dishes served in an open-air stall style restaurant;   Management/Flags Co., Hikaru Onkai;   Number of employees/service 4, kitchen 5, part-time 4, totaling 13

中国レストラン & カフェ/*Chinese Restaurant & Cafe*

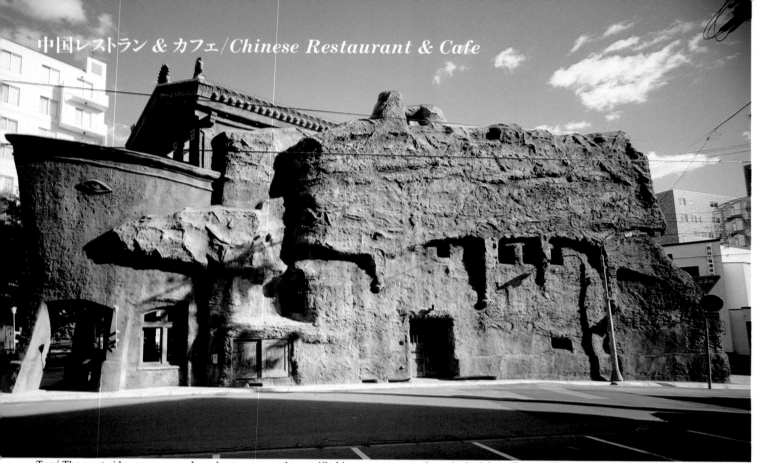

Top/ The west side appearance. In order to express the petrified image, a stone sculptor invited from England finished the surface with concrete. The nearby children have name this building a "haunted house."

上/西面外観をみる　石化したイメージを表現する
ためイギリスより石彫の専門家をよび　コンクリ
ートをハツっている　近所の子供たちはこの建物
を "幽霊屋敷" と命名

右/南面外観をみる　建築はローマに影響を与えた
オリエントのエトルリア文明の様式を基本として
いる

Right/ The south side appearance. The architecture is modeled after the style of Etrurian civilization in the Orient that had affected Rome.

札幌市中央区南8条西4丁目１　Phone/011-521-3300

L'arca di Noé
Nishi 4-1, Minami 8-jyo, Chuo-ku, Sapporo city, Japan
Phone/011-521-3300

撮影/安達　治

上/北側入口脇の鉄砲階段より1階カフェをみる　ここから物語が始まる
下/中2階個室のシャンデリア

Top/ The 1st floor cafe viewed from the starcase beside the north side entrance. The story begins from here.
Bottom/ The chandelier of a mezzanine private room.

上/中2階より階段上部の吹抜けと天窓をみる
下/1階南側入口に面したラセン階段と吹抜けシャンデリア

Top/ The stairwell and skylight above the staircase, viewed from the mezzanine.
Bottom/ The spiral staircase facing the 1st floor south side entrance and the stairwell chandelier.

2階レストラン全景をみる
The entire scene of the 2nd floor restaurant.

南側入口レジ脇よりみた1階カフェのカウンター席をみる
The counter seat area of the 1st floor cafe viewed from beside the south side entrance register.

壁面が描かれた2階レストランのソファ席をみる
The sofa seat area with wall paintings in the 2nd floor restaurant.

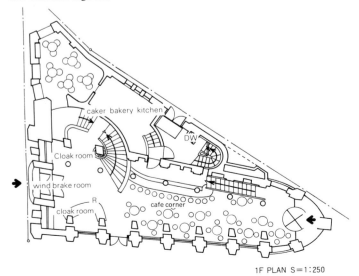

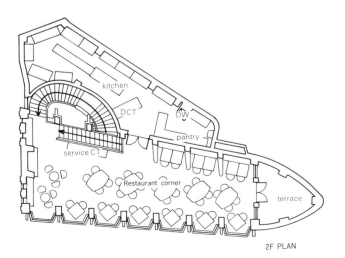

1F PLAN S＝1:250

2F PLAN

ノアの箱舟

このプロジェクトは　エリア開発をしているクライアントの〝札幌の長期観光名所になり得るビルをプロデュースしてくれ〟という依頼から始まった。

そして　英国人の建築家ナイジェル　コーツとぼくのコンビの仕事を見ているので　ブランソン　コーツ　アーキテクチャーに建築を担当させた。ぼくはナイジェル　コーツに　過去と未来を対話させた21世紀に向けたイメージを求めたいとコンセプト　ディレクションした。彼は見事に　石化してしまったノアの箱舟という力強いテーマのドローイングを描いた。箱舟の建築デザインは　エトルリア文明の影響を受けている。この文明は　西洋文明の基になっているローマ文明に影響を与えた。異なった豊かな文明だが　彼らの起源をたどるとオリエント人である。

ぼくは　西洋をたどって行くと東洋であると勝手に解釈し　楽しんでいる。

トラスウォールにより造られた岩山の岩肌は　4種類に分けられ　自然の部分　岩石の部分　人間がかかわり始めた部分　文明により掘られた部分などに分けられている。古代芸術を再現するため　石の彫刻家を英国より招へいし　コンクリートを石に見えるようにしてしまった。このプロジェクトは　日本のチーム(建築家　施工業者)と海外チーム(画家　彫刻家　陶芸家　ガラス職人)の　3年間の汗の結晶である。

〈シー・ユ・チェン/シー・アイ・エー〉(88-12)

企画:シー・アイ・エー/シー・ユ・チェン
設計:ブランソン・コーツ・アーキテクチャー/ナイジェル・コーツ
協力:建築/弾設計　構造/ケースリー建築研究所　設備/ジェット企画設計　壁画/アダム・ロー　スチュワート・ヘルム　岩山及び壁面彫刻/リチャード・サーモン　ノア　夫婦像/マーク・クイン　シャンデリア/トム・ディクスン
施工:建築/辰村組
　　　内装/川原木建築設計

構　　造:SRC造
規　　模:地下1階　地上2階
面　　積:敷地/230.09㎡　建築/182.81㎡　床/地下1階　166.13㎡　1階187.81㎡　2階160.29㎡　合計511.23㎡(内　厨房83.55㎡)
工　　期:1987年12月中旬〜1988年10月8日

施設概要:開店/1988年10月13日　営業時間/午前11時30分〜午前2時　定休日/なし　客席数/150席　客単価/4750円　客回転数/1.4回　メニュー/北海うにと豆腐煮つけ1800　焼きビーフン800　ゆば野菜巻き揚げ700　海の幸の包餅2000　若鶏の湖南風炒め2000　蒸しタラバ蟹のソース添え3600　帆立て貝のレモンソースかけ2400　コーヒー500〜550　ウーロン茶400〜600　ビール500〜600　カクテル700〜950　ウイスキー(スコッチ)S700〜1100　ワイン(ボトル)2500〜5000　経営/㈱ジャスマック　従業員数/サービス10人　厨房11人　パート　アルバイト11人　合計32人

L'arca di Noé

This project started with the request of the client, who is engaged in area development, for "producing a building that can be a long-range tourist spot in Sapporo."

Since the client saw a piece of work completed by my combination with Nigel Coates, an English architect, he requested Branson Coates Architecture to undertake this architecture.

I placed a concept direction before Nigel Coates that I would like to pursue an image towards the 21st century through a dialogue between the past and future. In reply, he presented a powerful, wonderful drawing based on the theme – petrified L'arca di Noé. His architectural design of this ark is influenced by the Etrurian civilization. This civilization had influenced the Roman civilization that is the basis of the Western civilization. Although it is a different civilization, it was very rich, and its origin, when traced back, is found to be the Orient. I am amusing myself thinking that, when tracing the West back to its origin, we reach the East.

The surface of the rocky mountain created by trass wall is divided into four types – natural part, rocky part, part that began to be affected by man, and part digged by civilization. In order to reproduce the ancient art, a stone sculptor was invited from England. He finished the concrete so that it looks like stone. This project is an outcome of three years' efforts of Japanese team (architect and contractor), and foreign team (painter, sculptor, ceramist and glass artist).

Design: Nigel Coates

Structure : SRC
Scale　　 : 1 under and 2 stories above the ground
Area　　 : Site/230.09 m²;　Building/182.81 m²;　Floor/1st basement 166.13 m², 1st floor 187.81 m², 2nd floor 160.29 m², totaling 511.23 m² (including kitchen 83.55 m²)
Term of construction: In the middle of December, 1987 to October 8, 1988
Facilities : Opening/October 13, 1988;　Open time/11:30 a.m. to 2:00 a.m.;　Fixed close/nil;　Number of guest seats/105;　Unit price per guest/4,750 yen;　Turnover of guests/1.4 times;　Menu/Chinese dishes cooked by utilizing rich marine products of Hokkaido, as well as cafe service;　Management/Jasmac Co.;　Number of employees/service 10, kitchen 11, part-time 11, totaling 32

材料仕様
屋根/コンクリート下地銅板 t＝5瓦棒葺き　雪止めルーフヒーター　外壁/コンクリート下地トラスウォール特殊樹脂モルタル　開口部/木製建具及びスチール建具　外部床/特殊樹脂モルタル　一部鉄平石貼り
〈1階　カフェ〉床/タイル貼り　壁&梁型/吹き付けモルタル掻き落とし仕上　天井/コンクリート下地聚楽塗装
〈中2階個室　2階レストラン〉床/中2階:塗床　2階:楢材フローリング　壁&天井/コンクリート下地聚楽塗装及び吹き付けモルタル掻き落とし仕上

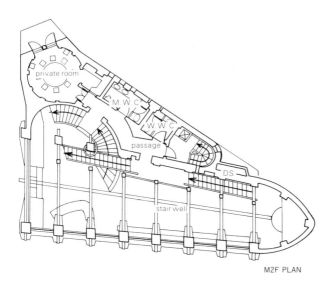

M2F PLAN

国道55号線よりみた南面外観

The south side appearance viewed from the Highway No. 55.

国道55号線よりみた南面外観（夜景）

The south side appearance (night scene) viewed from the Highway No. 55.

ウェーブ コート

徳島県阿南市宝田町平岡902-10　Phone/0884-22-7373

撮影/大竹静市郎

Wave Court

902-10, Hiraoka, Takarada-cho, Anan city, Tokushima, Japan
Phone/0884-22-7373

国道に面したアプローチから西端に配されたアネックスとその頂部のタワーを
みる

The annex placed at the western end from the approach facing the highway, and its top tower.

ネーミングの通りにウェーブが幾重にも重なったフォルムの北側外観
The north side appearance featuring waves upon waves, as the name suggests.

２階入口ホールからみた中央吹抜けとブリッジ
The central stairwell and bridge viewed from the 2nd floor entrance hall.

西側入口よりホールとその上部吹抜けをみる　右側がグッズコーナー　左は
カジュアルブティック コーナー
The hall and its upper stairwell viewed from the west side entrance.
The goods corner in the right side and casual boutique corner in the
left side.

パントリー側からみた２階レストラン客席Ａ　天井吊りのステンレスメッシュとカウンターテーブルにもウェーブの意匠が表現されている
The 2nd floor restaurant's guest seat area A viewed from the pantry side; the ceiling-suspended stainless mesh and counter table are also designed after waveshapes.

２階レストランのＶＩＰルームから中央吹抜け方向をみる　　　　　The central stairwell area viewed from the VIP room of the 2nd floor restaurant.

ウェーブ コート

ロードサイドではまだ少ない複合店舗建築である。1階が物販　2階が
レストラン　アネックスがケーキとアイスクリームのテイクアウトとな
っている。
敷地のある阿南市郊外の国道55号線沿いは単調で　アイデンティティの
喪失された風景であり　これにインパクトを与え　風景と商業施設のダ
イナミズムを創り出す必要性を感じた。ダイナミズムは高感度の商品
店舗形態　そして空間である。現在の社会状況で　生活や店舗に最も不
可欠なものは時間を含めた空間。空間のダイナミズムは自然の豊饒さで
あり　私にとっては敷地近くの故郷である。大地　水　火　風　空の宙と一
体化した過去の空間感覚の記憶の抽出が　この建築空間に置換されたの
かも知れない。　　　　　　　　〈歌　一洋/歌　一洋建築研究所〉(88-02)
企画：藤井　正　宮本　知　歌　一洋
設計：歌　一洋建築研究所
協力：構造/野村哲夫
　　　設備/ティーエーシー設備設計
施工：大林組四国支店

構　　　造：S造
規　　　模：地上2階　一部屋根裏
面　　　積：敷地/1,458.79㎡　建築/465.25㎡　床/1階　396.34㎡　2階
　　　　　267.82㎡(内　厨房41.10㎡)　屋根裏　27.13㎡　合計　691.29㎡
工　　　期：1987年7月25日～1987年10月24日

施設概要：開店/1987年10月25日　営業時間/1階　物販コーナー　午前11
　　　　　時～午後9時　2階　レストラン　午前11～午後10時　定休日
　　　　　/なし　客席数/2階　レストラン72席　客単価/1階　物販コ
　　　　　ーナー5000円　2階　レストラン1500円　客回転数/2階　レ
　　　　　ストラン2回　メニュー/2階　レストラン　淡の海の幸サラ
　　　　　ダ1500　淡牛ヒレ肉のグリエマスタード風味3000　鴨胸肉のポ
　　　　　ワレグロゼイユソース(2人分)3500　コーヒー300　ぶどうジ
　　　　　ュース450　経営/㈲フジイグループ　藤井　正　従業員数/1
　　　　　階　物販コーナー　サービス6人　2階　レストラン　サービ
　　　　　ス6人　厨房3人　パート　アルバイト6人　合計21人

Wave Court

"Wave Court" is a composite shop building, and this type of building
is less found along the roadside. The 1st floor is occupied by com-
modity shops, while the 2nd floor is occupied by a restaurant, and
the annex is used for confectionery/ice cream takeout.
The area along the Highway No. 55 in the suburbs of Anan City,
where this building is situated, features monotonous scenery devoid
of identity, I felt it necessary to give an impact to it by creating dynamism between commercial facilities and the scenery. The dynamism
consists in high sense goods, shop style and space. In today's social
condition, space is essential to life and shops, together with time. The
dynamism of space consists in richness of nature, and to me, in my
hometown near the site of "Wave Court." Those elements, which
have been extracted from my memory of past space sense fused with
land, water, fire, wind and sky, might have taken shape in this architectural space.

Design: Ichiyo Uta

Structure : S
Scale 　　 : 2 stories above the ground (loft in part)
Area 　　 : Site/1,458.79 m²; Building/465.25 m²; Floor/1st floor
　　　　　396.34 m², 2nd floor 267.82 m² (including kitchen
　　　　　41.82 m²), loft 27.13 m², totaling 691.29 m² (including
　　　　　41.10 m²)
Term of construction: July 25 to October 24, 1987
Facilities : Opening/October 25, 1987;　Open time/1st floor (shop-
　　　　　ping corner) 11:00 a.m. to 9:00 p.m., 2nd floor (restau-
　　　　　rant) 11:00 a.m. to 10:00 p.m.; Fixed close/nil; Number
　　　　　of guest seats/2nd floor (restaurant) 72;　Unit price per
　　　　　guest/1st floor (shopping corner) 5,000 yen, 2nd floor
　　　　　(restaurant) 1,500 yen;　Turnover of guests/2nd floor
　　　　　(restaurant) 2 times; Menu/2nd floor (restaurant) seafood
　　　　　salad, meat dishes, etc.;　Management/Fujii Group Co.,
　　　　　Tadashi Fujii;　Number of employees/1st floor (shopping
　　　　　corner) service 6, 2nd floor (restaurant) service 6, kitchen
　　　　　3, part-time 6, totaling 21

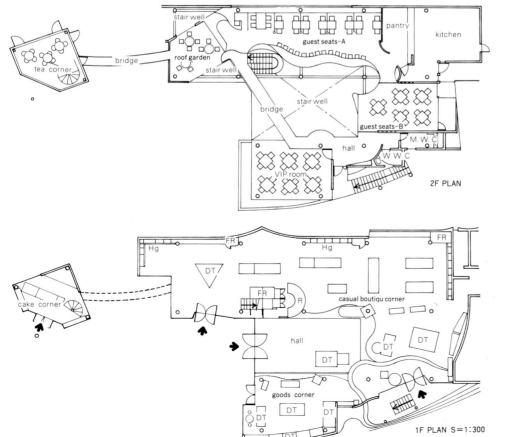

1F PLAN S=1:300

2F PLAN

材料仕様

屋根/断熱木片セメント板t=55下地長尺カラー鉄板
t=0.4瓦棒葺き　一部平葺き　外壁/グラスウール
t=100下地スチールスパンドレルt=0.35　石綿板
t=63樹脂系酢酸ビニールペイント吹き付け　鉄骨
&サッシ：塩化ゴム塗装　外部床/豆砂利洗い出し
アスファルト塗装　モルタル金鏝押さえ　床/1階売
り場：コンクリート直押さえ下地フレキシブルタイル
貼りt=3　PCVラミネート床材t=3無釉タイル
貼り200角　1階コート：豆砂利洗い出し　モルタル
金鏝押さえの上にウレタン塗装　2階/楢材フローリ
ングt=15　OSウレタン仕上h=60　壁/PBt=
12ジョイント工法下地ビニールクロス貼り&スエー
ド貼り　小波スレートt=6.3下地EP　天井/梁とデ
ッキプレートあらわしOP　断熱ガラス不織布AE
P　ステンレスメッシュ吊り　一部PBt=12ジョ
イント工法下地EP　家具/塩路材染色ウレタン塗装
什器楢合板ポリウレタン塗装　塩地材染色ウレタン
塗装

1階イベント広場兼駐車場へ通じるアプローチ進入路からみた東側外観
The entire east side appearance viewed from the approach way leading to the 1st floor event plaza/parking lot.

南側外観をみる　傾斜地に建つため2階
テラスが進路と同じレベルになる

The south side appearance. Since the building stands along an incline, the 2nd floor terrace lies at the same level as the road.

シーバル

香川県綾歌郡宇多津町2719-1　Phone/0877-46-1500

撮影/川元　斉

Sea-Bal
2719-1, Utazu-cho, Ayauta-gun, Kagawa, Japan
Phone/0877-46-1500

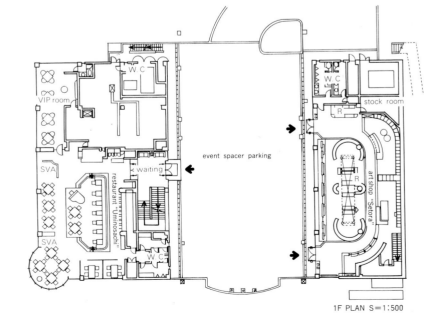

1F PLAN S=1:500

シーバル

ここは地元市民憩いの場として「坂出観光センター」が開業していたが 瀬戸大橋開通を期にイメージを一新 新たなコンセプトの元にこの「シーバル」が企画された。

建物配置は 営業時間の異なるショップとレストランを別棟とし 来客の目的動線を明確にし この2棟は大橋（ブリッジ）で結ばれている。

外観は自然の中の人工を意識した直線で構成し 柱梁の構造体を仕上げの一部として扱い ブリッジにつながるテラスは この架構により空間を区画している。外装に45角の白を基調としたタイルを用い 架構にはめ込まれた大型ガラスで立面をまとめ インテリアはシンプルなものとし 素材の質感を重視し材料を選択した。　〈大都 隆／日建設計〉(88-06)

企　画：プラン ドゥ
設計監理：日建設計大阪
施　工：鹿島建設

構　　造：RC造
規　　模：地下1階 地上2階
面　　積：敷地/3,636.36㎡ 建築/983.51㎡ 床/地下1階 533.20㎡ 1階 884.85㎡ 2階 494.55㎡ 合計 1,912.60㎡（内 厨房201.3㎡）
工　　期：1987年9月3日～1988年3月15日

施設概要：開店/1988年3月30日 営業時間/カフェ 午前10時～午後10時 レストラン 午前11時～午後3時 午後5時～10時 ショップ 午前10時～午後9時 定休日/なし 客席数/カフェ 88席 客単価/カフェ 800円 レストラン 5000円 客回転数/カフェ 平日3回 日曜・祭日6回 レストラン 平日1.5回 日曜・祭日2回 メニュー/カフェ（海適カフェ パズ）：パズ特製サンド500 テリーヌ1000 海老と帆立てのプロシェット1000 コーヒー各種400 500 ソフトドリンク各種400～500 レストラン（欧卓料理レストラン 海の四季）：(昼の食事)シェフの気まぐれ2800 海の四季スペシャル5000 (夜の食事)マダム5000 グルマン7000 プレジタン1万 食前酒500～700 ワイン各種（ボトル)2000～1万 取扱商品/ショップ（ファイングッズ 瀬戸羅)：陶磁器 漆木工品 金工 染織物 竹細工 ショップ（生活アートショップ セトラ)：ライフスタイル グッズ インポート グッズ インテリア グッズ ラッピング アート雑貨 経営/㈱シーバル 従業員数/カフェ&レストラン サービス10人 厨房14人 合計24人

Sea-Bal

Here, "Sakaide Kanko Center" has been open as a place for recreation of community inhabitants. On the occasion of the completion of Seto Ohashi (Seto Big Bridge), the center's image has been totally renewed to bring "Sea-Bal" into being with a new concept.

The shop and restaurant buildings are separated, as they differ in open time, but they are connected by a bridge, so that guests can easily select either of them.

Conscious of artificiality amidst nature, the appearance is composed of straight lines, and the structural beams and pillars are used as part of finish. The terrace leading to the bridge segments the space. The exterior employs 45 x 45 mm white tone tiles, and large sheets of glass are fitted to the framework for cubic presentation. The interior has been simply designed by selecting materials whose quality is suitable to this purpose.

Design: Nikken Sekkei Ltd., Plan Do Incorporated

Structure : RC
Scale : 1 under and 2 stories above the ground
Area : Site/3,636.36 m²; Building/983.51 m²; Floor/1st basement 533.20 m², 1st floor 884.85 m², 2nd floor 494.55 m², totaling 1,912.60 m² (including kitchen 201.3 m²)
Term of construction: September 3, 1987 to March 15, 1988
Facilities : Cpening/March 30, 1988; Open time/Cafe 10:00 a.m. to 10:00 p.m., Restaurant 11:00 a.m. to 3:00 p.m., 5:00 p.m. to 10:00 p.m., Shop 10:00 a.m. to 9:00 p.m.; Fixed close/nil; Number of guest seats/Cafe 88, Restaurant 82; Unit price per guest/Cafe 800 yen, Restaurant 5,000 yen; Turnover of guests/Cafe – Weekday 3 times, Sunday & Holiday 6 times, Restaurant – Weekday 1.5 times, Sunday & Holiday 2 times; Menu/Cafe ("Kaiteki Cafe Pas") – special sandwiches, terrine, seafoods, coffee, various soft drinks; Restaurant (European table dish restaurant "Umi-no-Shiki") – course dishes (lunch, dinner) centering around seafoods, various types of wine; Articles dealt with/Shop ("Fine Goods Setora") – chinaware, lacquered woodworks, metalworks, dyed clothes, bamboo works; Shop ("Living Art Shop Setora") – lifestyle goods, imported goods, interior goods, wrappings, miscellaneous pieces of art; Management/Sea-Bal Co.; Number of employees/Cafe & Restaurant – service 10, kitchen 14, totaling 24

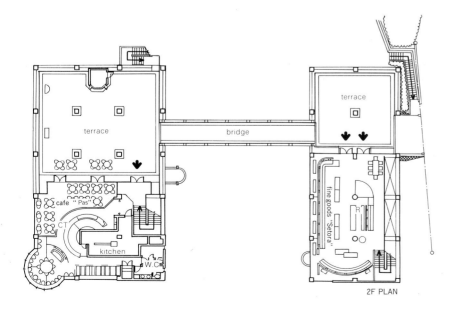

2F PLAN

材料仕様

屋根/コンクリート下地アスファルト露出防水 三角フレーム：スチール加工シルバーペンキ内設照明入り 外壁/コンクリート下地磁器質タイル貼り45角 外部建具：窓 アルミ焼き付け塗装 出入りロ ステンレス鏡面加工 外部床/豆砂利洗い出し サインタワー/ステンレス焼き付け塗装アッパーライト照明 〈地下1階「シーバルホール」内装〉床/じゅうたん 壁/モルタル下地EP一部クロス 天井/PB下地寒冷紗EP
〈1階 欧卓料理レストラン「海の四季」内装〉床/大理石 楢フローリング じゅうたん 壁/モルタル下地EP 腰壁/楢材染色仕上 天井/PB下地寒冷紗EP
〈1階 生活アートショップ「セトラ」内装〉床/フローリング&ビニールタイル 壁/モルタル下地EP 天井/RC型枠外しEP PB下地寒冷紗EP
〈2階 海適カフェ「パズ」内装〉床/ビニールタイル模様貼り フローリング 壁&天井/1階「海の四季」と同じ
〈2階 四国ファイングッズ「瀬戸羅」内装〉床/ビニールタイル 壁/モルタル下地EP 柱形：モザイクタイル下地 天井/RC型枠外しEP

中央イベント広場兼駐車場から"飲食棟"をみる   "Eating & Drinking Building." viewed from the central event plaza/parking lot.

"ファイングッズ"の売場をみる   The selling corner of "Fine Goods."

"飲食棟"地階1階「シーバルホール」　コンサートなど多目的に使用できる
"Sea-Bal Hall" at the 1st basement of "Eating & Drinking Building"; can be used for multi purposes, such as concert.

北側飲食棟2階「海適カフェ・パズ」の円形テーブル席
"Cafe Pas" at the 2nd floor of the north side "Eating & Drinking Building."

西棟「ザ シャパー イメージ」の外観をみる

The appearance of the west building "The Sharper Image."

ザ ネクスト ワン

大阪市西区立売堀4丁目11-11　Phone/06-533-1904

撮影/福本正明

北側外観をみる

The north side appearance.

The Next One
4-11-11, Itachibori, Nishi-ku, Osaka city, Japan
Phone/06-533-1904

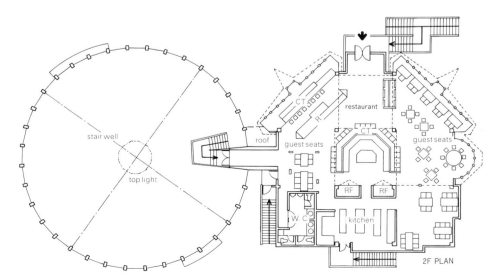

ザ ネクスト ワン

大阪市西区 地下鉄 阿波座駅前 新なにわ筋の角に アメリカの風を
伝える建物「ザ ネクスト ワン」の誕生である。宅配便のフットワーク
㈱の新業態開発ショップで アメリカで年間3,300万部 直営店 48店舗
をもつカタログ販売の大手「ザ シャーパー イメージ」の日本での一号
店である。
このコンセプトは 日本での一号店づくりというよりは クライアント
の母体会社である日本運送の本社跡地利用計画という開発事業が目的で
あり 開発のコンセプトは その立地の不利をいかに克服するかという
ことから 他の業種との複合化を考えたという。その結果 同グループ
がハワイで営むフランス料理「パパドレ」 フットワークスポーツレーシ
ングチームのドライバー鈴木亜久里をコーディネーションとしたスポ
ーツマインド カジュアル ショップ「ギアボックス」のそれぞれの第一号店
を複合させ「ザ ネクスト ワン」は生まれた。3年間で20店舗展開を目標
にしている。
〈香川英行/ディ ブレイン研究所〉(88-09)
設計:西棟基本設計/ザ シャーパー イメージ
　　実施設計　東棟設計/コムデス

構　　造:Ｓ造
規　　模:地上2階
面　　積:敷地/1,875.22㎡　建床/723.19㎡　床/ 1階671.26㎡
　　　　　　2階 326.78㎡(内 厨房38㎡)　合計 998.04㎡
工　　期:1988年6月4日

施設概要:開店/1988年6月4日　営業時間/ショップ(ザ シャーパー イ
　　　　　メージ):午前11時〜午前2時　ショップ(ギアボックス):午前
　　　　　11時〜午前2時　レストラン(パパドレ):午前11時〜午後2時
　　　　　午後5時〜午前2時　定休日/なし　客席数/レストラン(パパ
　　　　　ドレ):102席　客単価/ショップ(ザ シャーパー イメージ):1
　　　　　万5000〜2万円　ショップ(ギアボックス):8000円　レストラ
　　　　　ン(パパドレ):5000円　取扱い商品/ショップ(ザ シャーパー
　　　　　イメージ):フィットネス商品 スポーツ用品 時計 貴金属
　　　　　バッグ ステーショナリーなど200〜250品目　ショップ(ギアボ
　　　　　ックス):Tシャツ5400　ポロシャツ8800　ブルゾン2万6000
　　　　　カーディガン1万2800　ワンピース9600　メニュー/レストラ
　　　　　ン(パパドレ):日替ランチ1300　カルパッチョ850 地中海風前
　　　　　菜盛り合わせ1300　活オマール海老グリエ2400　牛フィレ肉の
　　　　　パイ包み焼き2300　ワイン2300〜経営/フットワーク㈱　従業
　　　　　員数/ショップ(ザ シャーパー イメージ):サービス5人(ギア
　　　　　ボックス):サービス2人　レストラン(パパドレ):サービス5
　　　　　人　厨房6人　パート アルバイト6人　合計24人

The Next One

At a corner of Shin-Naniwasuji in front of Subway Awaza Station, Nishi Ward, Osaka, the American style building "The Next One" came into being. This is a new-type shop developed by the home delivery service chain Network Co., and is the first shop in Japan of the leading American catalog sales "The Sharper Image" chain that has a yearly circulation of 33 million copies and 48 shops under direct control.
Rather than opening the first shop in Japan, the current construction project is more intended to utilize the old site of the head office building of Nihon Unso, the client's parent company. In the development concept, to overcome the disadvantageous location, a composite system with other types of business has been formulated. As a result, "The Next One" was combined with the 1st shop in Japan of "Papadore" – French restaurant being managed by the group in Hawaii – and also the 1st shop of sports minded casual shop "Gearbox" opened with Aguri Suzuki, Footwork Sports Racing Team's driver as a coordinator.
They intend to open 20 chain shops for three years to come.

Design: The Sharper Image

Structure : S
Scale　　: 2 stories above the ground
Area　　 : Site/1,875.22 m²; Building/723.19 m²; Floor/1st floor 671.26 m², 2nd floor 326.78 m² (including kitchen 38 m²), totaling 998.04 m²
Term of construction: March 24 to May 28, 1988
Facilities : Opening/June 4, 1988; Open time/Shop ("The Sharper Image") – 11:00 a.m. to 2:00 a.m., Shop ("Gearbox") – 11:00 a.m. to 2:00 a.m., Restaurant ("Papadore") – 11:00 a.m. to 2:00 p.m., 5:00 p.m. to 2:00 a.m.; Fixed close/nil; Number of guest seats/Restaurant ("Papadore") 102; Unit price per guest/Shop ("The Sharper Image") – 15,000 to 20,000 yen, Shop ("Gearbox") – 8,000 yen, Restaurant ("Papadore") – 5,000 yen; Article dealt with/Shop ("The Sharper Image") – fitness goods, sports ware, watches, precious metals, bags, stationery, etc. totaling 200 to 250 items; Shop ("Gearbox") – T-shirts, polo shirts, blouson, cardigans, one-piecers; Menu/Restaurant ("Papadore") – French dishes, lunch menu available; Management/Footwork Co. Number of employees/Shop ("The Sharper Image") – service 5, ("Gearbox") – service 2, Restaurant ("Papadore") – service 5, kitchen 6, part-time 6, totaling 24

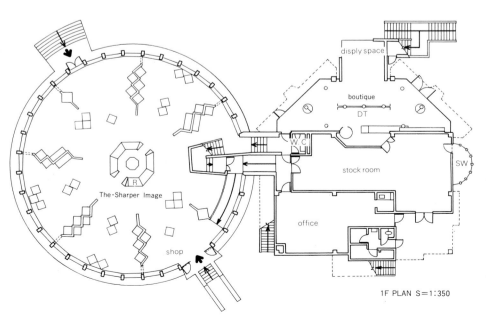

1F PLAN S=1:350

材料仕様
屋根/カラー鉄板一文字葺き　外壁/ＡＬＣ板 t=100樹脂系
塗材鏝押さえ　ラスモルタル下地擬石貼り　外部床/磁器質
タイル貼り100角　インターロッキングロック
〈1階 「ザ シャーパー イメージ」〉床/土間コン金鏝押さ
えカーペット貼り　壁/モルタル金鏝押さえＥＰ　天井/
ＢＰ t=12ＥＰ　家具/什器:アメリカから直輸入
〈1階 「ギアボックス」〉アンダーフェルトカーペット敷
一部人造石貼り300角　壁/ＰＢ t=12ＶＰ　一部アルミ t
=1.6アルマイト加工パネル貼り　天井/ＰＢ t=12ＶＰ
間接照明:アルミアルマイト加工ルーバー落込み　ディスプ
レイテーブル/メラミン化粧板　アルミ t=1.6アルマイト
加工　アルミパンチング板 t=12アルマイト加工　フレー
ム/ステンレスＦＢ
〈2階 「レストラン パパドレ」〉床/人造大理石貼り　ア
ンダーフェルトカーペット敷　長尺ビニール床材　楢フロ
ーリング貼り　壁/ＰＢ t=12クロス貼り＆レンガタイル貼
り　スタッコ仕上　丸柱(φ500)/モザイクガラスタイル貼
り　天井/ＰＢ t=12クロス貼り　カウンタートップ/ブビ
ンガ材＆御影石　楢材

223

「ザ シャーパー イメージ」売り場をみる

"The Sharper Image" selling corners.

東棟と西棟の間にあるモニュメント
The monument between the east and west side buildings.

2階・シーフードレストラン「パパドレ」
The 2nd floor seafood restaurant "Papadore."

「パパドレ」の開口部側ソファ席をみる　　　　　　　　The sofa seat area in the opening side of "Papadore."

1階・ブティック「ギアボックス」をみる　　　　　　　The 1st floor boutique "Gearbox."

正面外観をみる　前面の庇は大きな弧を描いて　山中湖の水平線と共鳴し　湖畔との環境的調和を図っている
The front appearance. The front penthouse drawing a large arc echoes with the horizontal line of Lake Yamanaka, keeping an environmental harmony with the lakeside.

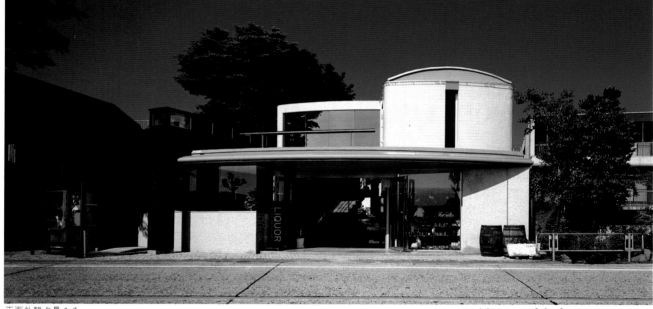

正面外観夕景みる

A night scene of the front appearance.

ブージー

山梨県南都留郡山中湖村山中98　Phone/0555-62-1511

Boozy
Yamanaka, Yamanakako-mura, Minamitsuru-gun, Yamanashi, Japan
Phone/0555-62-1511

撮影/小山　孝

正面入口より店内中央部の階段廻りをみる　左がリカーショップコーナー　右側がスーベニールショップコーナー
The staircase area in the center viewed from the front entrance.　The liquor shop corner in the left side, and souvenir shop corner in the right side.

２階のスーベニールショップの吹抜
け階段廻り

The stairwell/staircase area of the 2nd floor souvenir shop.

山中湖は 別荘地として知られ 観光客やスポーツを楽しむ若者たちで
にぎわいを見せている。その湖畔に「ブージー」はある。前面には山中
湖 背後には富士山がそびえ その雄大な自然のなかにリカー＆スーベ
ニールの店としてオープンした。
土産物の購買層は 主に10〜20代前半の若者たちであり 午前中から夕
方にかけて訪れる。一方 酒類の購買層は20代以上であり 時間帯も夕
方から夜にかけてとなる。このズレを解決するために リカーコーナー
とスーベニールコーナーとの空間を分離した。二つのコーナーを角度を
持たせて配置することにより 山中湖に向かって開かれた空間をつくり
出した。
リカーコーナーは 酒樽のイメージから内外とも米松仕上げ スーベ
ニールコーナーは 石とタイルによって軽快で明るいイメージを持たせた。
大きな弧を描いて突き出した庇は 山中湖の水平線と共鳴し 湖畔と店
内の調和を生み出している。 〈高橋洋一/高橋建築事務所〉(88-11)
設計:高橋建築事務所
施工/井出工業

構　　造:Ｓ造
規　　模:地上2階
面　　積:敷地/1,219.17㎡　建築/163.47㎡　床/1階 159.03㎡　2階
　　　　44.51㎡　合計 203.54㎡
工　　期:1988年1月8日〜4月29日

施設概要:開店/1988年4月29日　営業時間/午前9時〜午後10時(土曜と
　　　　8月は午前0時まで)　定休日/毎週木曜日(ただし 7月 8月
　　　　はなし)　取扱い商品/和 洋酒全般　土産物　経営/㈲富士田屋
　　　　従業員数/2人　パート アルバイト2人　合計4人

Boozy

Lake Yamanaka is known as a villa resort, crowded with cheerful
tourists or young people who enjoy sporting. Standing by Lake
Yamanaka, "Boozy" opened as a liquor & souvenir shop in the grand
nature – Lake Yamanaka in front of the shop and Mt. Fuji towering
behind.
Souvenir shoppers are mainly teens and those in their 20's who come
to the shop from morning till evening, while liquor shoppers are older
than 20 years who come to the shop from evening till night. In order
to solve the time gap, the liquor corner and souvenir corner were
separated from each other with a certain angle so that space open to
Lake Yamanaka has been created.
To express an image of cask, both exterior and interior of the liquor
corner have been finished with American pine, while the souvenir
corner has been finished with stone and tiles to present a cheerful,
bright image.
The penthouse projected drawing a large arc echoes with the horizontal line of Lake Yamanaka, bringing a harmony between the lake
side and interior.

Design: Yoichi Takahashi

Structure : S
Scale : 2 stories above the ground
Area : Site/1,219.17 m²; Building/163.47 m²; Floor/1st floor
159.03 m², 2nd floor 44.51 m², totaling 203.54 m²
Term of construction: January 8 to April 29, 1988
Facilities : Opening/April 29, 1988; Open time/9:00 a.m. to 10:00
p.m. (Saturday and August – 0:00 a.m.); Closed
regularly on/every Thursday (July and August – nil);
Article dealt with/Japanese and Western liquors in gener-
al, various types of souvenir; Management/Fujitaya Co.;
Number of employees/staff 2, part-time 2, totaling 4

材料仕様
屋根/カラー鉄板瓦棒葺き　外壁/モルタル下地特殊面状ラスタータイル貼り　米松防腐保護色塗料　御影石本磨き貼り　外部床/ピンコロ石敷　サイン/スチールメラミン焼き付け塗装
床/1階:御影石本磨き貼り　楢フローリング貼り　2階:木下地カーペット敷　幅木/マンガシロOP h=100　壁/木下地模様吹き付け塗材　天井/PB t=9下地寒冷紗VP　R天井:
合板下地寒冷紗VP　照明器具/ダウンライト　レジカウンター　什器/米松集成材OSウレタン塗装

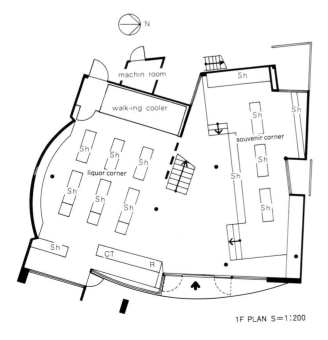

1F PLAN S=1:200

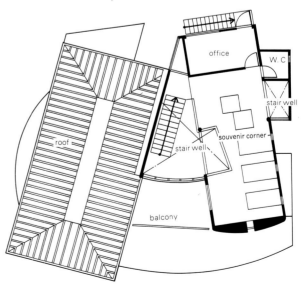

2F PLAN

正面外観をみる　中央に2階テラスへの階段が形成され　開放的なイメージでまとめている
The front appearance. The staircase leading to the 2nd floor terrace is formed in the center, giving an open image.

2階テラスより楓の木のある吹抜け中庭を見下ろす
Looking down upon the courtyard in the stairwell, where a maple tree stands, from the 2nd floor terrace.

2階テラス席をみる　グリーンと白のコーディネーションがカラーポリシー
The 2nd floor terrace seat area, accented with green and white co-ordination.

軽井沢　サムタイムハウス

長野県北佐久郡軽井沢町

撮影/平沢写真事務所

Karuizawa Sometime House
Karuizawa-machi, Kitasaku-gun, Nagano, Japan

1階フロア中央のビッグテーブル席をみる　フロア半分は吹抜けの中庭を形成し　レストスペースとともに　パフォーマンス　ステージともなる
The big table seat in the center of 1st floor; half side of the floor forms a courtyard in the stairwell, and together with the rest space, it also serves as a performance stage.

1階のインフォメーションコーナー壁面をみる　アートスペースとして各種展示が行なわれる
The wall surface at the 1st floor information corner; various pieces of artistic work are displayed on the wall surface that serves as an art space.

軽井沢 サムタイムハウス

軽井沢が避暑地として見い出されてから　百年余。このリゾート地にさわやかな夏のひとときを提供して「日本たばこ産業」のイメージアップと　日本たばこの理解と共感を深めてもらうことを目的とした建物が「サムタイムハウス」です。

高原のリゾートという点から　この環境のもつ快適性——自然　清涼　新鮮　健康　自由　休息　解放——と同じレベルの空間を表現することをデザインコンセプトにしました。

たばこの煙がこもるような世界ではなく　文化性の高い　ファッションブランド的なイメージをもつ軽井沢に調和した　大きな広がりとさわやかな空気を創造し　建築自体にサイン機能をもたせています。

通りに面した所に大きな階段を設けて　街の人々に呼びかけをし　この階段の線の流れを　2階のルーバーへとつなげることで　青く澄みきった大空へと広がっていきます。そして　1階は8mの楓の木をおいた吹抜けの中庭にして　緑の木漏れ日に高原を感じ　2階のステージは多彩なパフォーマンスステージとしての役割をもつことで　人々の出会いの場になるでしょう。〈緑と人と空間〉そして　くつろぎの軽い一服感との一体化を「サムタイムハウス」の形にしました。

〈小川幸子／エスティーデザイン〉(86-09)

企画：日本たばこ産業　電通　電通映画社
設計：エスティーデザイン
協力：照明／海藤春樹
施工：小林工芸社

構　　造：S造
規　　模：地上2階
面　　積：敷地／330.64㎡　建築／150.29㎡　床／1階 150.29㎡（内 厨房9
　　　　　㎡）　合計 227.09㎡
工　　期：1986年5月20日〜6月30日

施設概要：開店／1986年7月18日　営業期間／1986年7月18日〜8月17日
　　　　　営業時間／午前9時〜午後8時（金曜 土曜は午後9時30分まで）
　　　　　取扱い商品／たばこ：特製サムタイム220　たばこ各種 グッズ：
　　　　　Tシャツ1800　灰皿600　メニュー／コーヒー500　ビール400
　　　　　オードブル500　経営／日本たばこ産業㈱　従業員数／サービス
　　　　　6人　厨房4人　合計10人

Karuizawa Sometime House

A hundred odd years have passed since Karuizawa was found to be a summer resort. By offering a pleasant summer time at this resort, "Karuizawa Sometime Resort" intends to improve the image of "Nihon Tabako Sangyo" and thereby deepen consumers' understanding and sympathy for Nihon Tabako.

In view of the nature of highland resort, I decided to make it my design concept to express a space parallelling the comfortable elements of the surrounding environment – nature, refreshment, freshness, health, freedom, rest and liberation.

I wished to create a world not clouded with tobacco smoke, but a world harmonizing with Karuizawa that is rich with cultural and fashionable brand images, by creating an expansive space filled with refreshing air. The building itself is designed as a sort of sign.

A large staircase installed at a place facing the street serves as an appeal to inhabitants, and the flow of the staircase lines is connected to the 2nd floor louver, then leading to the clear, blue sky. A maple tree 8 m high stands at a stairwell courtyard at the 1st floor, so that you can feel a highland atmosphere with sunlight shining through the leaves of trees. The 2nd floor stage serves as a place for performance where people can communicate with each other. ＜Green, Man and Space＞ and a pleasant smoke – these elements have been united into "Sometime House."

Design: Shoichi Tsukahara

Structure : S
Acale : 2 stories above the ground
Area : Site/330.64 m²; Building/150.29 m²; Floor/1st floor 150.29 m², 2nd floor 76.80 m² (including kitchen 9 m²), totaling 227.09 m²
Term of construction: May 20 to June 30, 1986
Facilities : Opening/July 18, 1986; Open period/July 18 to August 17, 1986; Open time/9:00 a.m. to 8:00 p.m. (Friday and Saturday – till 9:30 p.m.); Articles dealt with/various types of tobacco, T-shirts, ashtrays; Menu/coffee, beer, hors d'œuvre; Management/Nihon Tabako Sangyo Co.; Number of employees/service 6, kitchen 4, totaling 10

材料仕様
ルーフテラス／防水下地スノコ（ラワン足場板）　敷塗装仕上　外壁／耐水合板貼りEPローラー仕上　床／コンクリート舗石板300角　ワックス仕上　壁／ラワン合板＝9下地EPローラー仕上　天井／ラワン合板 t＝5.5下地　EPローラー仕上　ビッグテーブル／集成材CL仕上　ショーケース／方立：スチール t＝2メラミン焼き付け　棚板／透明ガラス t＝6

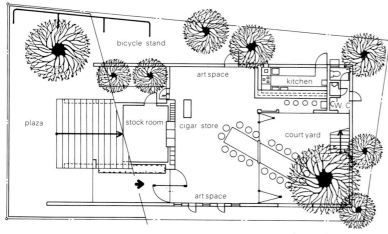

1F PLAN S＝1:250

2F PLAN

エントランスよりみたスペース全景　奥のステージバーは一段高くなった位置にあり　舞台美術の大道具的な構成
The entire space scene viewed from the entrance.　The inner stage bar lies a step above the ground, serving as something like a stage set.

ファサード全景　手前にフローリストがオープン

The entire facade scene; a florist opened in your side.

レ　スィルコンスタンス

東京都港区赤坂6丁目10-44

撮影/香川康之

Les Circonstances
6-10-44, Akasaka, Minato-ku, Tokyo, Japan

ステージバーよりテラスをみる
The terrace viewed from the stage bar.

天候の許す限り可動テントはオープン
The moving tent is open, as long as the fine weather holds.

レ スィルコンスタンス

"街の景色に溶けあったカフェテラス" 私たちが目新しさや流行ではなく
都会の生活の中で息を抜けるスペースをつくろうと思い立った時　辿り
着いたイメージはまさにそれであった。
ダブルデッカーとテントを使ったカフェテラス。ゆったりとしたオープ
ンスペースを現在の都心で確保するために　仮設のテントは非常に有効
な武器となってくれた。ビルの建設予定地の有効利用。その目的とスペ
ースの確保という　難しい問題の隙間にテントはピッタリとはまってく
れた。
メニュー構成は　朝から夕方までのヘルシーフード＆ドリンクと夜のフ
ランスの酒　シャンパーニュ（シャンパン）を中心にした2本立。特にシ
ャンパーニュのグラス売りがメイン。　　　〈及川有正／ホワイト〉(88-09)
企画：ホワイト
設計：設計組織エー・ディー・エイチ
施工：建築／稲垣興業
　　　内装／万造工務所

構　　造：鉄骨膜構造
規　　模：平屋
面　　積：敷地／289.83㎡　建築／154.80㎡　床／54.80㎡（内　厨房7.56㎡）
工　　期：1988年6月22日～7月5日

施設概要：開店／1988年7月9日　営業期間／1988年7月9日～9月30日
　　　　　営業時間／午前8時～午前0時　客席数／80席　客単価／2000円
　　　　　客回転数／4回　メニュー／シャンパン13種　グラス1300～2000
　　　　　ボトル2500～7500　コーヒー400～500　ヨーグルト400　チー
　　　　　ズ1000　キャビア6000　ミネラルウォーター400
　　　　　経営／㈱レスィルコンスタンス　従業員数／サービス5人
　　　　　厨房3人　パート アルバイト6人　合計14人

Les Circonstances

"Cafeterrace melting into the street scenery." This was exactly the image we have reached when we wished to create a space where we can relax in an urban life, not merely pursuing novelty or fashion.
The cafeterrace using a double decker and tent. In order to secure a leisurely open space in Tokyo today, the temporary tent proved to be a very useful tool. Effective utilization of a planned building construction site. Securing the space for this purpose. In the difficult situation, the tent fitted ideally.
The menu contains healthy foods & drinks from morning to evening, and French wine and champagne at night. This shop specially sells a glass of champagne.

Design: Makoto Watanabe

Structure : Steel-frame membrance structure
Scale　　 : 1 story above the ground
Area　　　: Site/289.83 m²;　Building/154.80 m²;　Floor/54.80 m²
　　　　　　(including kitchen 7.56 m²)
Term of construction: June 22 to July 5, 1988
Facilities : Opening/July 9, 1988;　Open period/July 9 to September 30, 1988;　Open time/8:00 a.m. to 0:00 a.m.;　Number of guest seats/80;　Unit price per guest/2,000 yen;　Turnover of guests/4 times;　Menu/13 types of champagne, coffee, yogurt, cheese, caviar, mineral water;　Management/Les Circonstances Co.;　Number of employees/ service 5, kitchen 3, part-time 6, totaling 14

材料仕様
屋根＆外壁／可動式テント　外部床／アスファルト舗装
〈ステージバー〉床＆壁／フローリングの上にOP　天井／PBt＝9下地OP

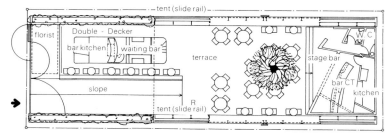

PLAN S＝1：300

入口よりビーチをみる　周りのビルとのギャップで不思議な気分に誘われる
The beach viewed from the entrance. Allured into a strange atmosphere due to the gap from the surrounding buildings.

ポールポジション

代官山

東京都渋谷区猿楽町222-7

撮影/香川康之

Pole Position Daikanyama
222-7, Sarugaku-cho, Shibuya-ku, Tokyo, Japan

エントランスよりみたファサード
The facade viewed from the entrance.

234

ポールポジション 代官山

味の素㈱はアイソトニックドリンク"テラ"を通じてのモーターサイクルロードレース活動で若いターゲットをとらえてきたが ファン層をさらに広げるために "都会的なスポーツ感覚"をもつスペース展開をしようという試みが「ポールポジション 代官山」である。
ミスマッチと思われるような モータースポーツの持つエキサイティングな気分と リゾートの持っている "リラクセーション"を共存させたスペースづくりがコンセプトとなった。ショップのスローガンは "レーシング リゾート"としても 施設内は "ひと夏だけの不思議なビーチ"にしたてようという企画になった。具体的には レーシングチーム グッズを扱うショップと冷たい飲みものが飲めて くつろげるテラスとビーチを組み合わせた。　　　　　〈後藤陽次郎/スタッフ生活総合研究所〉(88-09)

企画総合:プロデュース:スタッフ生活総合研究所
設計:加田空間設計事務所
協力:サイン/ウエストブラザーズ

構　　造:S造
規　　模:平屋
面　　積:敷地/446㎡　建築/41㎡　床/41㎡
工　　期:1988年 6 月 1 日～ 6 月17日

施設概要:開店/1988年 6 月18日　営業期間/1988年 6 月18日～ 8 月27日
　　　　　営業時間/午前11時～午後 7 時　メニュー/カフェ:スポーツドリンクなど　清涼飲料水 9 種 100～　取扱い商品/ショップ:"アジノモト ホンダ レーシング チーム"のオリジナルウェア 小物 その他/バイクの展示　参加レースの予定と結果の掲示 情報交換ボード　ヘッドホン　ラジオの貸し出し　経営/味の素㈱　従業員数/ 5 人

Pole Position Daikanyama

Ajinomoto Co. has captured the heart of young people by motorcycle road racing activities through isotonic drink "Terra." "Pole Position Daikanyama" is an attempt to offer a space having an "urban sporty sense" for a wider group of fans. Our intention in concept making has been to create a space where an exciting mood associated with motor sports and "relaxation" associated with resort can coexist, although these two may usually be regarded as being a mismatch.
Thus, we decided to pursue a "racing resort" as the shop slogan, while turning the inside into a "strange beach for only a summer." Concretely, a shop selling racing team goods has been combined with a terrace & beach where you can drink cold drinks, while relaxing.

Produce : Staff Corp
Design　: Harutoshi Kada

Structure : S
Scale　　: 1 story above the ground
Area　　 : Site/446 m²; Building/41 m²; Floor/41 m²
Term of construction: June 1 to June 17, 1988
Facilities : Opening/June 18, 1988;　Open period/June 18 to August 27, 1988;　Open time/11:00 a.m. to 7:00 p.m.;　Menu/ cafe – 9 types of soft drinks, such as sports drinks; Articles dealt with/Shop – original wear of "Ajinomoto Honda Racing Team," fancy goods; Others/motor bicycle exhibition, notice of race entry schedule and race results, information exchange board, headphone/radio sets lended;　Management/Ajinomoto Co.;　Number of employees/5

材料仕様
屋根/錫引鉄板葺き　外壁/工事現場用仮囲いスチールOP　庭/砂　テラス/栂材板貼り　サイン/スチール板にシルクプリント　床/合板貼りOP　壁/PB下地VP　天井/PB下地VP　明天井/透明アクリル板貼り　照明器具(外部)/工事現場用マルチハロゲンランプ　家具/デッキチェア　テラスチェア　テラステーブル　テラスカウンター　以上すべてオリジナル　スチールパイプ　栂材

ショップをみる　　The shop.

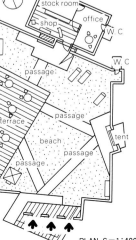
PLAN S=1:400

235

クラブハウスとステージ全景　風車や魚などのイラストが遊び心を誘う　またＤＪブースでは各大学の学生の放送研究会等のネットワークでＤＪを交代で行なっている
The entire club house/stage scene. Illustrations of windmills, fish, etc. make us playful. At the DJ booth, DJ is performed, in turn, by broadcasting study groups at various universities, etc. which form a network.

ロケーションは片瀬江ノ島海岸
Located at Katase Enoshima Beach.

パナソニック　クラブ　ハウス

神奈川県藤沢市片瀬江ノ島西海岸

撮影/香川康之

Panasonic Club House
Katase-kaigan, Fujisawa city, Kanagawa, Japan

スロットルレーシング脇よりテラスをみる

The terrace viewed from beside the throttle racing corner.

パナソニック クラブ ハウス

「パナソニック クラブ ハウス」は首都圏の高感度ヤングにイメージアピールする情報発信基地として 松下電気産業㈱が湘南 江ノ島片瀬海岸に '88年に作ったサマーハウス。

イベントとの連動による高いパブリシティー効果を図るため ハウスとイベントステージのデザインイメージを統一することができ 楽しい空間が広がった。

イベントハウスのおもしろさは 短時間で打ち上げられる花火がイベントであるならば ハウスは毎日がお祭り気分の屋台であり 他より何かアピールするものがあれば 興味をそそられ 中まで入って来てくれる。ましてビーチがその舞台となれば 遠くから注目度は高くなり 視覚的デモンストレーションとしての意味も大きいと思う。

〈小川幸子/エスティーデザイン〉(88-09)

設計:エスティーデザイン
協力:イラスト/伊藤桂司
施工:丹青社

構　造:鉄骨造
規　模:平屋
面　積:建築/ハウス 119.82㎡　ステージ 85.95㎡　床/ハウス119.82㎡(内 厨房6.13㎡) ステージ 81.45㎡ 合計 201.27㎡
工　期:1988年 6 月 6 日〜30日

施設概要:開店/1988年 7 月 1 日　営業時間/1988年 7 月 1 日〜 8 月28日　営業時間/午前 9 時〜午後 5 時　客席数/20席　メニュー/缶ビール350〜400 ソフト缶ドリンク150 取扱い商品/T シャツ1000〜2800 カセットテープ400〜 経営/松下電器産業㈱ 従業員数/サービス 3 人 厨房 1 人 パート アルバイト 5 人 合計 9 人

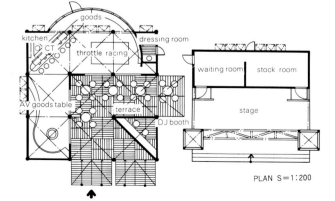

上/カウンター席をみる
下/スロットルレーシングとグッズ売り場をみる
Top/ The counter seat area.
Bottom/ The throttle racing and goods corners.

Panasonic Club House

"Panasonic Club House" is a summer house created in 1988 at Katase Beach, Enoshima, Shonan, by Matsushita Electric Industrial Co., as an information despatching station with images appealing to the sensitive young in the Metropolitan area.

In order to achieve a high publicity effect in conjunction with an event, the house and event stage were designed with an image uniting both. As a result, an amusing space has come into being.

If an event is likened to fireworks displayed in a short time, the event house may be likened to an open stall where you can enjoy a festive mood everyday. If passers-by see something appealing there, they will be interested and come in. Since the beach serves as its stage, it will draw attention from far away. Thus, it will also be meaningful as a visual demonstration.

Design: Shoichi Tsukahara

Structure : Steel-frame structure
Scale   : 1 story above the ground
Area   : Building/house 119.82 m², stage 85.95 m²; Floor/house 119.82 m² (including kitchen 6.13 m²), stage 81.45 m², totaling 201.27 m²
Term of construction: June 6 to June 30, 1988
Facilities : Opening/July 1, 1988; Open period/July 1 to August 28, 1988; Open time/9:00 a.m. to 5:00 p.m.; Number of guest seats/20; Menu/canned beer, canned soft drinks; Articles dealt with/T-shirts, cassette tapes; Management/Matsushita Electric Industrial Co.; Number of employees/service 3, kitchen 1, part-time 5, totaling 9

PLAN S=1:200

材料仕様
屋根/耐水合板 t =12 A E P　外壁/耐水合板 t =12 A E P　ガラスFix　外部床/合板 t =15 A E P　サイン/合板切文字A E P　A E Pシルクスクリーン　床/合板 t =15 A E P　スノコ敷 A E P　壁/鉄骨 A E P　合板 A E P　一部網入り型板ガラスFix　透明ガラスFix　天井/合板 A E P　D Jブース:乳半白アクリル板 t =4　照明器具/スポットライト

●この索引の施設名　店名　事務所名　所在地　電話番号などのデータは開業(開店)時　及び「月刊商店建築」に掲載時のものです。現在変更されている場合もありますのでご了承下さい。
商店建築社

■撮影者・50音順

撮影者名／スタジオ名／所在地／電話／掲載ページ